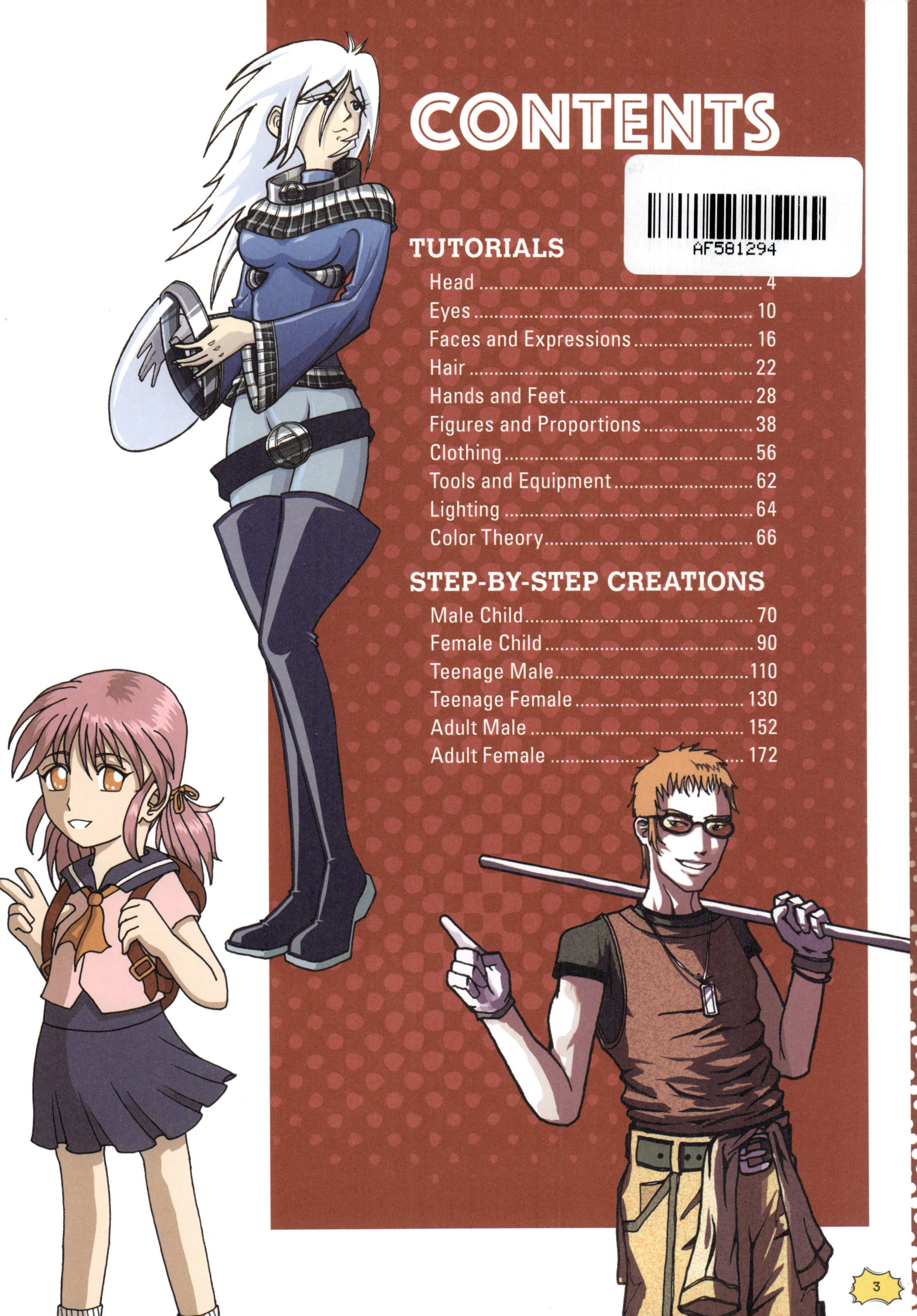

CONTENTS

TUTORIALS

STEP-BY-STEP CREATIONS

HEAD

Although manga is a very distinct form of artwork, it is based on the fundamental skills of basic figure drawing and knowledge of anatomy. Too often many beginners launch straight into the more famous aspects of the manga style, such as the exaggerated facial features and the lustrous hair, and upon completing their drawing realize that something does not look quite right. It is very important to have some knowledge about how the overall head of a character is put together, as it forms the "canvas" for the face, allowing you to place facial features accurately. Knowing how to construct a head from first principles will mean that you can effectively portray a character from almost any angle. The human head comes in many different sizes and shapes. However, all heads are formed from a skull, which can essentially be represented by a sphere with a lower jaw.

BUILDING BLOCKS

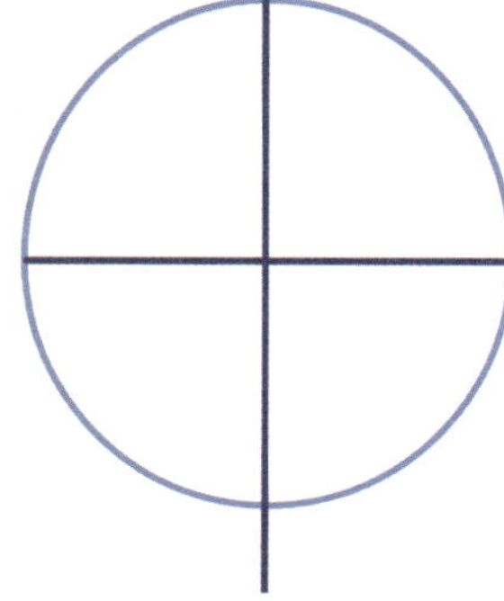

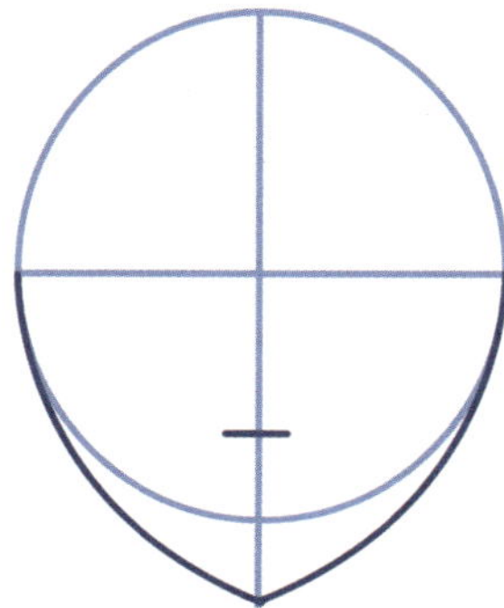

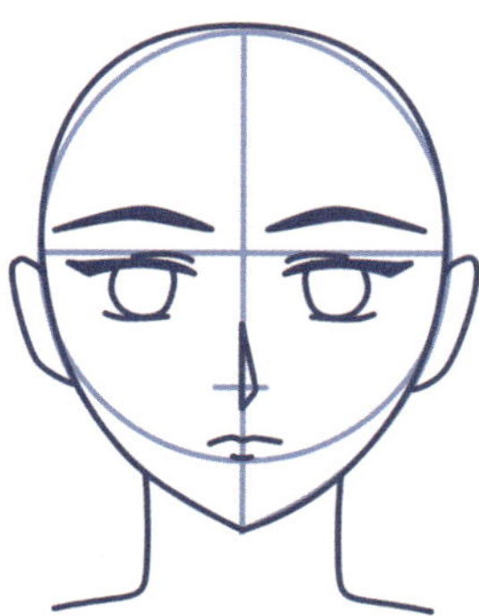

1. Draw a circle for the upper part of the head. Draw a cross over it, splitting the circle into quarters. The vertical line represents the center line of the head and face. The horizontal line represents the upper eye socket line.

2. Draw curved lines from the sides of the face to the bottom of the vertical line. These lines map out the chin and jaw. Draw another horizontal line in between the eyeline and the point of the chin, roughly equidistant from the two. This helps place the nose.

3. Using these lines as a rough guide for the placement of features, add in the details of the eyes, nose, ears, mouth, and neck. The ears are at a similar level to the eyes and are spaced evenly on the sides of the head. The mouth is approximately halfway between the bottom of the nose and the chin.

MANGA SKETCHBOOK

SWEATDROP STUDIOS

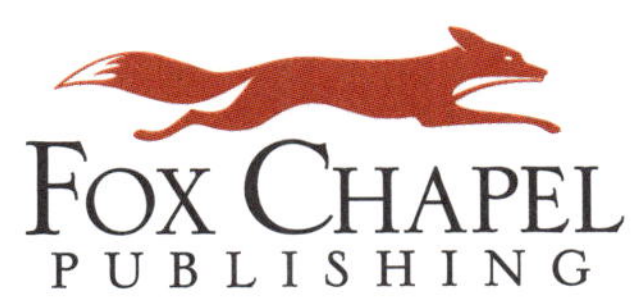
FOX CHAPEL PUBLISHING

CONTRIBUTORS

HEAD CONTRIBUTORS

Sonia Leong – Sweatdrop Editor, Author of *Beginning Manga* and *The Complete Guide to Drawing Manga*

Tutorials: Head, Figures and Proportion, Clothing; Step-by-Step Creations: Male Child Alternative 1, Teenage Female

Selina Dean

Tutorials: Faces and Expressions, Figures (Exaggerated Proportion Sets), Clothing example, Accessories, Chibis/Super-Deformed Characters; Step-by-Step Creations: Female Child, Teenage Male Alternative 2

Hayden Scott-Baron

Tutorials: Clothing example, Lighting, Color Theory; Step-by-Step Creations: Teenage Male, Adult Male Alternative 2, Adult Female Alternative 2

Laura Watton

Tutorials: Hair, Hands and Feet, Clothing examples, Accessories examples; Step-by-Step Creations: Female Child Alternative 2, Adult Female

Emma Vieceli

Tutorials: Eyes, Clothing examples; Step-by-Step Creations: Male Child, Teenage Female Alternative 2, Adult Male

OTHER CONTRIBUTORS

Sam Brown – Adult Female Alternative 1
Carrie Dean – Teenage Female Alternative 1
Niki Hunter – Adult Male Alternative 1
Aleister Kelman – Teenage Male Alternative 1
Morag Lewis – Female Child Alternative 1
Wing Yun Man – Male Child Alternative 2

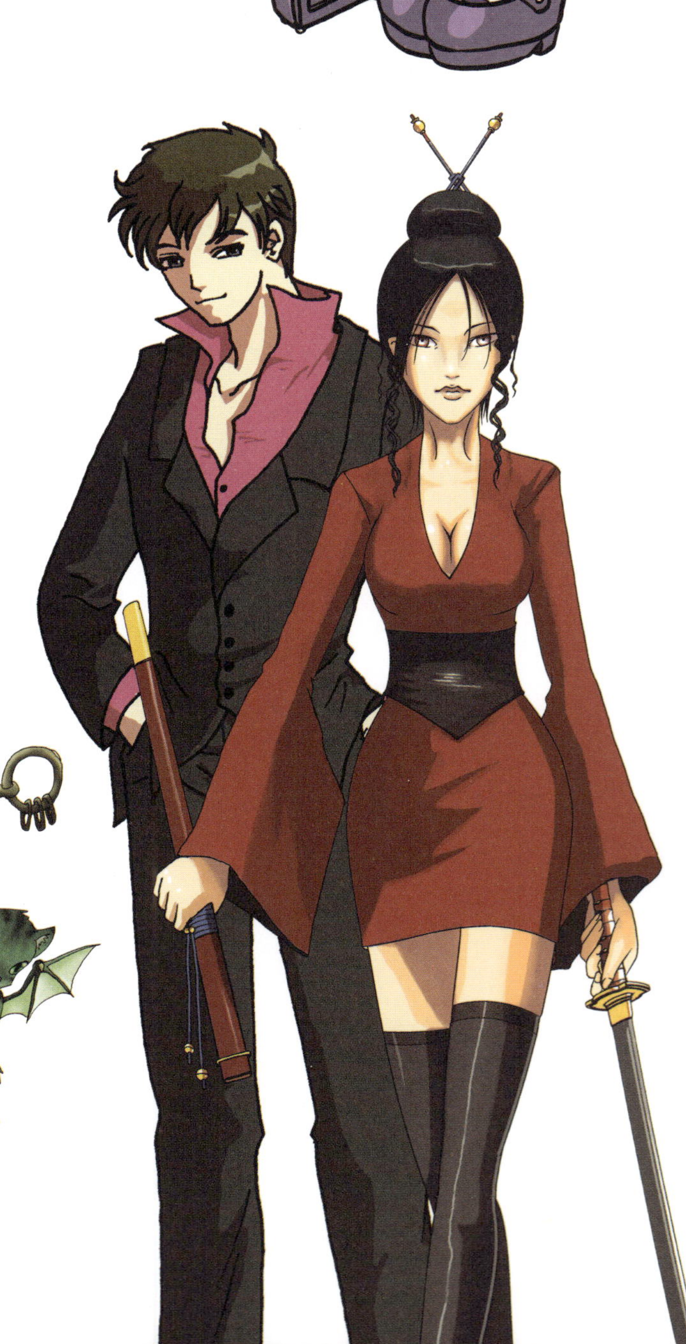

USEFUL TIPS

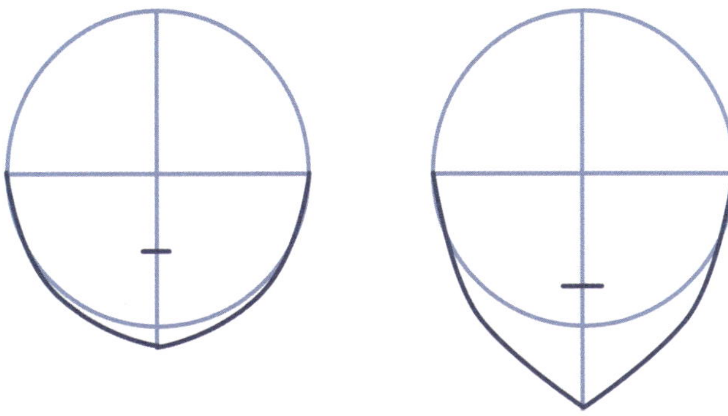

Note that the strength and length of the curve can vary for different faces, depending on how far you extend the vertical center line.

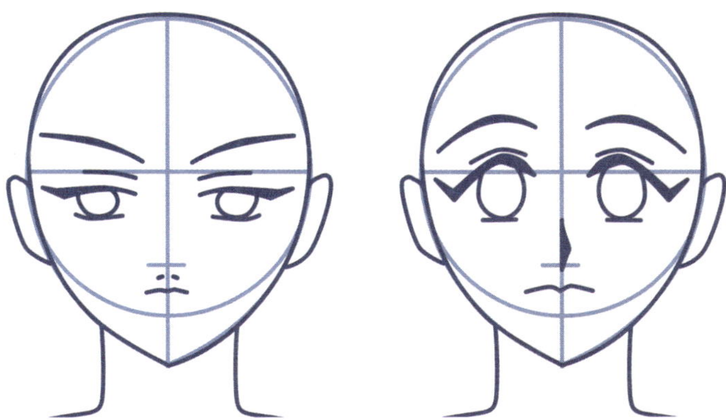

These guidelines are intended as a rough way of placing facial features. Depending on the type of character you are drawing, features can extend beyond these lines.

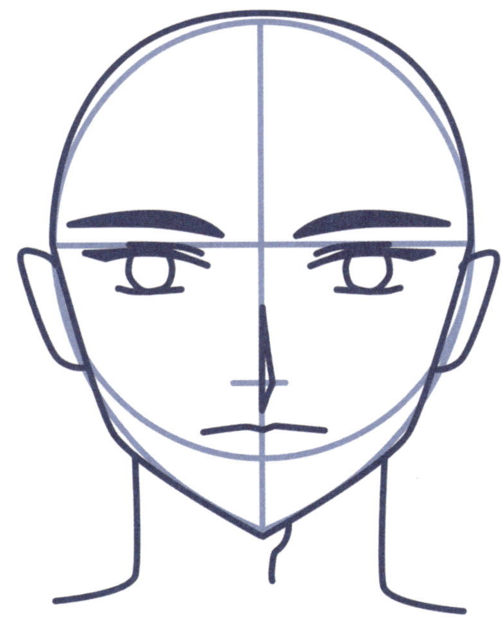

For a male face, make the neck thicker, the eyes narrower, the nose longer, and the jawline more angular. Don't forget the Adam's apple!

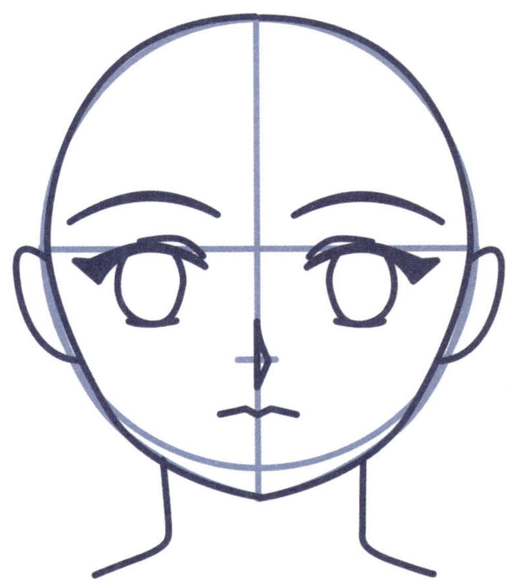

When drawing a child, the lower half of the head is more compact, making all the facial features much closer together. Draw a small, short nose and mouth, but keep the eyes large, as in real life. This conveys a sense of cuteness.

YOU TRY!

DIFFERENT VIEWS

To draw a side view, start with the forehead, then dip in slightly before drawing the nose. Below the nose, draw another dip into the lips, then chin. Note how the lips and chin are not far from the face's center line. Also observe the placement of the ear, slightly closer to the back of the head than exactly halfway.

Three-quarter views benefit most from guidelines – think in three dimensions when drawing the center line and eyeline. Take care with the side of the face – draw a slight dip below the temple, rounding out to the cheekbone. The jawline can then be round, sunken, muscular, etc., as appropriate.

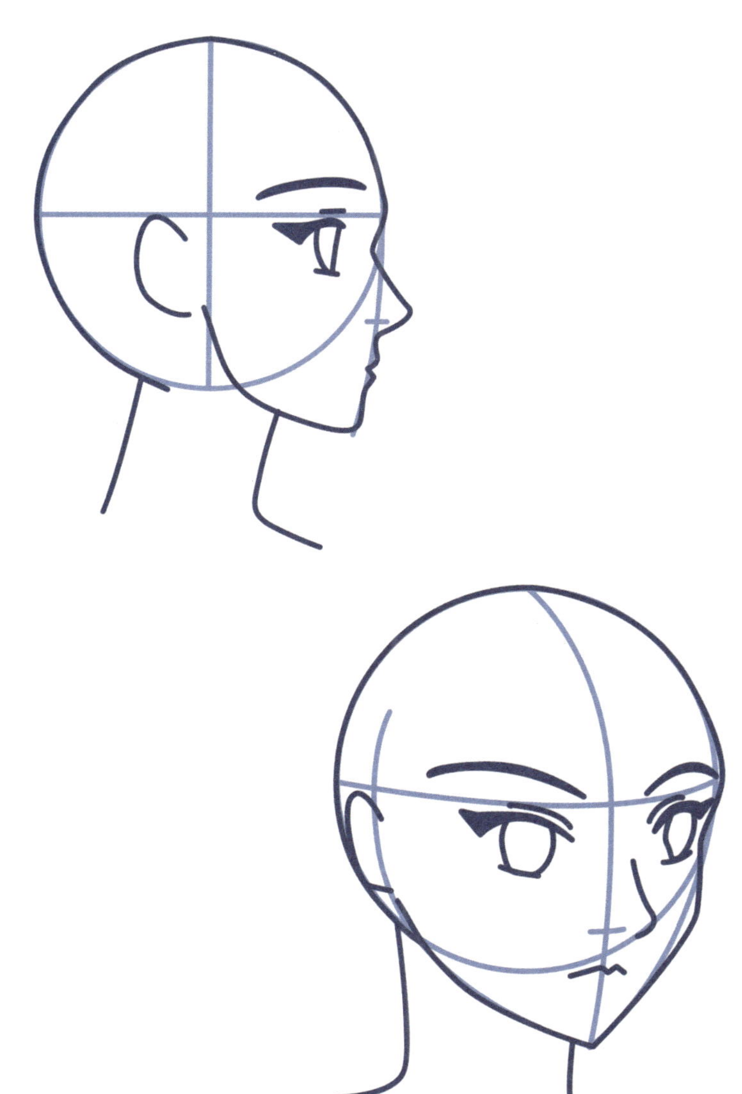

OVER TO YOU!

Here are various examples of different characters' heads from several viewpoints. These characters do not have the same facial proportions, as they range from male to female, young to old. By using the basic model, you can ensure all of the features are realistically placed at every angle the head is viewed from.

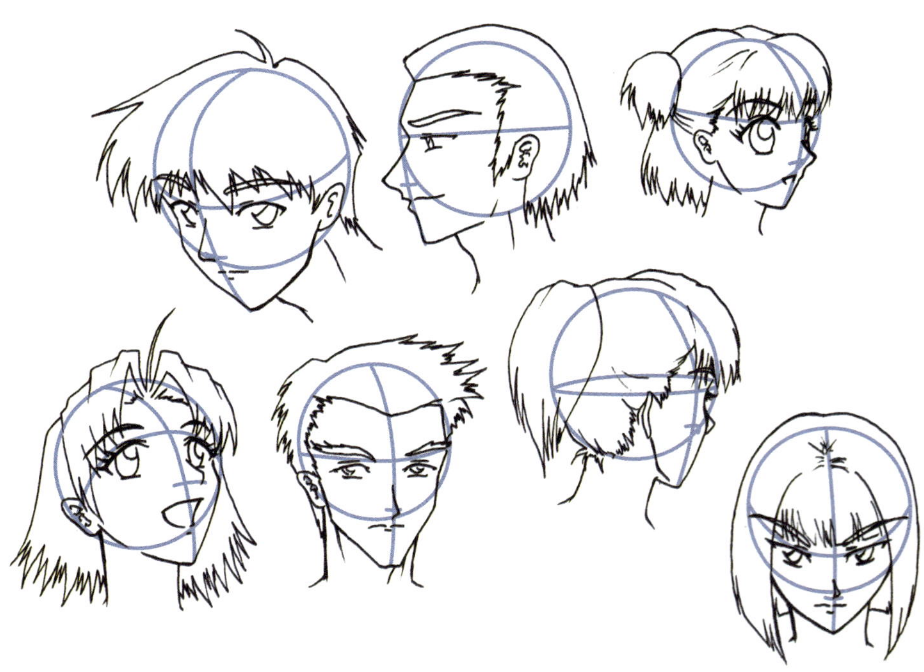

YOU TRY!

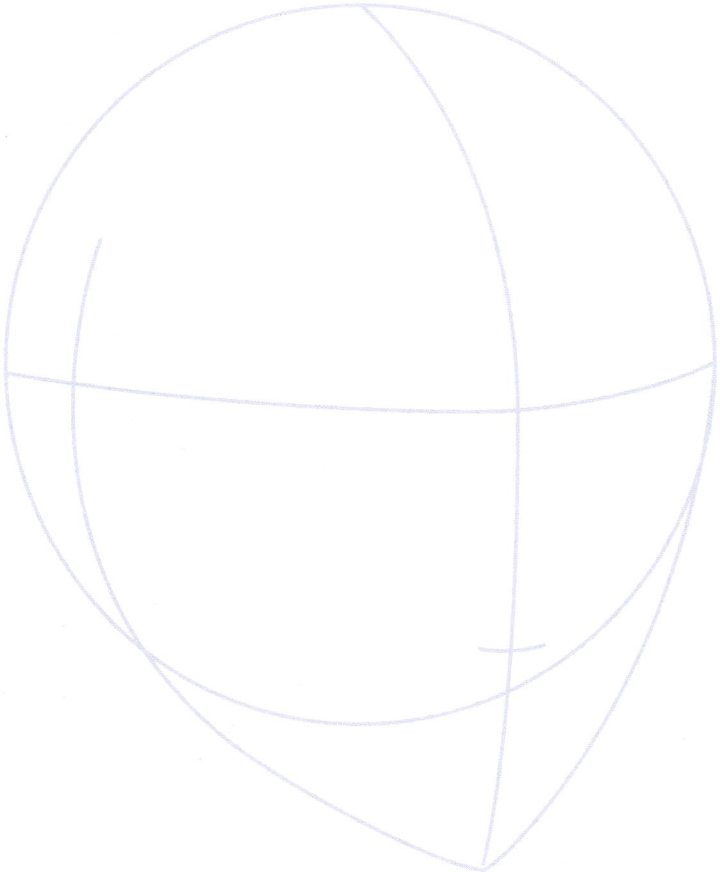

EYES

Large eyes are the most iconic feature of the manga aesthetic. However, there are many different approaches to drawing manga-style eyes, and each approach can radically change the way in which a character is perceived. Manga is all about individuality, so use the following guidance as stepping stones to developing your own unique style.

BUILDING BLOCKS

On the two-dimensional plane, an eye is made up of three sections: the upper line, the ball, and the lower line. These three simple parts can be molded into an infinite number of unique styles. Two very different examples are shown below and on page 12.

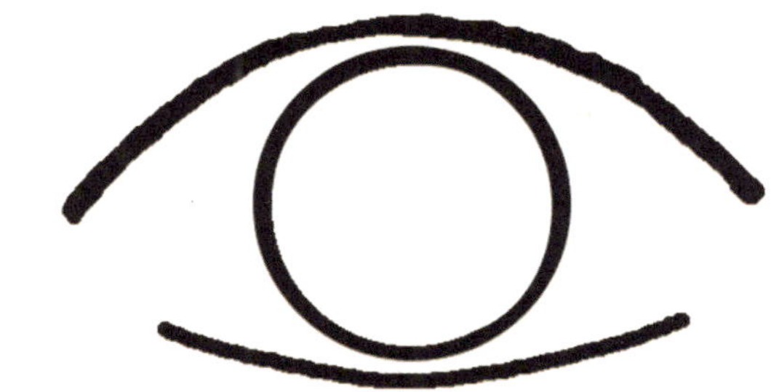

1. The upper and lower lines are elongated and flattened. An outside corner has been added and the two lines are almost touching, closing in the eye. The ball is partly obscured by the upper line, suggesting a hooded or glazed expression.
2. The upper lashes are curving down into the eye rather than upward as expected. This closes the eye in further.
3. A double line has been added inside the lower line for a three-dimensional perspective. A couple of extra lines added above the eye show the eyelid and even the start of the bridge of the nose.
4. Finally, a light source is added to increase the glazed look. The overall impression is of a closed and mysterious character.

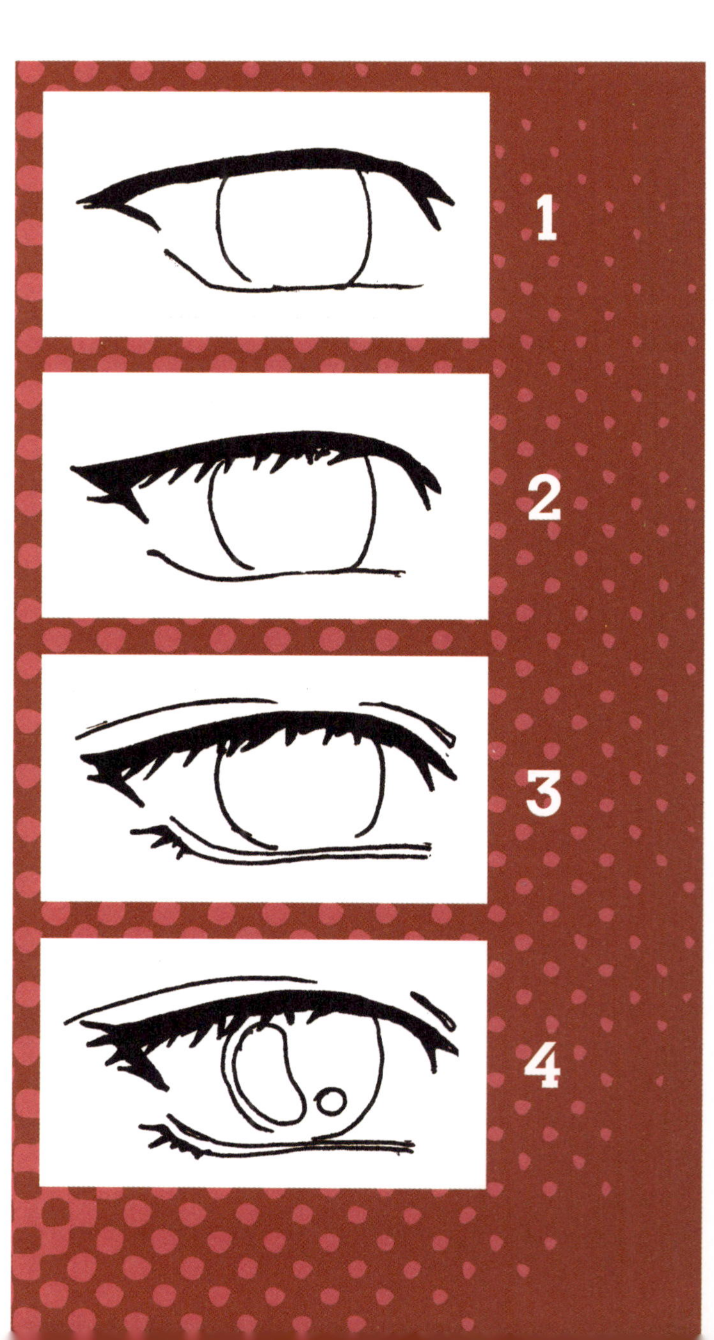

YOU TRY!

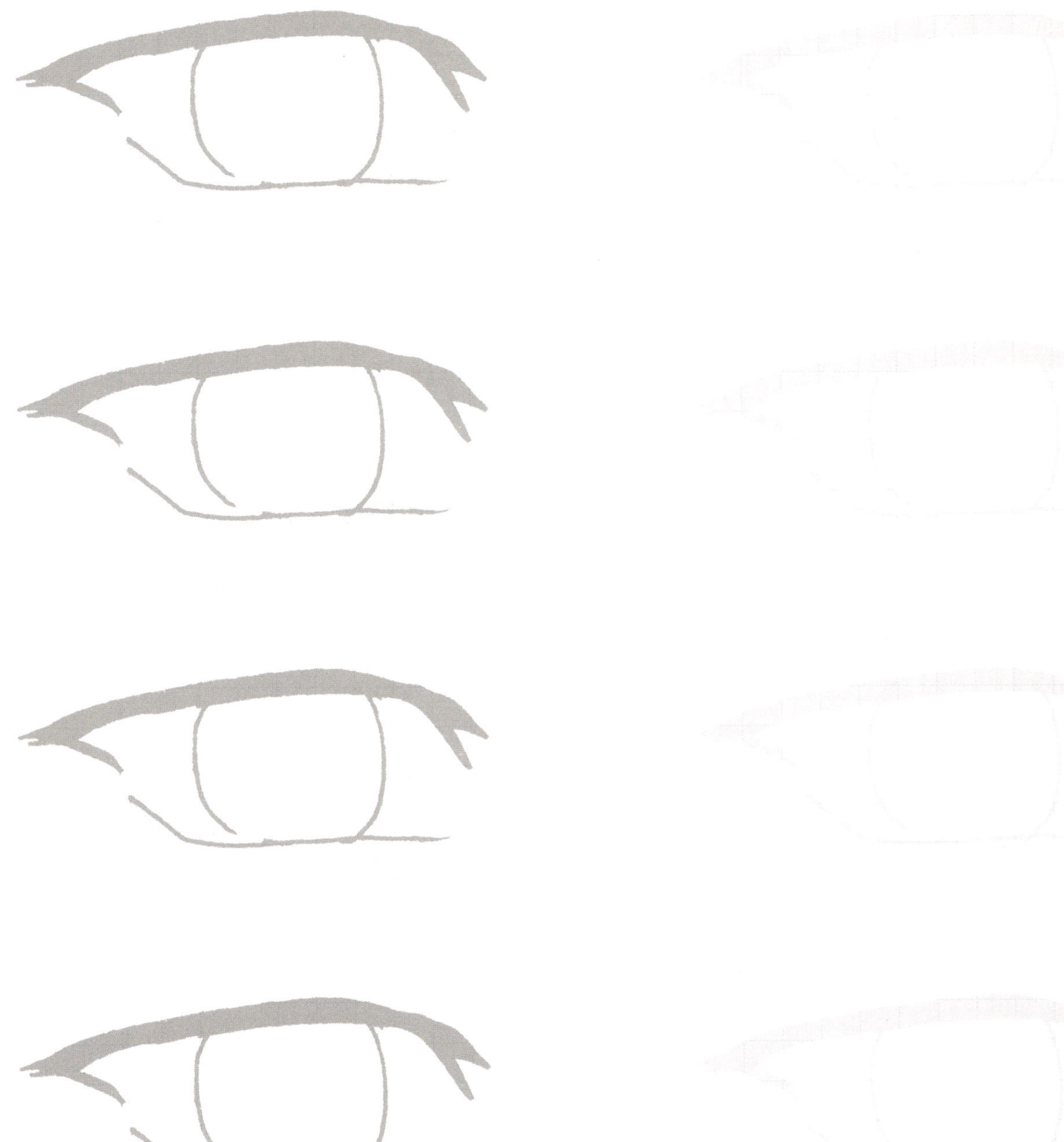

1. The upper line is arched rather than flattened and the lower line shortened. There is still an outside corner, but this time the two lines are further apart. The ball has been expanded upward and is fully visible.

2. A large and simple lash has been added to this eye, rather than the complex lashes of the first example.

3. The double lines are still in place.

4. This time, two simple light spots have been chosen. The impression here is one of wide-eyed wonder and brightness.

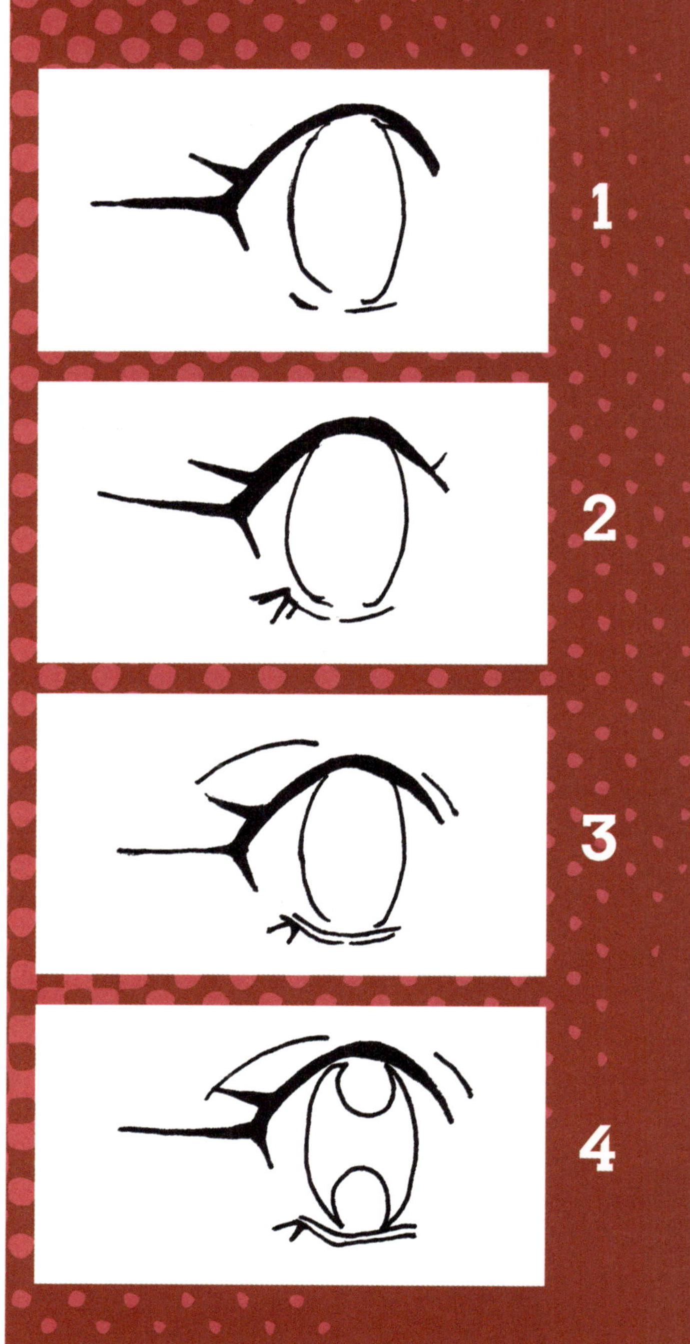

SIDE VIEW

When drawing an eye in profile, remember that the upper and lower lines originate from the outer corners of the eye.

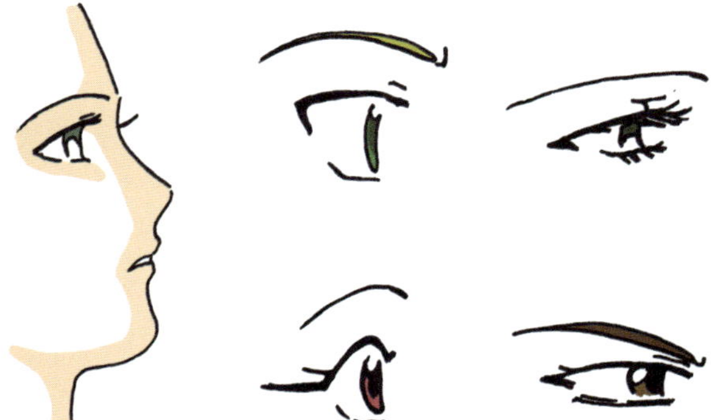

POSITIONING

As a general rule, when positioning eyes on a head, they are placed in line with the ears, halfway down the head (see step 1, page 4). A simple rule of thumb for distancing the eyes from each other in a straight-on view is to imagine an invisible third eye in the center. When drawn in a three-quarter position, the eye furthest from the viewer will seem slightly smaller, partly covered by the bridge of the nose.

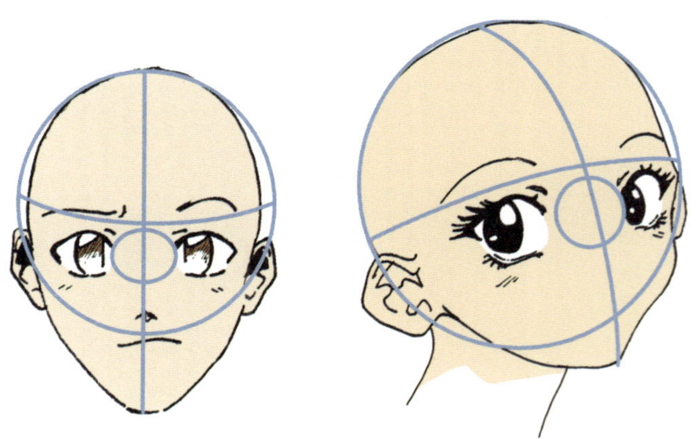

YOU TRY!

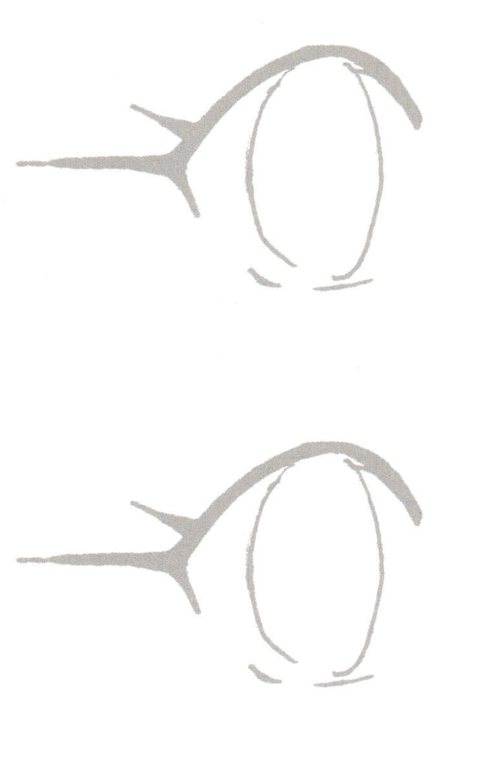

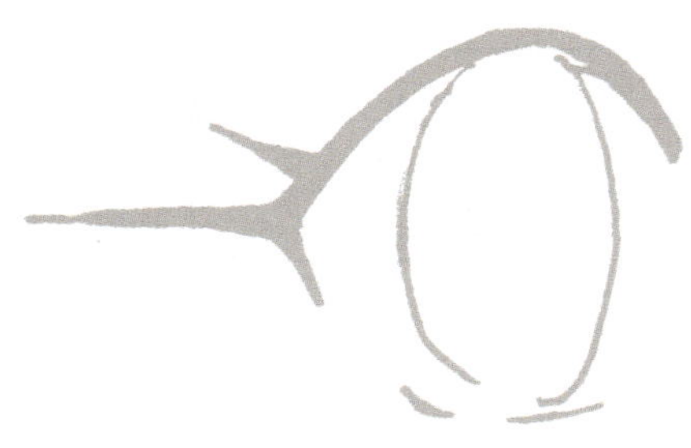

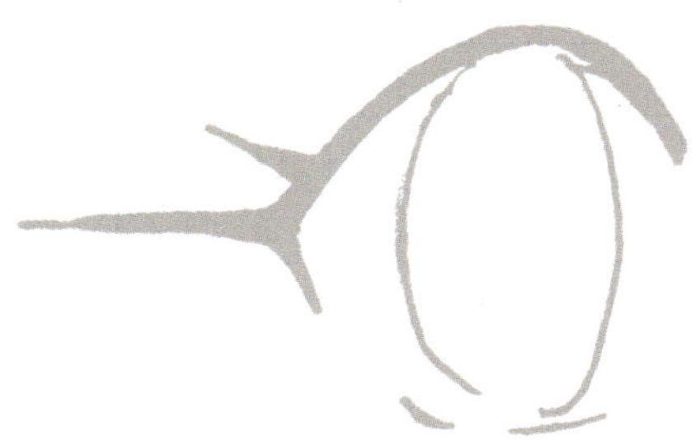

LIGHT SOURCE AND COLOR

As an additional touch, color and light are distinctive features of manga. Eyes offer the opportunity to go crazy with them – almost anything goes!

1. Large black pupils curl right around the iris. There is only a small light spot in each eye.
2. The large pupils have been colored a slightly darker shade than the iris, rather than traditional black. These large eyes reflect a lot of light back!
3. A gradient fill (a color fill that gradually blends) has been used – no pupil is visible at all.
4. An extreme amount of light spots has been added to accentuate the openness of the eyes, and the upper and lower lines have been dispensed with. This is all done for comic effect.

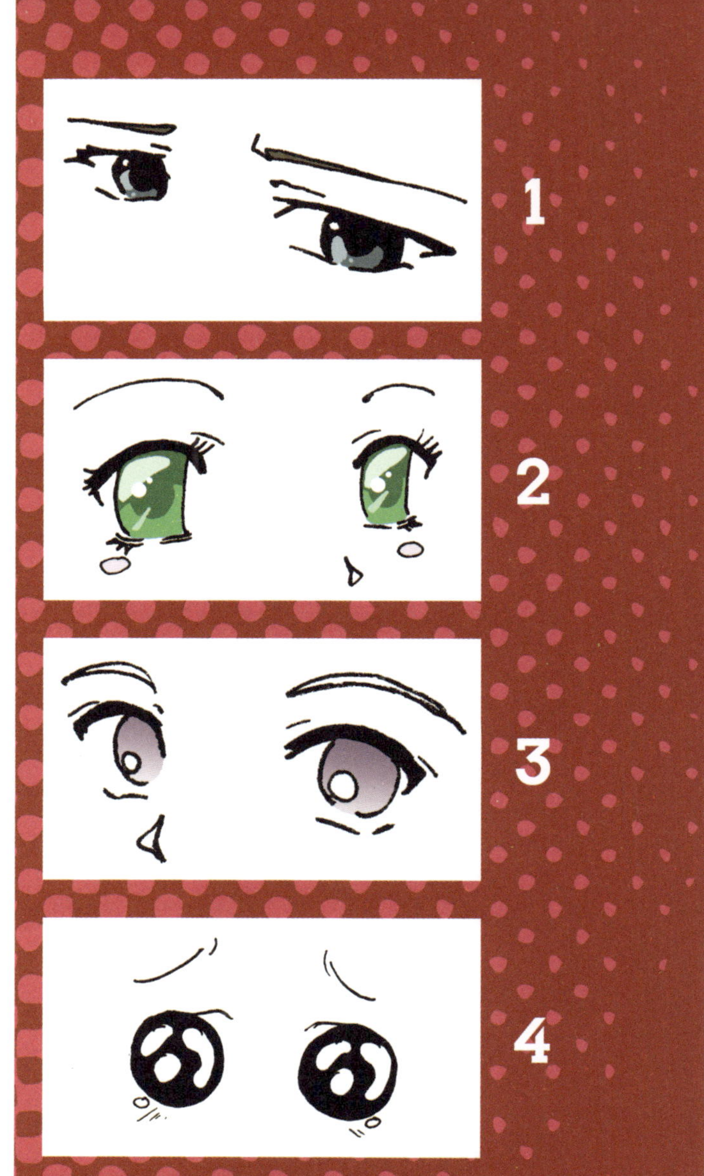

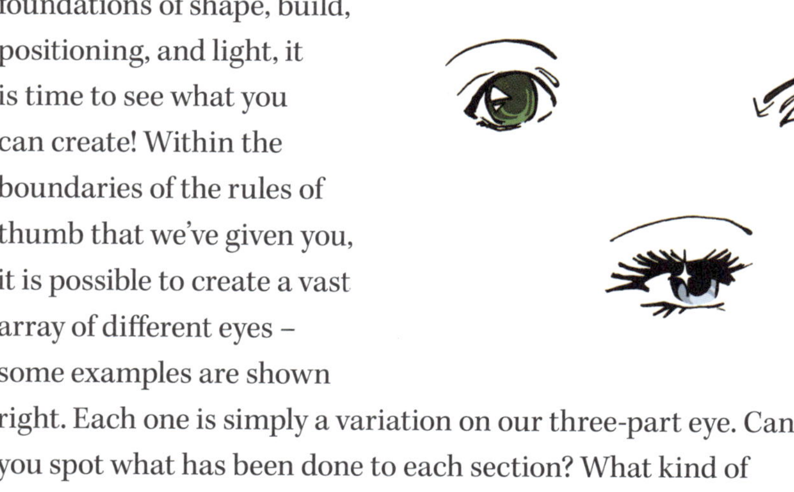

OVER TO YOU!

Armed with the basic foundations of shape, build, positioning, and light, it is time to see what you can create! Within the boundaries of the rules of thumb that we've given you, it is possible to create a vast array of different eyes – some examples are shown right. Each one is simply a variation on our three-part eye. Can you spot what has been done to each section? What kind of characters would have eyes like these?

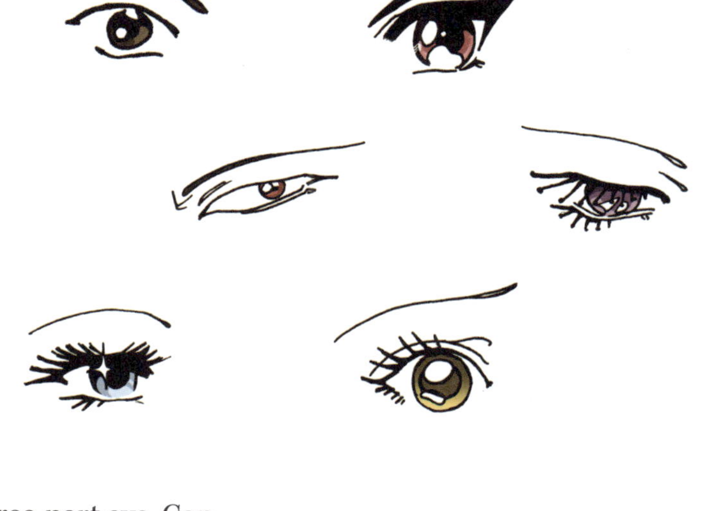

YOU TRY!

FACES AND EXPRESSIONS

On the most basic level, manga-style faces look very similar: they generally have tiny noses and huge eyes. But beyond the obvious similarities, there are many subtle nuances that you can use to build a unique style and individual characters.

EXPRESSIONS

An important aspect of achieving a genuine manga look with your characters is stylizing their expressions correctly. Many characters will have a set of common expressions, depending on their attitude and personality. For example, shy or stoic characters won't be seen with overly exaggerated expressions. Likewise, a happy or comedic character will lose its impact if you give it subtle features. Think about your character's personality and what kind of faces he or she would pull! Some examples are shown below.

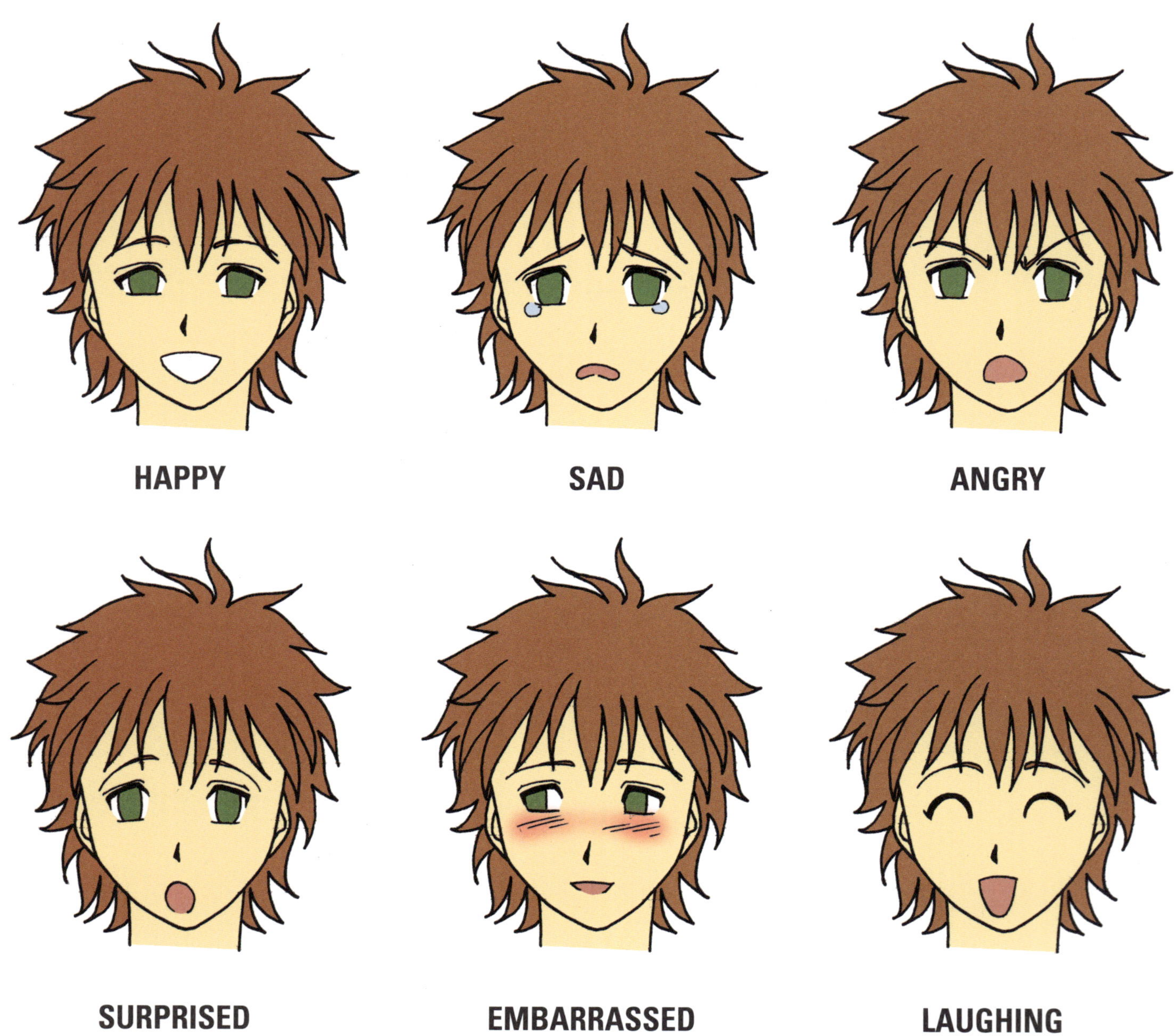

YOU TRY!

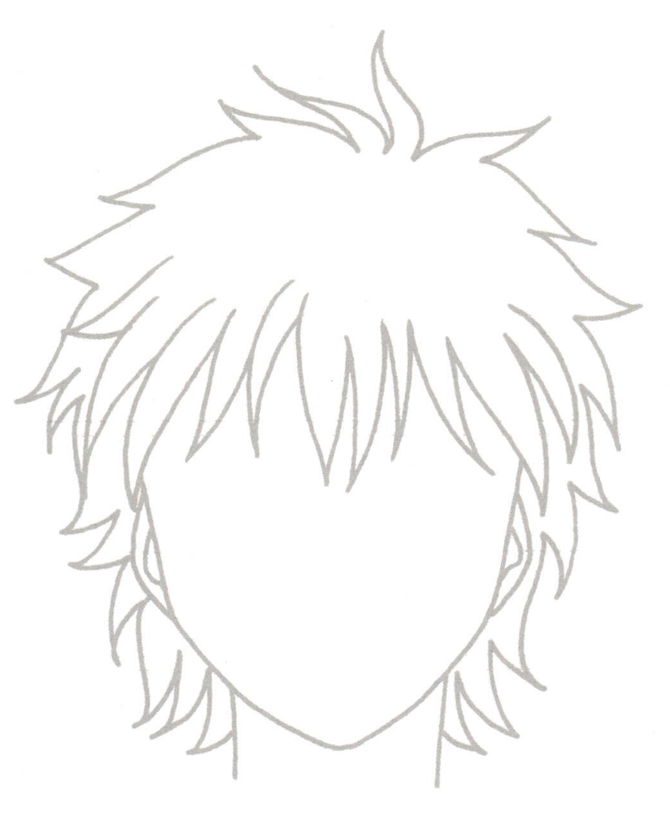

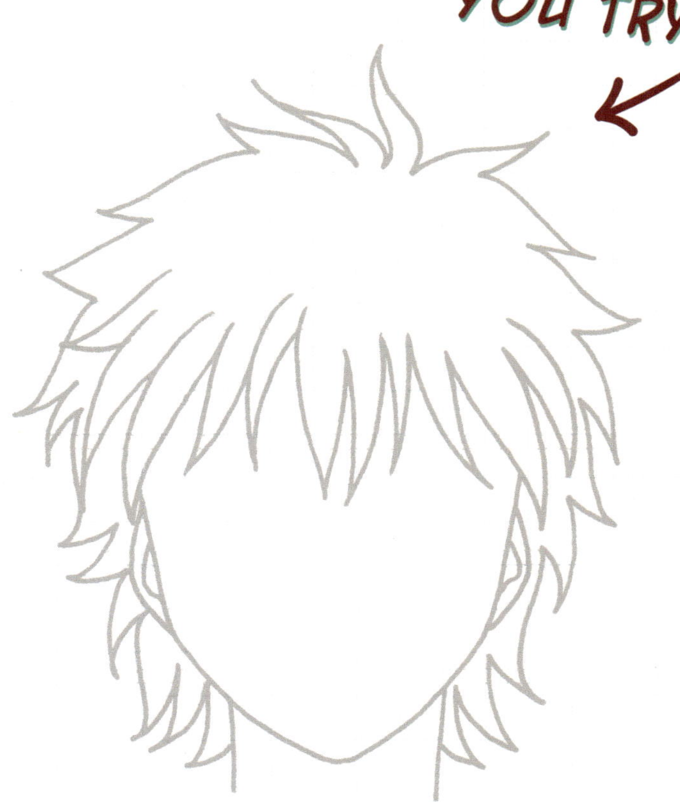

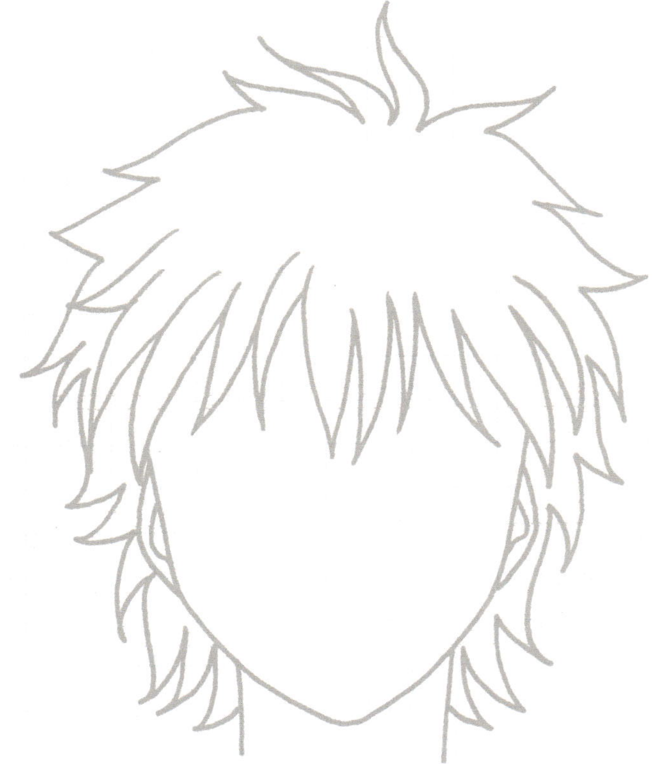

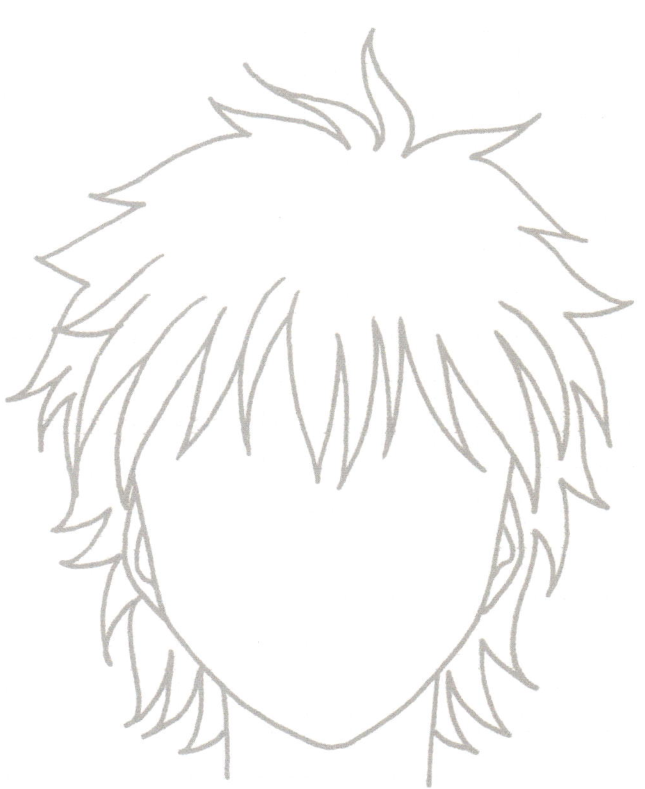

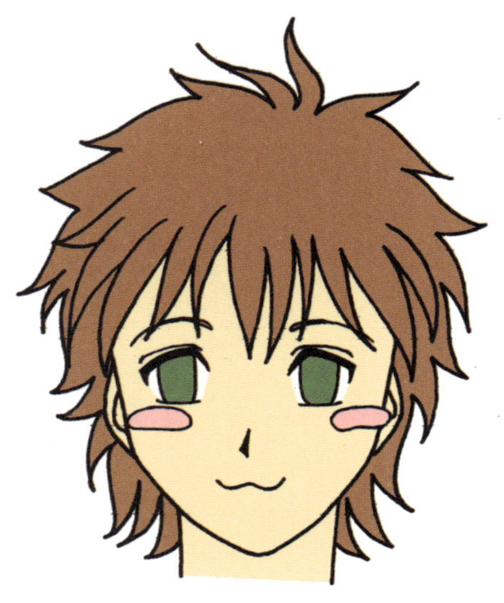

PLEASED

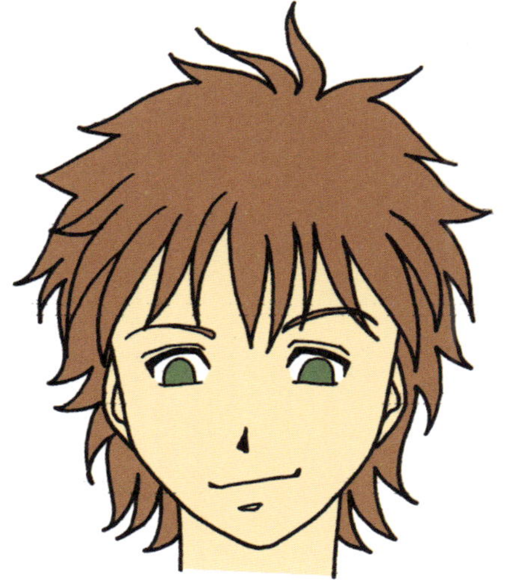

DEVIOUS

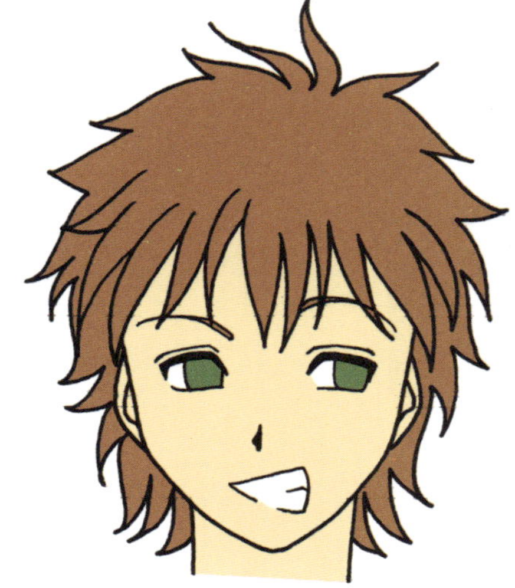

SARCASTIC

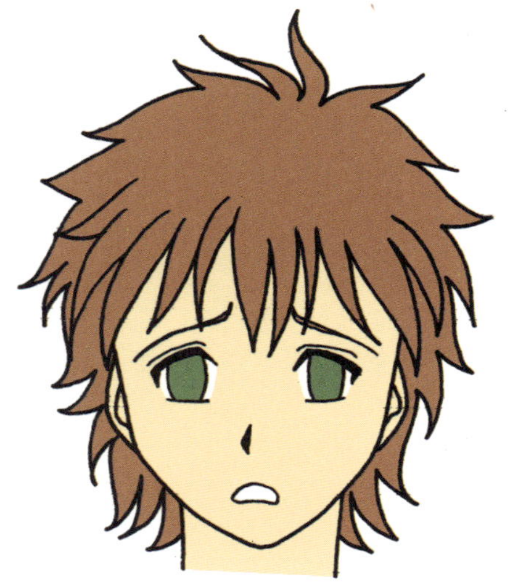

WORRIED

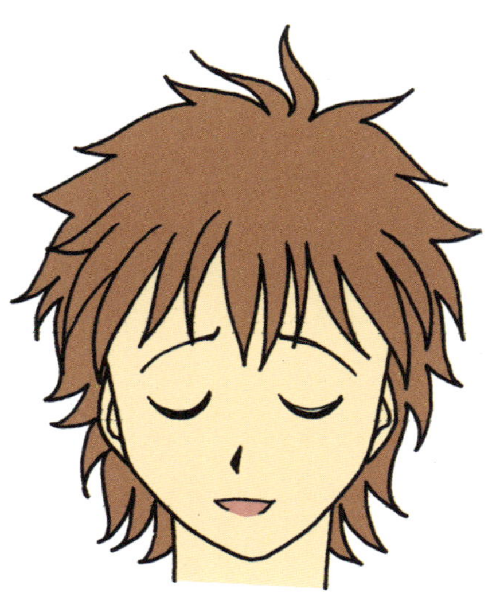

RELIEVED

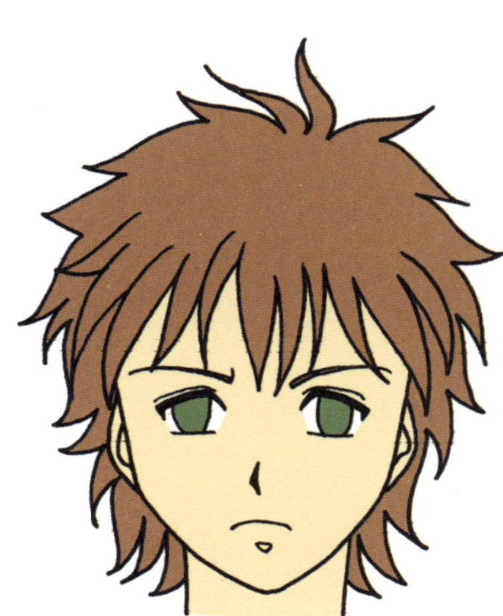

DETERMINED

EYES AND EYEBROWS

A lot of the emotion of a character is shown in the eyes and eyebrows. Even slight changes to the angle of the eyebrows can create a different expression.

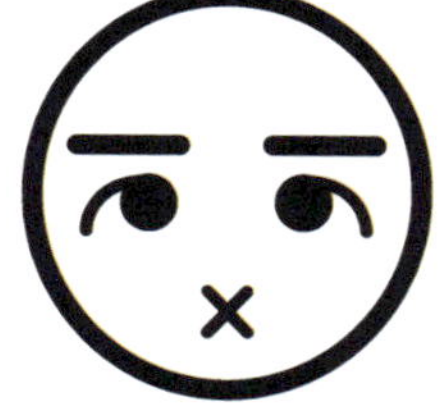

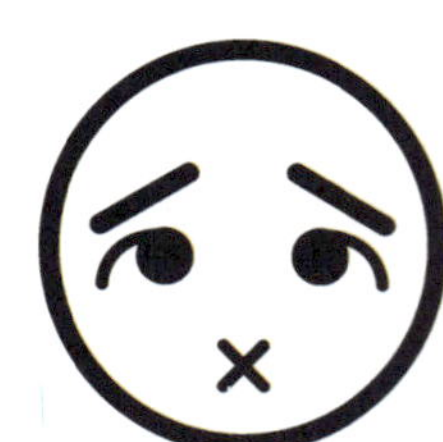

YOU TRY!

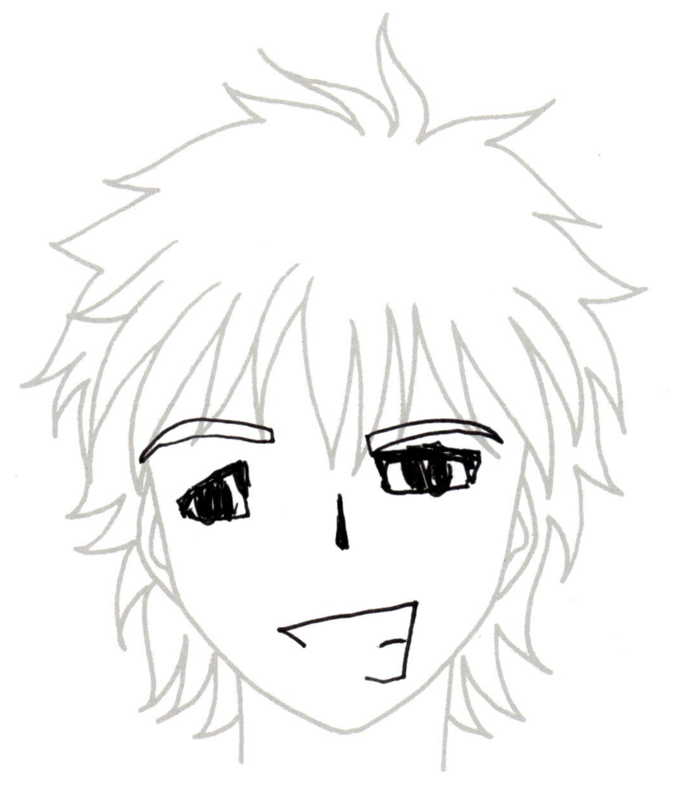

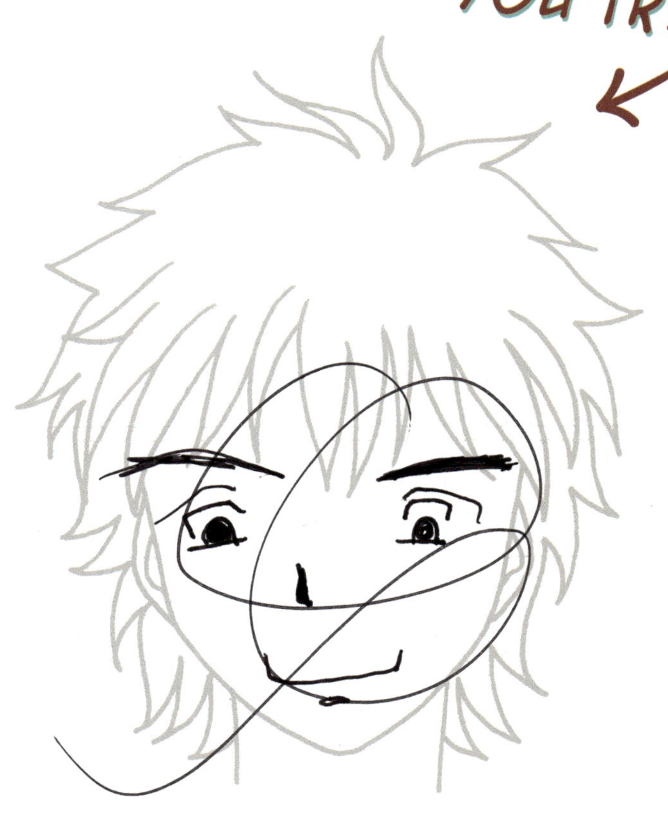

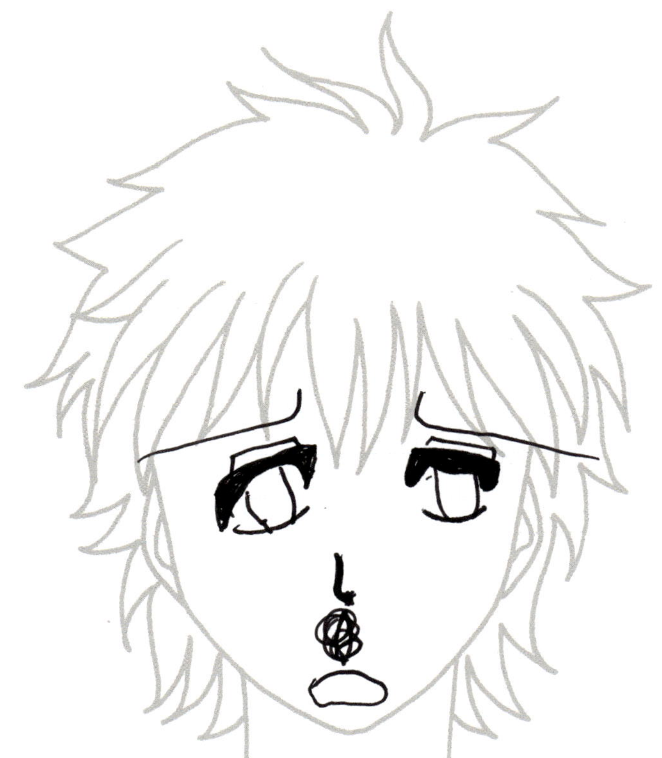

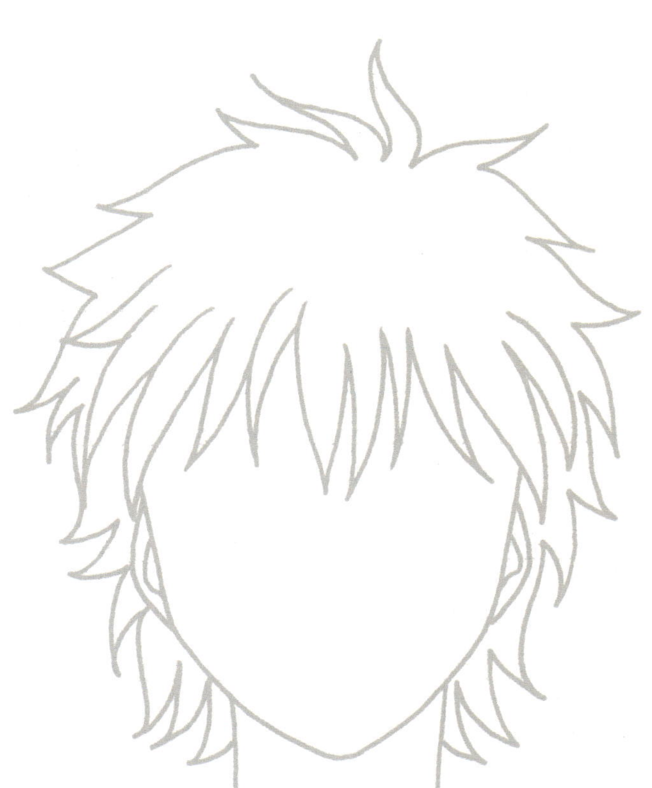

VISUAL GRAMMAR AND EXAGGERATED EXPRESSIONS

"Visual grammar" is a kind of illustrator's shorthand, iconic images used to quickly create a mood or just for comedic exaggeration. Here are some examples of visual grammar used to enhance characters' expressions, but be careful not to overuse them. These kinds of exaggerated expressions can look great in humorous or lighthearted drawings, but would be very inappropriate in serious or dramatic images.

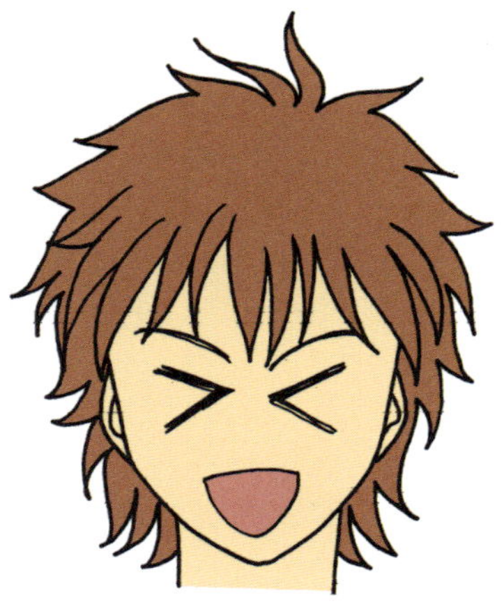

Happy – with eyes clasped shut and a huge grin. This is a very silly expression.

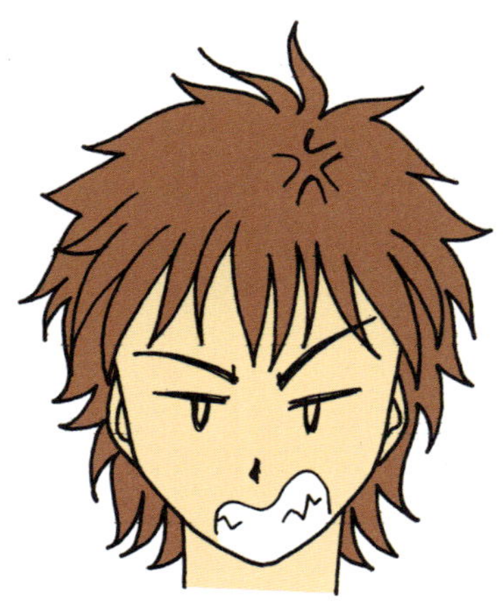

Angry – the throbbing vein on the character's head is a sign of anger.

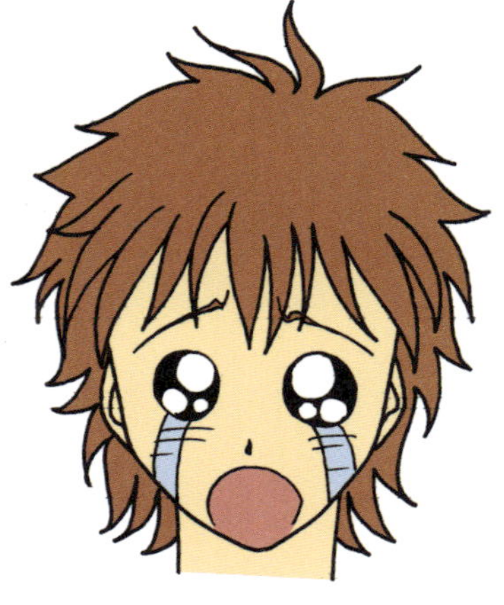

Sad – large, wet eyes and rivers of tears are usually a trademark of cuter characters.

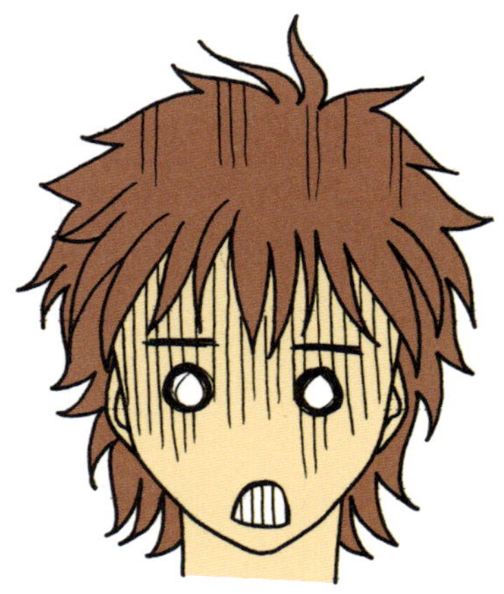

Shocked – the lines on the character's face give it a gloomy, doomed look.

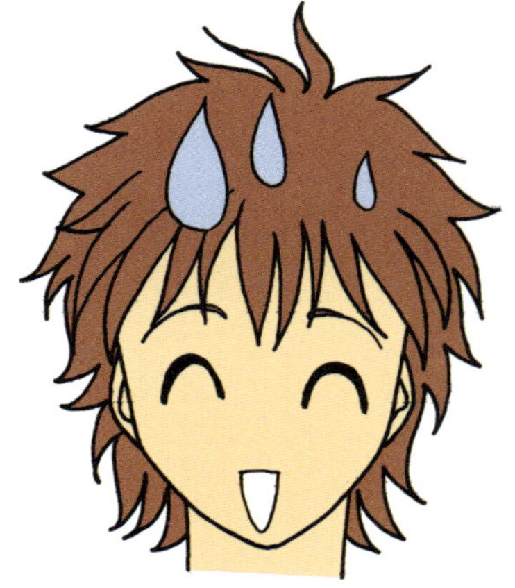

Embarrassed – large drops of sweat often appear above a character's head when they're embarrassed or exasperated.

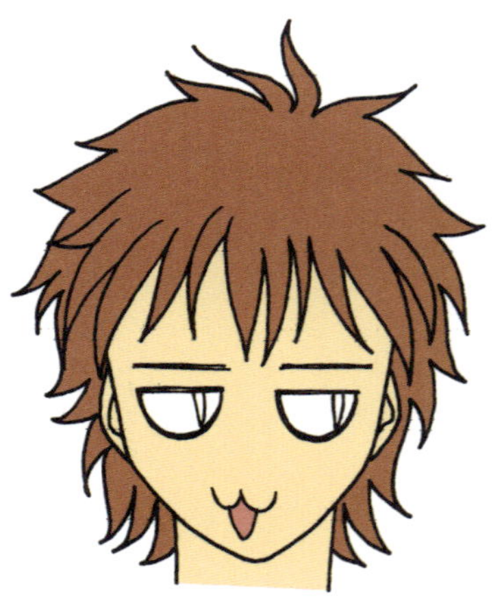

Mischievous – the catlike eyes and mouth make the character look sneaky and cunning.

YOU TRY!

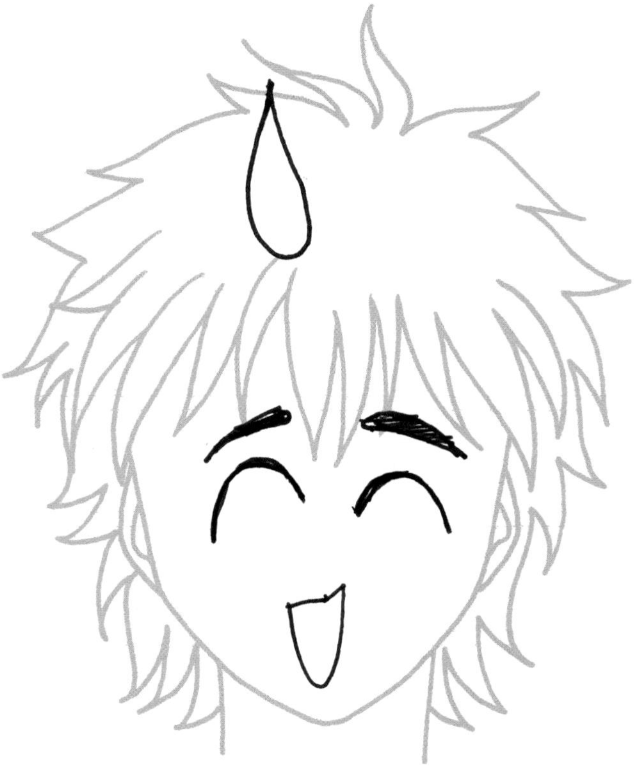

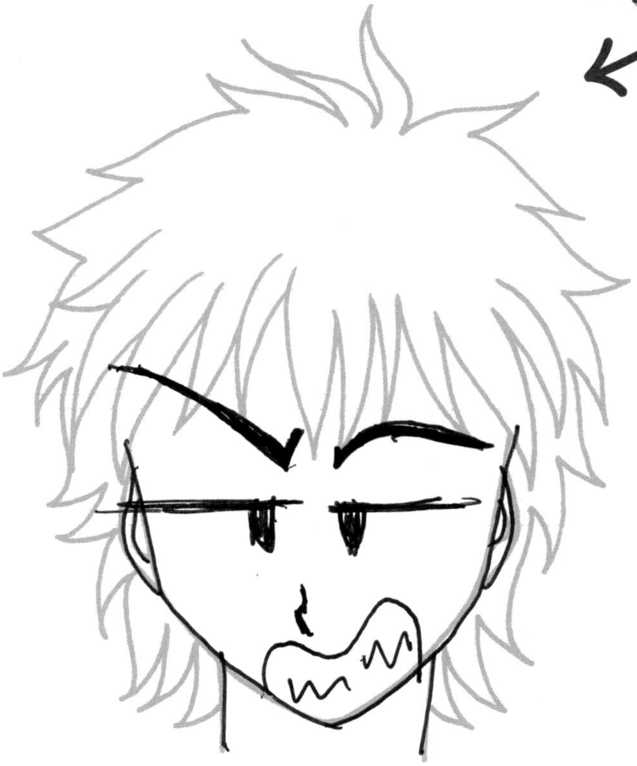

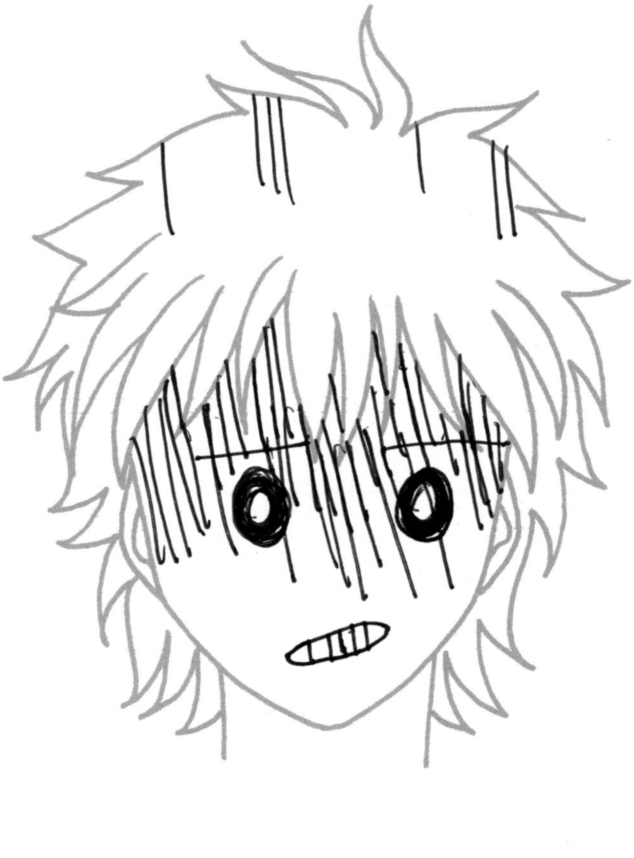

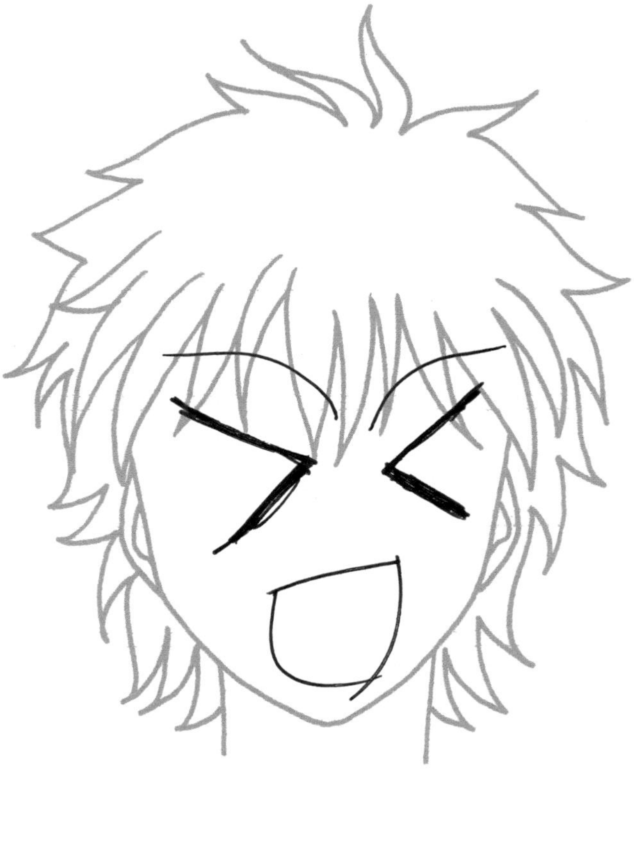

HAIR

Manga characters have very distinctive and brightly-colored hair. Their hair is noticeably of a different shape and style to their Western counterparts, and the varying colors used on manga characters' hair help differentiate each character from its peers. Hair is very expressive; many aspects of real-life hair – such as its flow, gravity, lift, and volume – are better represented in a three-dimensional style through adding details such as lines, shadows, and highlights.

PLACEMENT OF HAIR ON THE HEAD

It is important to put a few rules into practice when it comes to drawing manga-style hair to prevent the shape of the head from appearing incorrect and the hairstyle from looking amateur. Hair is often divided into chunky strands that taper off to a point. Try to draw with a flowing motion, and make sure the points all meet up to close the lines. All hair grows from a central point. Think about how your own hair grows, where your hair falls to one side, and where your part is, and try applying these to your characters for added realism.

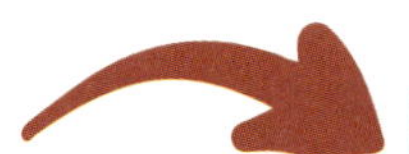

Look at these two examples. Make sure that the head is constructed correctly (see Head on pages 4, 5, and 8). The construction lines for the head are mapped out in light blue. The green lines depict an outer shell surrounding the characters' heads. This is where the bulk of the hair will rest on top of the head. Roughly speaking, there should always be an equal amount of space between the outline of the skull and the "boundary" of the hair.

The red lines mark out what you should try to avoid, namely:

- Drawing hair that is not proportional to the skull outline.
- Drawing hair too thickly or thinly on one side – this makes the skull look misshapen.
- Drawing spikes that are not fluid or not defined by points at their ends and roots.

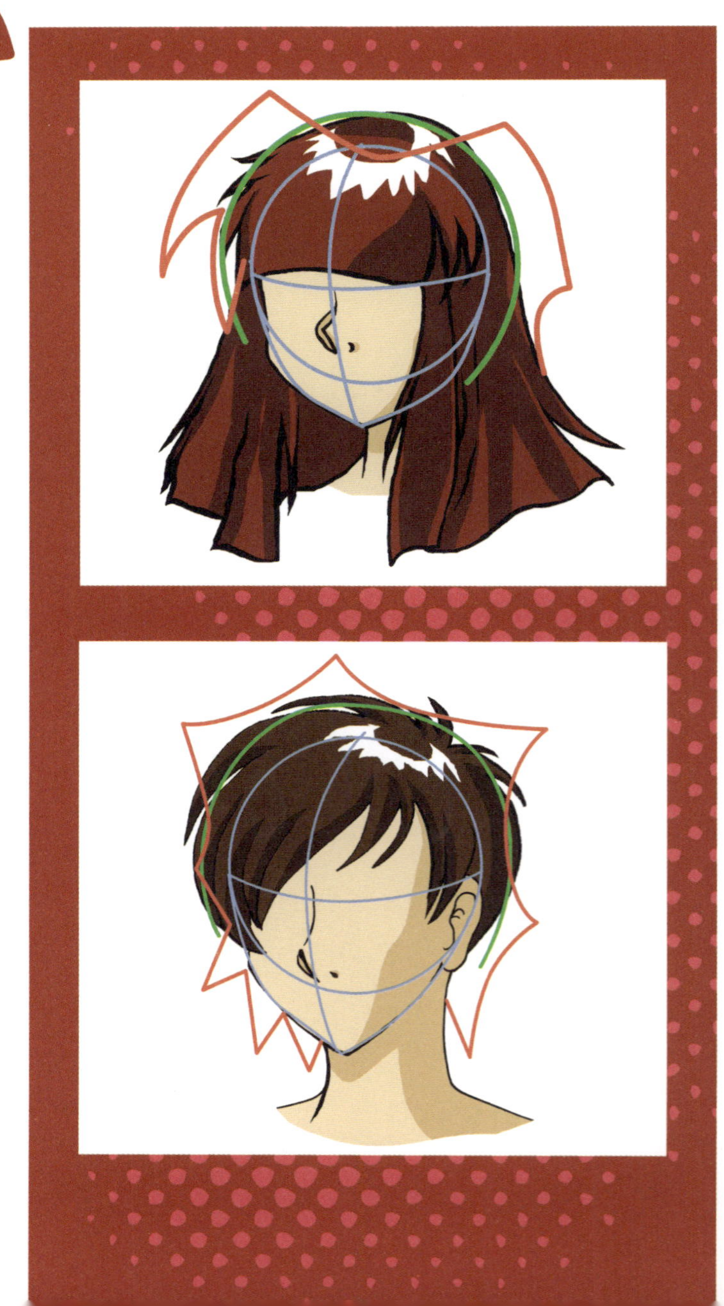

YOU TRY!

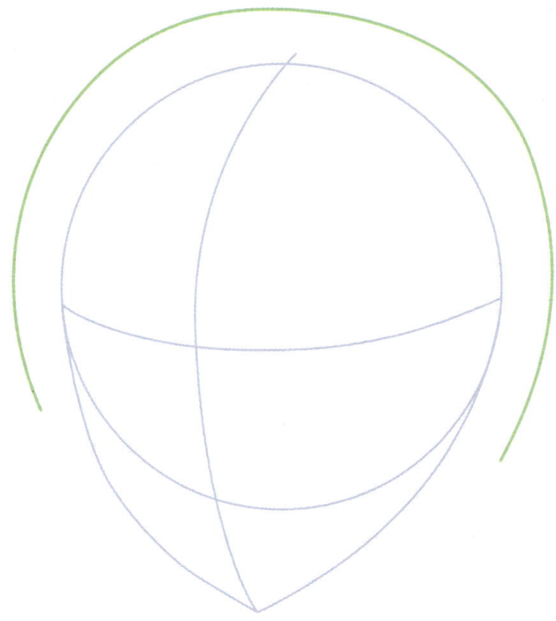

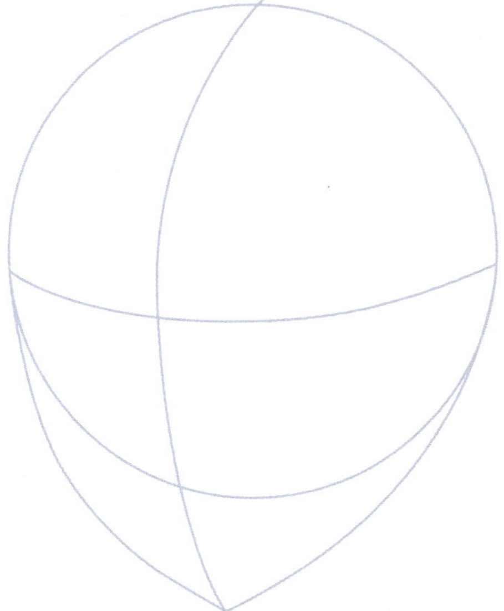

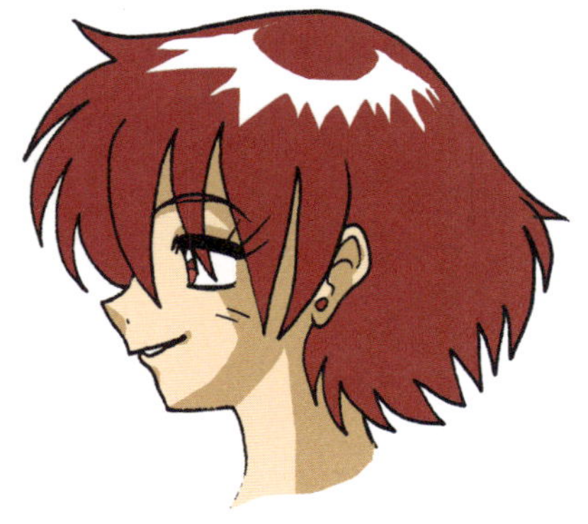
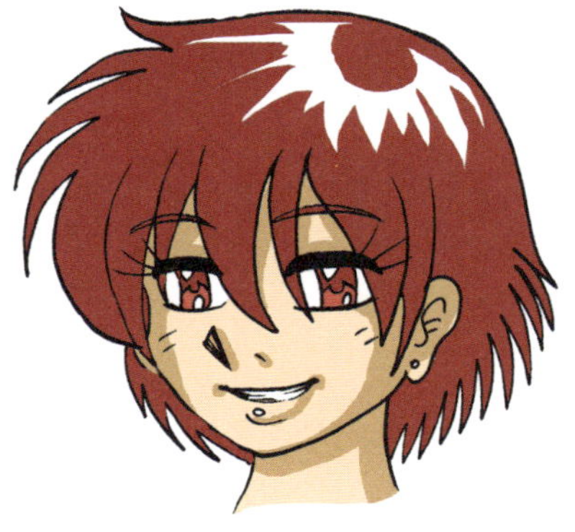
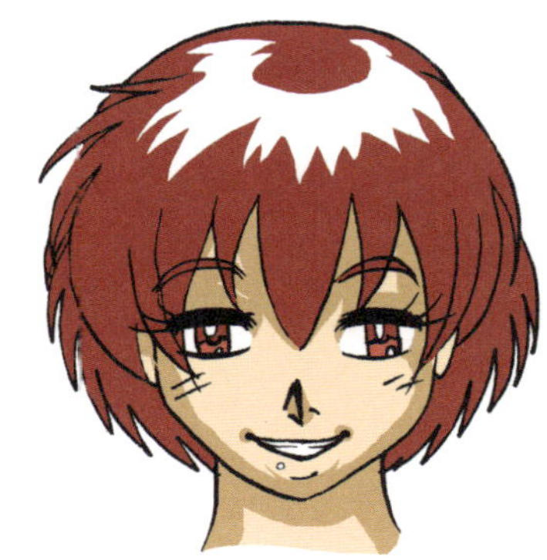

Here are several views of the same character so you can see how her hairstyle looks from various angles.

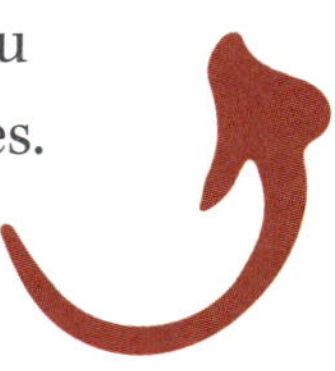

Would bangs make your character look serious? Is every strand of hair the same length? Does your character's hair flow outward in a triangular fashion or is it quite sleek and layered?

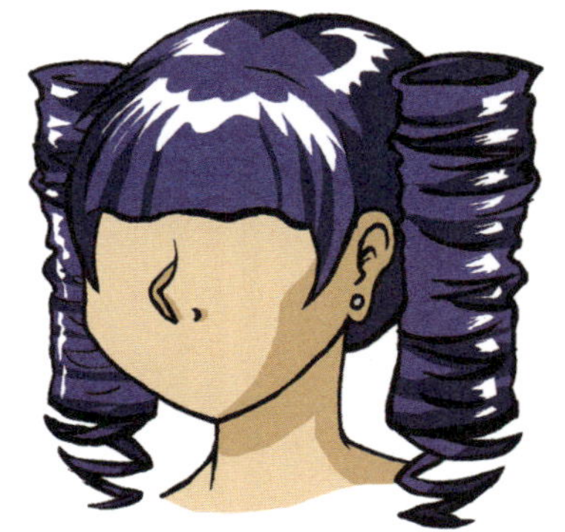
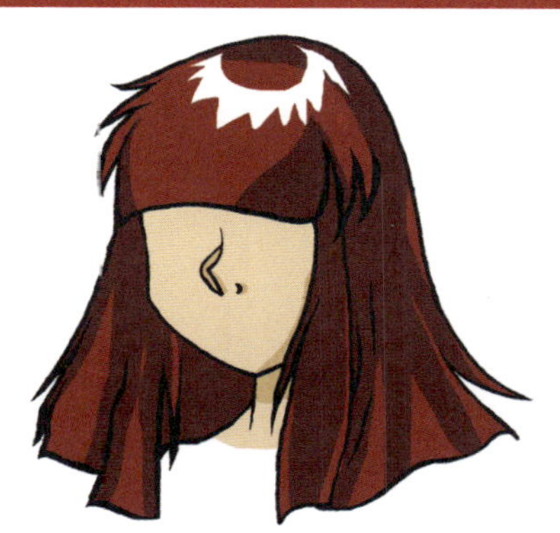

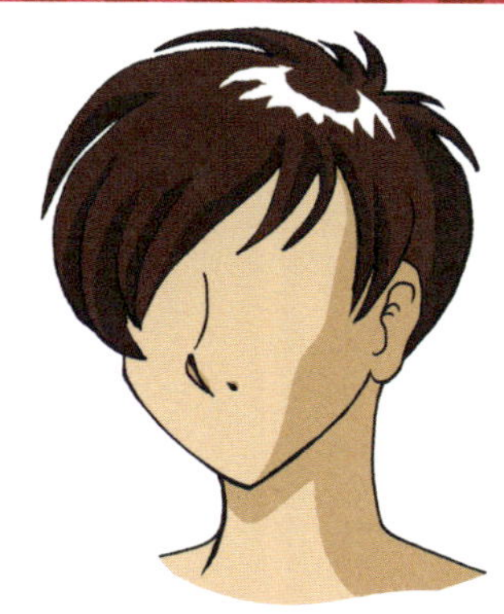
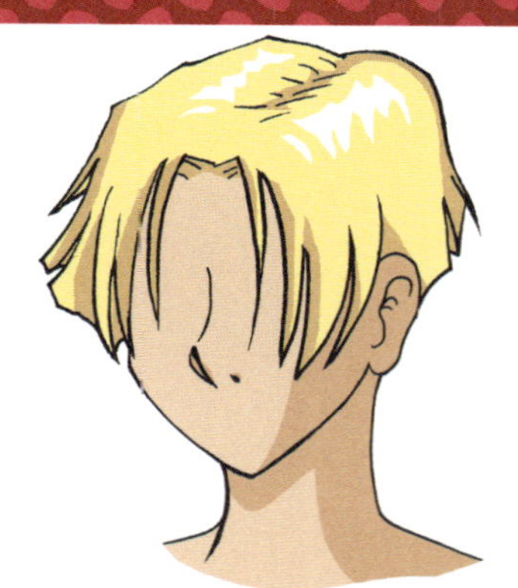

YOU TRY!

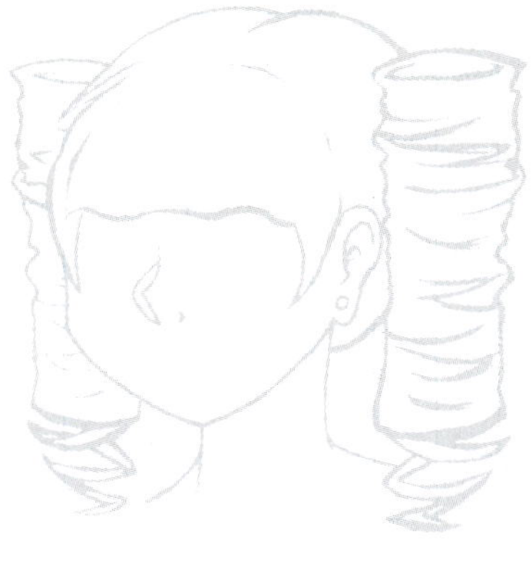

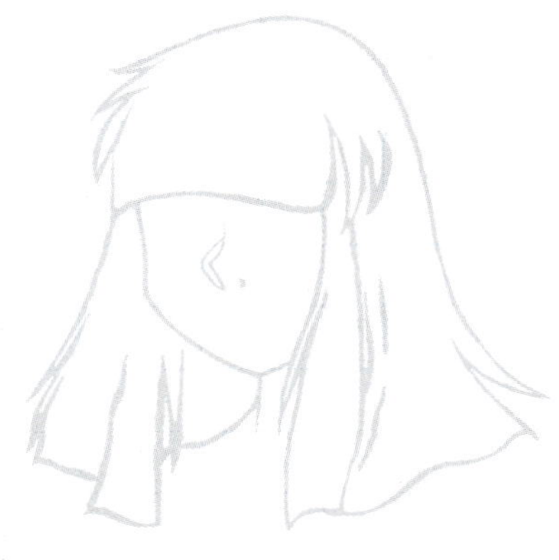

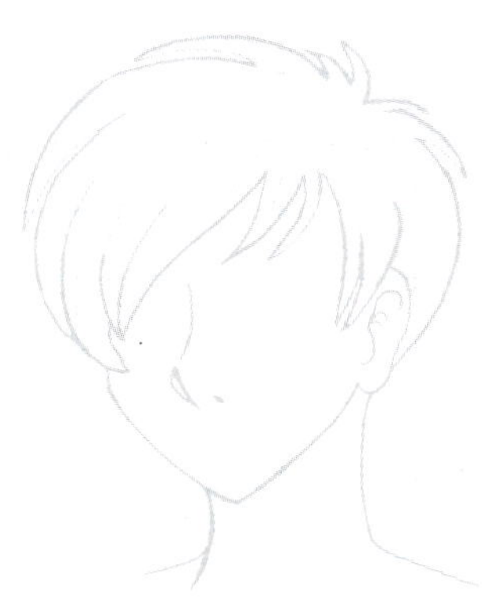

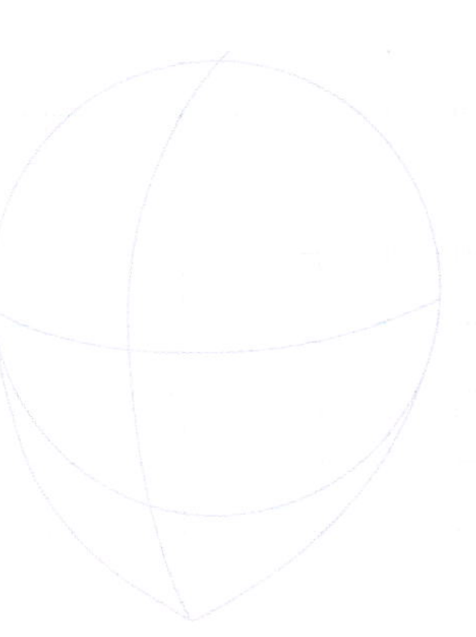

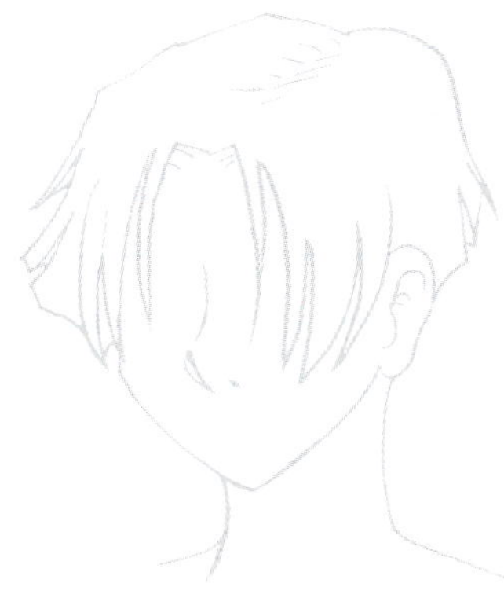

DIFFERENT STYLES FOR DIFFERENT CHARACTERS

Consistency of hair matters; if a character has thin hair, he or she could have a meeker personality. Thicker, chunkier hair suggests a more energetic nature. Sleek and straight suggests a fashion model, whereas messy hair is a sign of a more creative or active profession. The color of manga hair can be any shade of the rainbow! But your choice must say something about your character. If a character has bright pink hair, she may be a very energetic young girl. If a character has white hair, he may be spiritual or even very old! Make really modern manga characters by looking at what hairstyles are popular right now – try looking at hairstyle magazines.

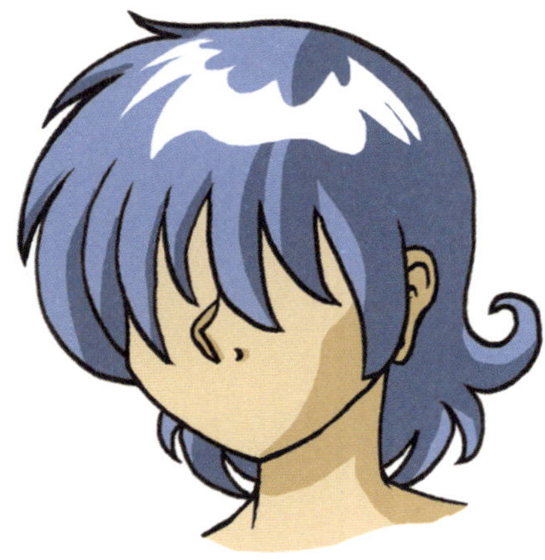

If your female character has short hair, she could be very sporty or tomboyish.

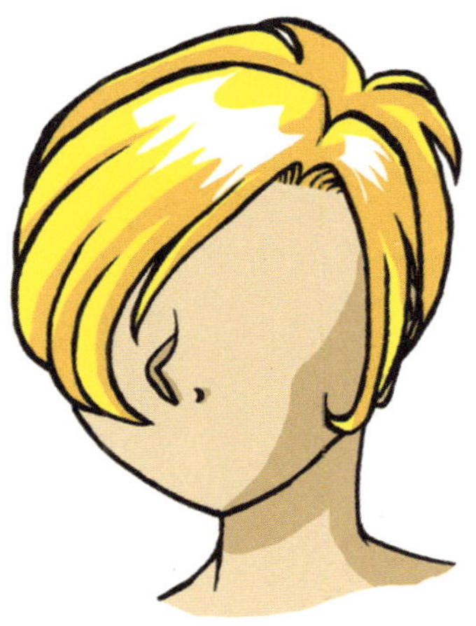

Here's another example of a short hairstyle that your character could have.

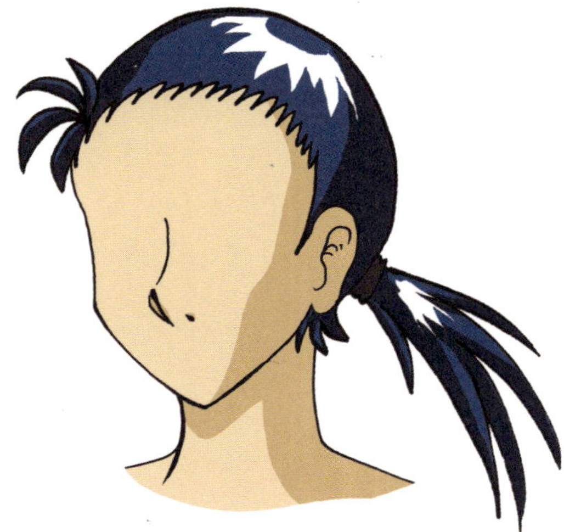

Hair that is closely shaven or very tightly tied back can be drawn closer to the skull.

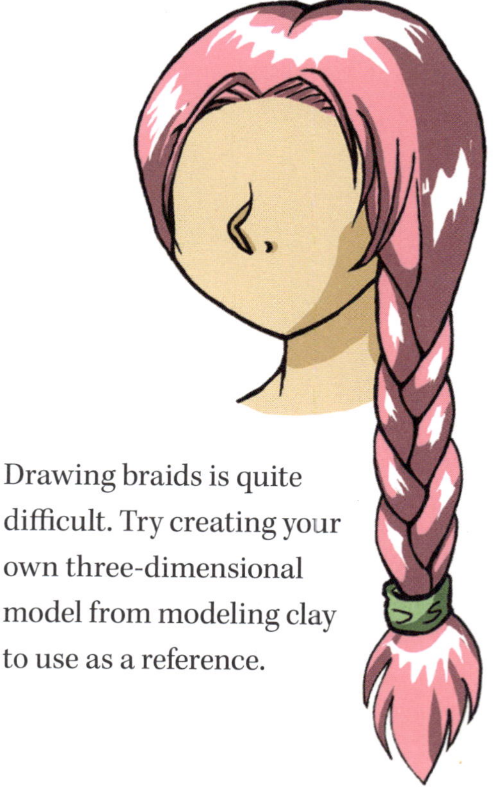

Drawing braids is quite difficult. Try creating your own three-dimensional model from modeling clay to use as a reference.

YOU TRY!

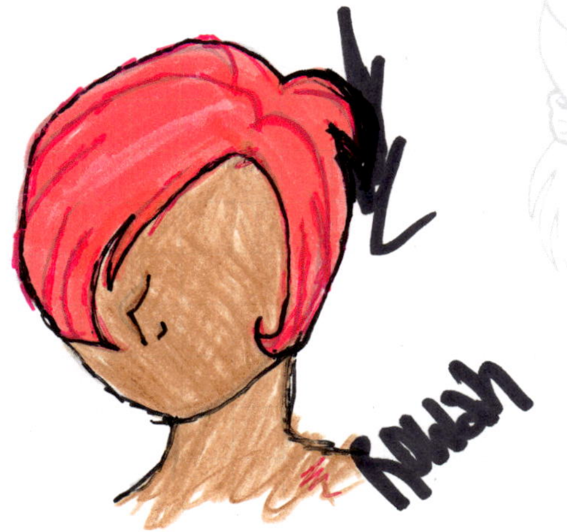

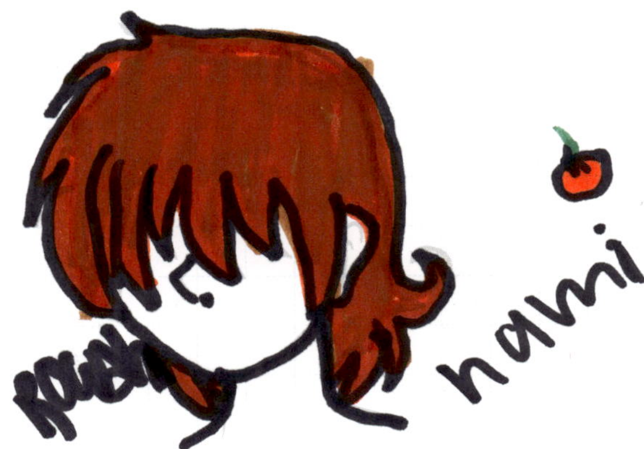

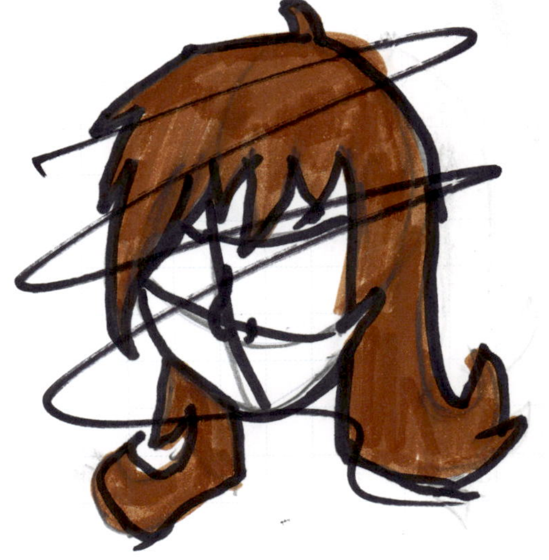

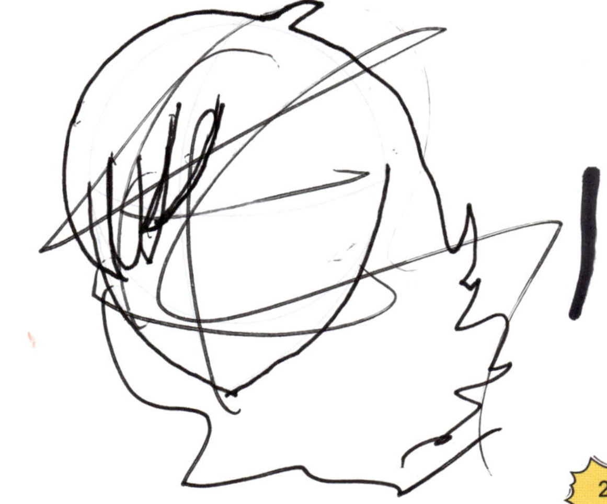

HANDS AND FEET

Drawing hands and feet may seem a little tricky at first, but it's important to depict hands and feet accurately. The good news is that this can be done quite simply.

HOW TO CONSTRUCT THE HAND

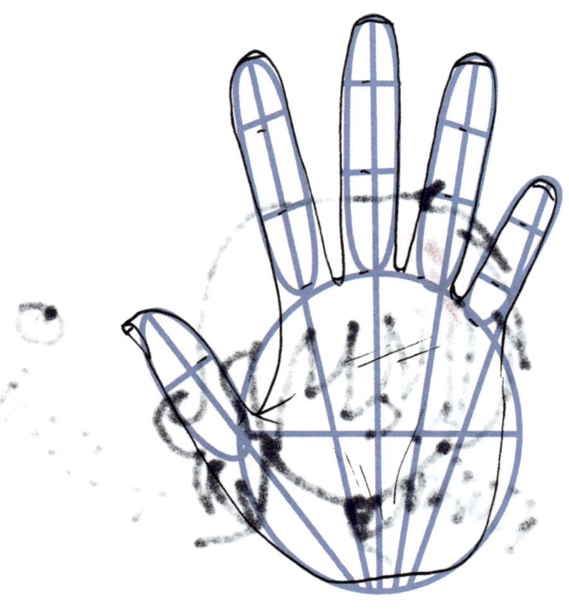

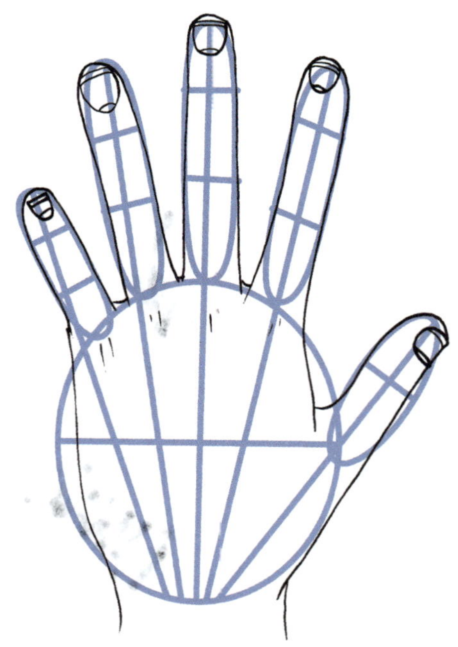

UNDERSIDE OF A LEFT HAND

Draw an oval, then draw a cross over it – this forms the palm of the hand. Extend the middle line upward as tall as the palm, then draw two guidelines on the right and on the left of the middle, all slightly splayed out, originating from the bottom of the palm.

The thumb is at a deeper angle and is a shorter, yet rounder, part of the anatomy.

Draw a long bubble that is almost the length of the oval. This will be the longest digit. Continue to draw long, oval bubbles, taking care to make sure the left digit is almost as high as the middle digit.

The third digit is slightly smaller than the second, and the little finger only reaches up to two-thirds of the length of the third digit.

Each finger is divided into three sections, the thumb into two. On a female, the tips of her fingernails may also be showing from this angle.

BACK VIEW OF A HAND

Follow the guidelines as detailed left, but the digits will be in reverse order when depicting the same hand. Take note of details such as knuckles and fingernails.

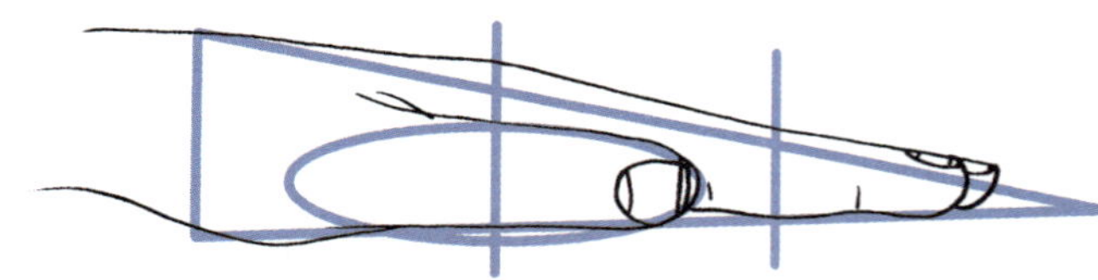

SIDE VIEW OF A HAND

Draw a thin and long triangle shape, with one edge angled higher than the other. Divide it into thirds. Draw a long balloon on the first division – this will be the thumb, and the division is the thumb knuckle. Note how the thumb joins the hand and the folds of skin that depict this.

YOU TRY!

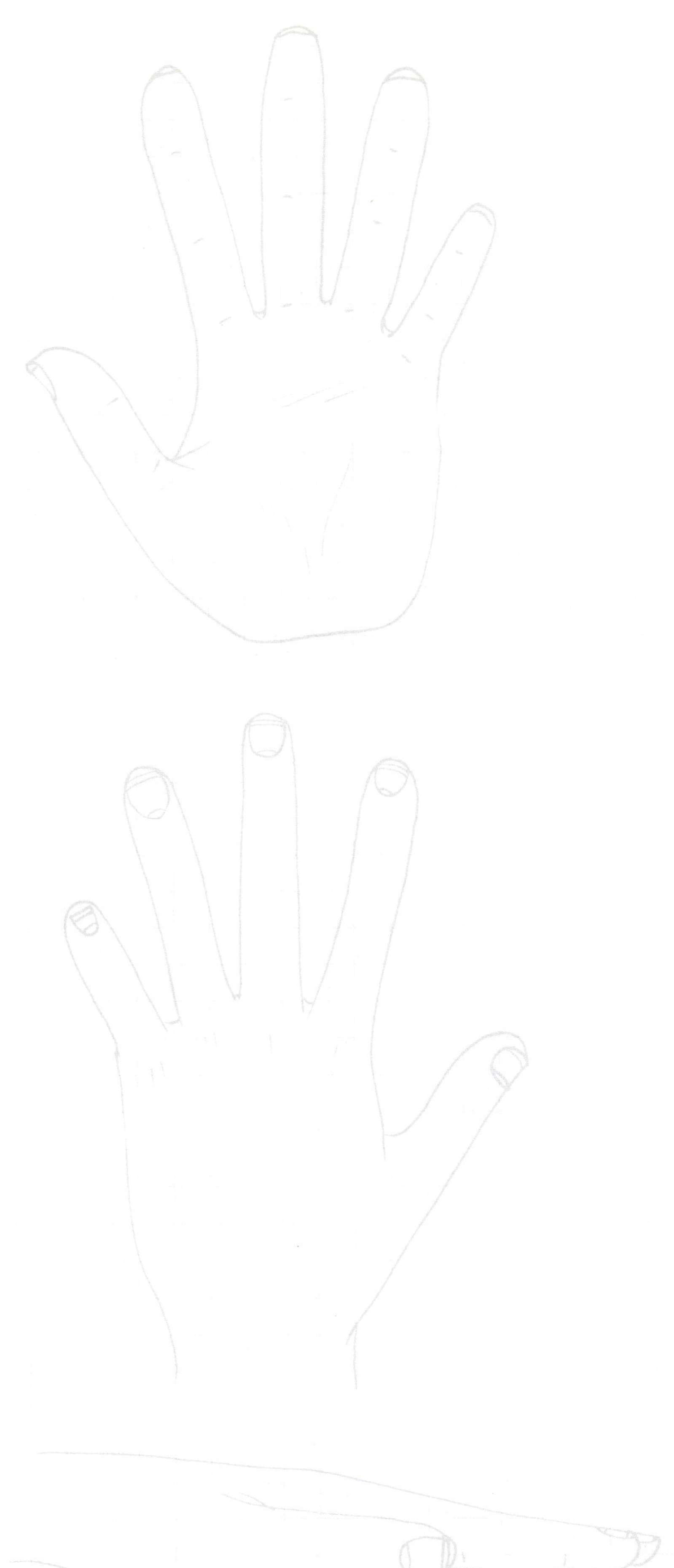

HOW TO CONSTRUCT THE FOOT

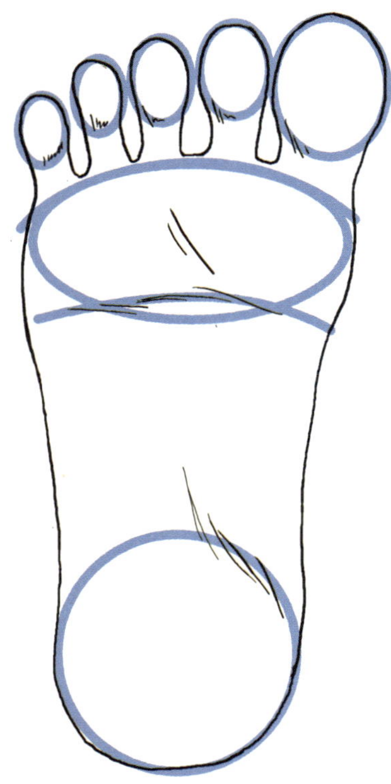

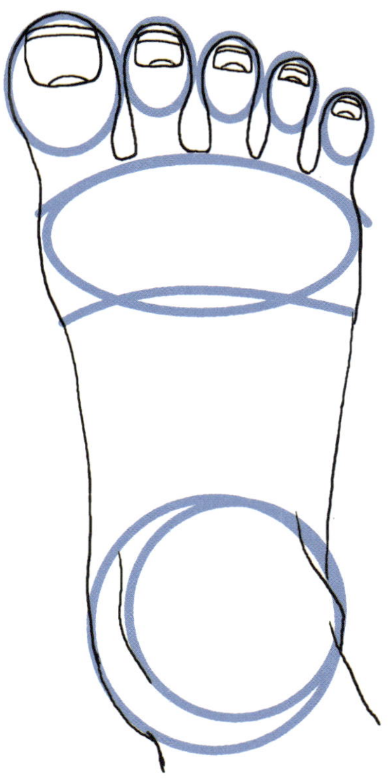

UNDERSIDE OF A RIGHT FOOT

Draw a circle and an oval that align vertically. Draw a curved line through the bottom of the oval. Join the edges of the circle and oval. Now draw five ovals hovering above the oval; these will be the toes. The big toe will be quite large in proportion to the others. The tallest toe will be the second toe, with the remaining three toes dropping in height as well as proportion. Join the toes to the foot with small inward-curving lines.

TOP OF A RIGHT FOOT

Follow the guidelines as detailed left, but the digits will be in reverse order. Draw toenails at the very tips of the toes, with the large toe's nail being much bigger than the other toes' nails. The ankle is slightly visible, so draw another circle above the heel and slightly to the outside of the foot.

SIDE VIEW OF A FOOT

Draw three circles – medium for ankle, large for heel, and small for ball of the foot. Draw a smaller oval to depict the big toe. Join these circles with inward-curving lines and create the bottom of the character's leg from the large circle.

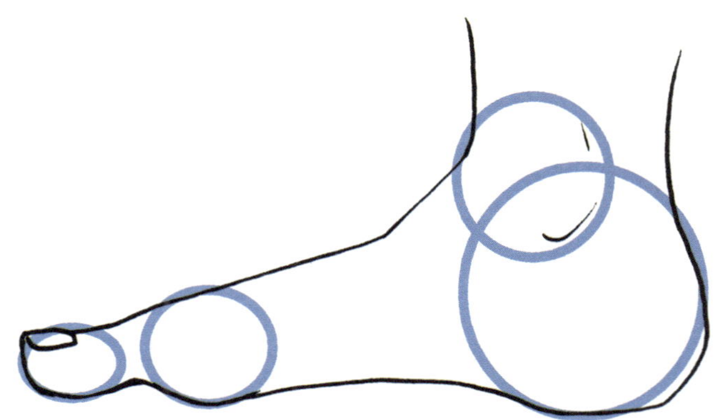

YOU TRY!

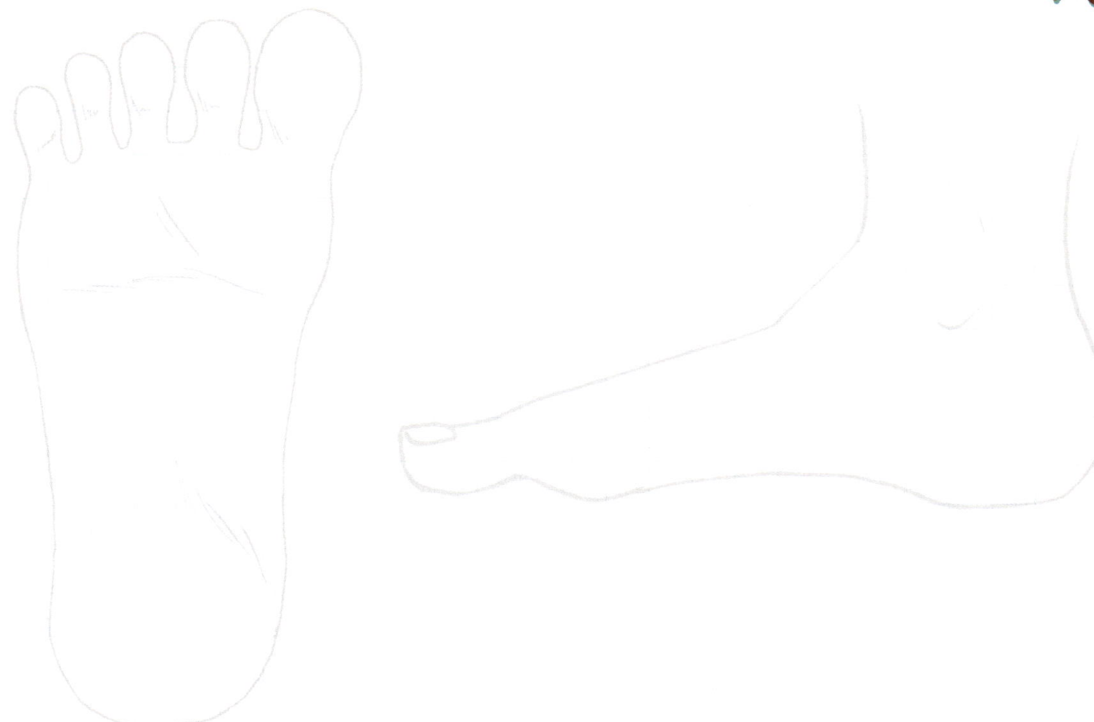

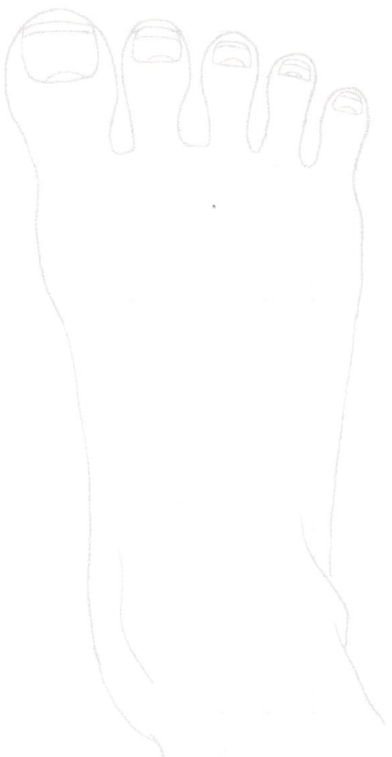

ADAPTING TO DIFFERENT CHARACTERS

Some aspects of these drawings will have to be changed to suit your character, depending on their gender, their size, their age, and so on.

Adult hands and feet are slightly more detailed to show signs of age and wisdom. Elderly characters will have very withered hands.

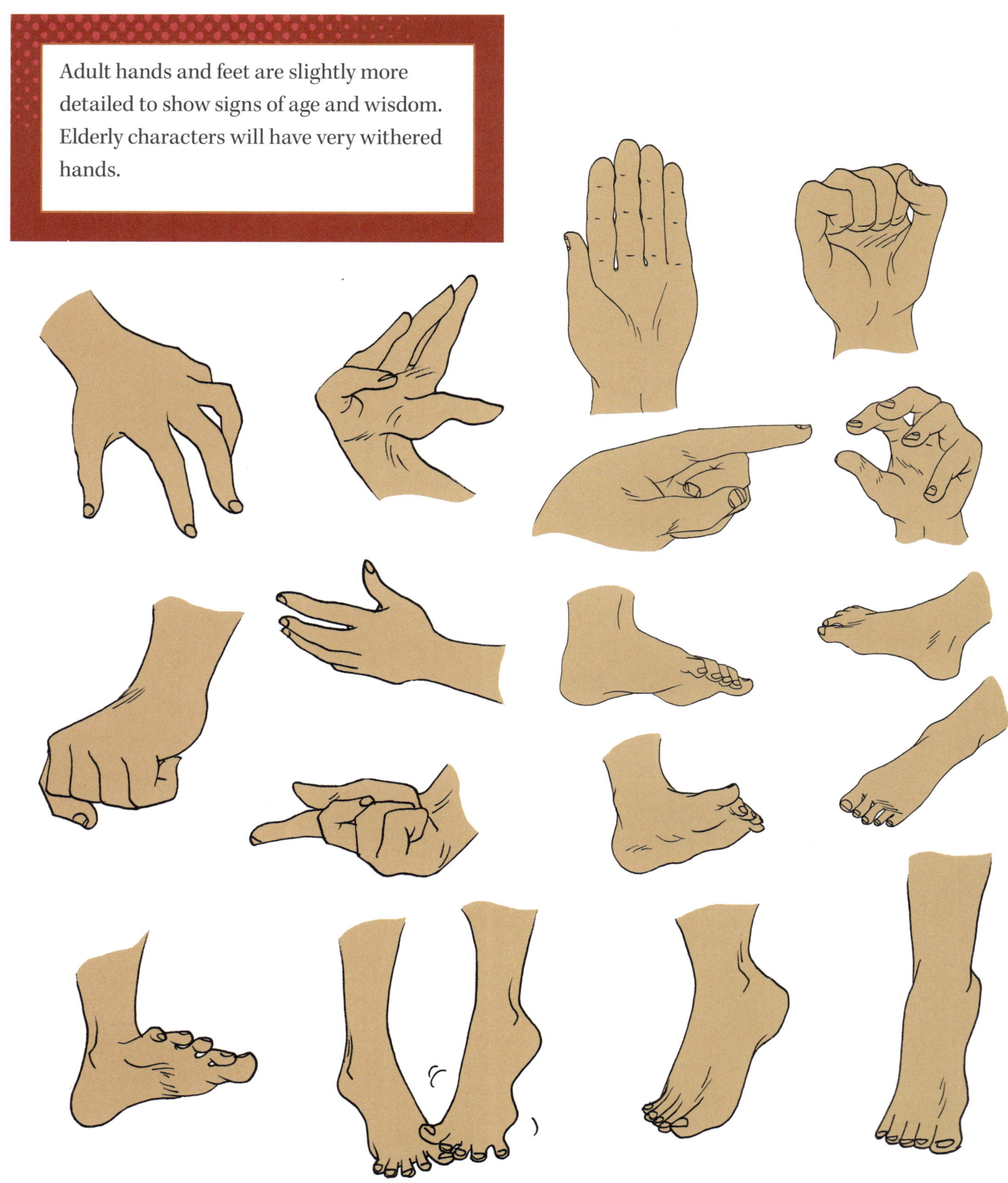

YOU TRY!

Teenagers' hands and feet can be depicted simply, to portray beauty and youthfulness.

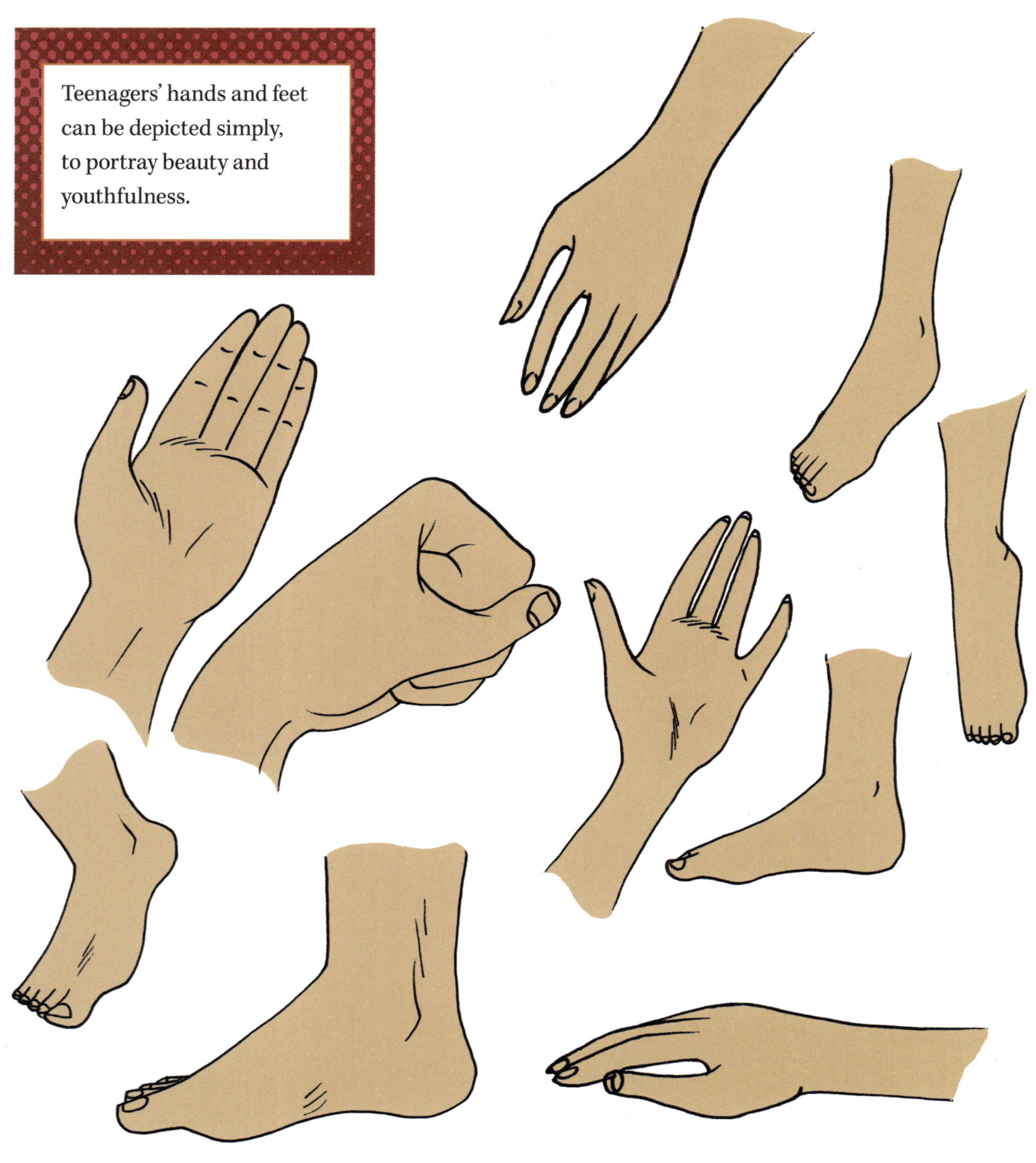

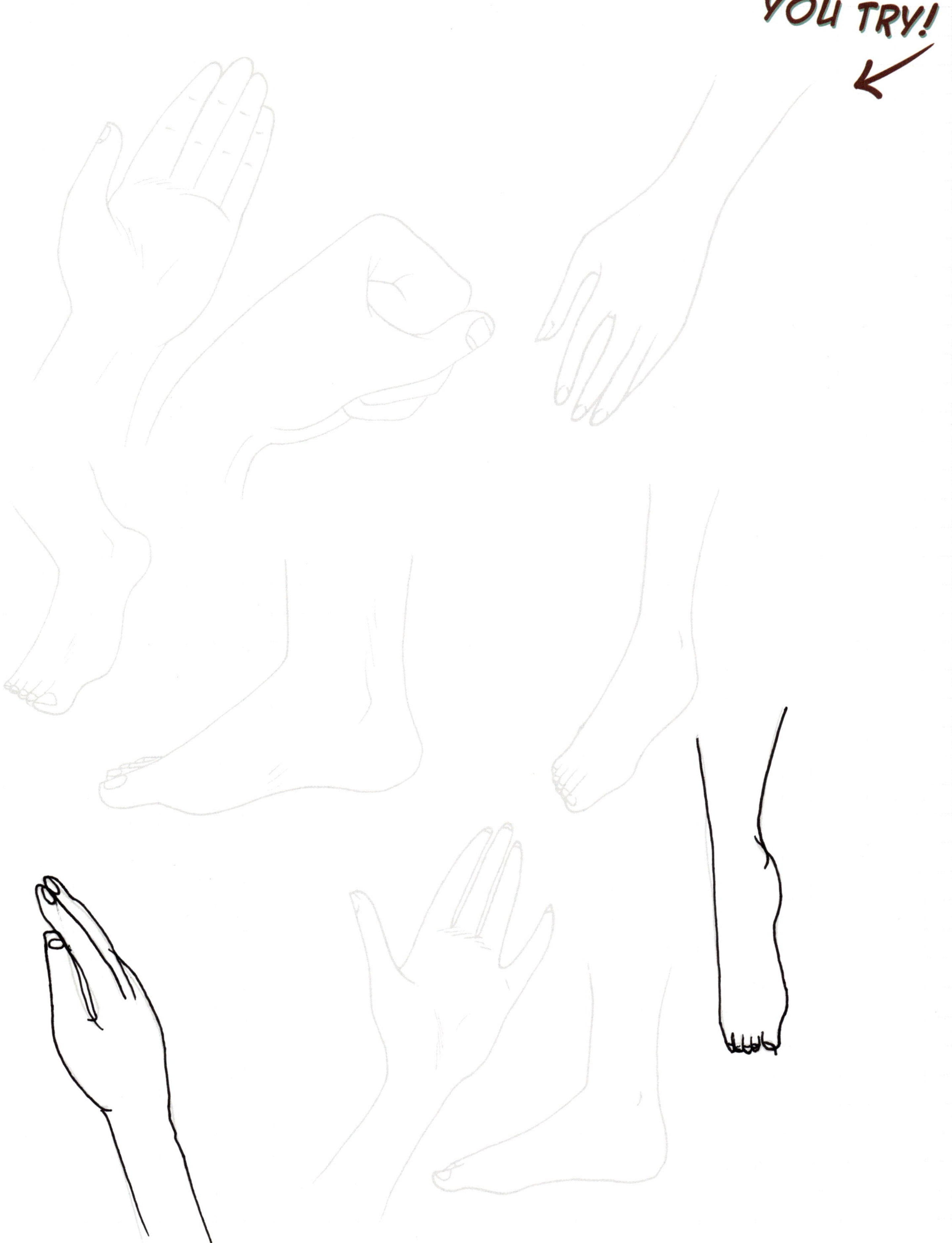
YOU TRY!

Children's hands and feet have cuter, stubbier proportions.

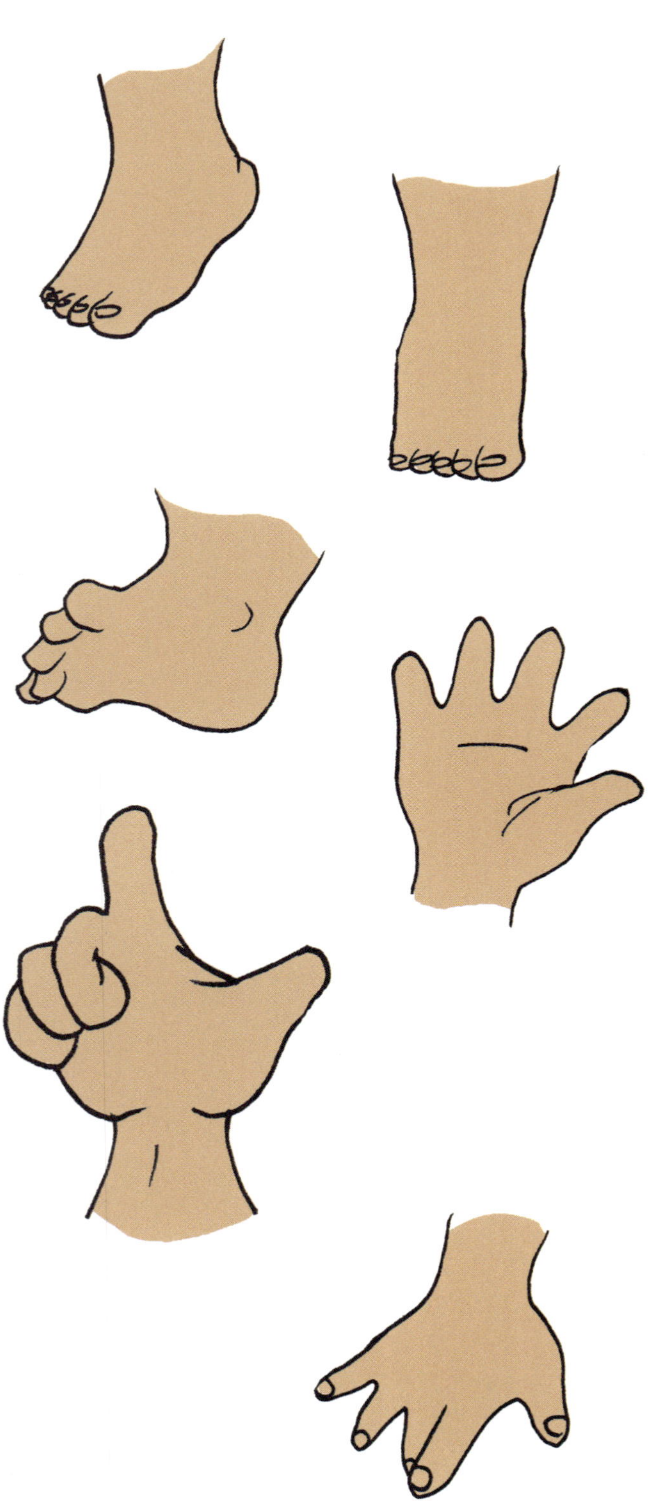

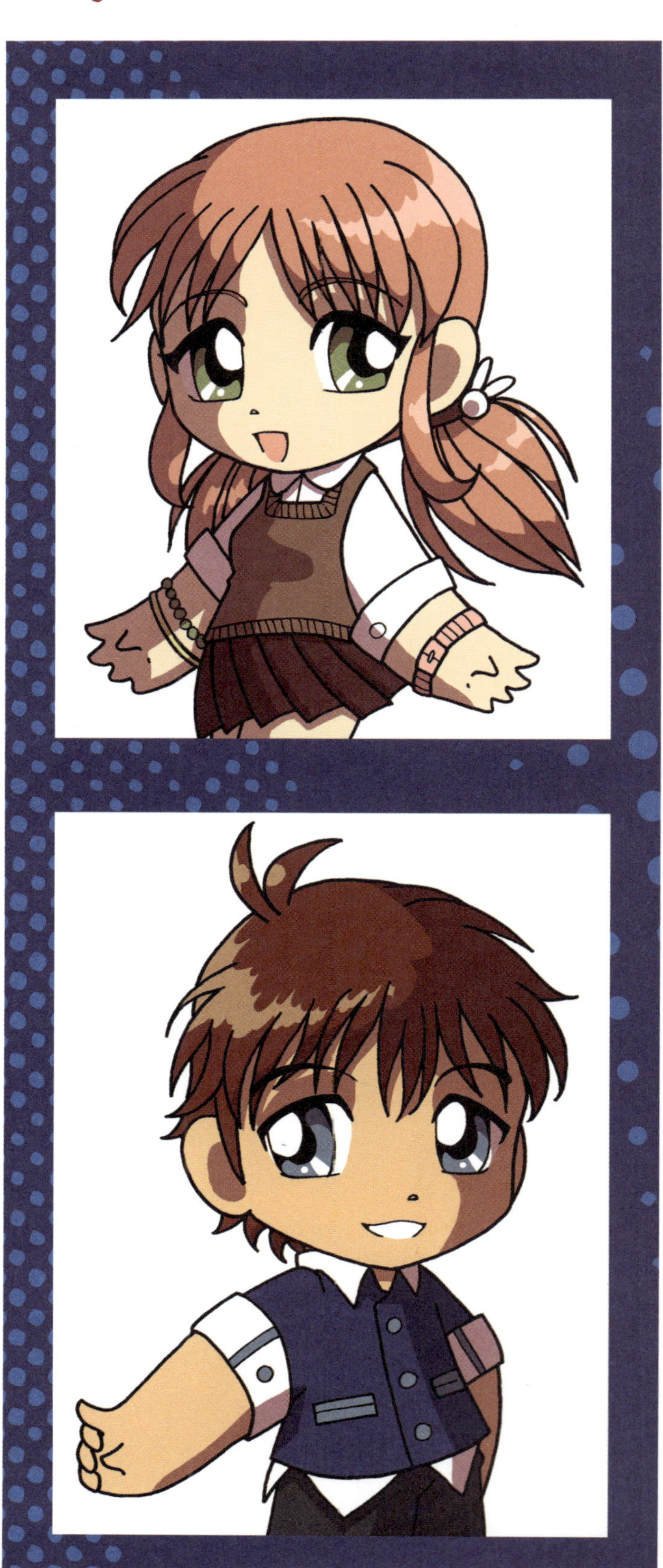

YOU TRY!

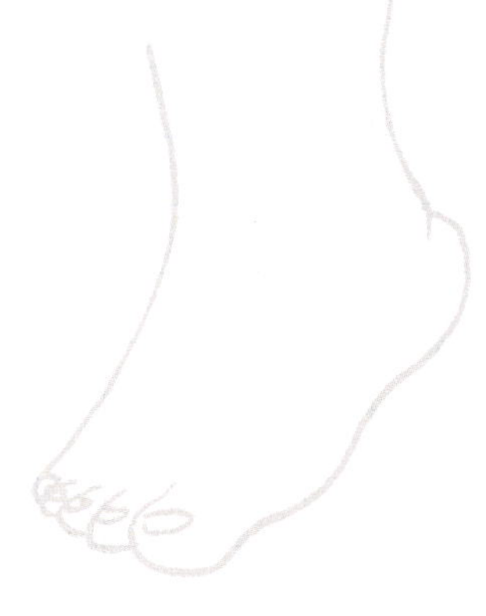

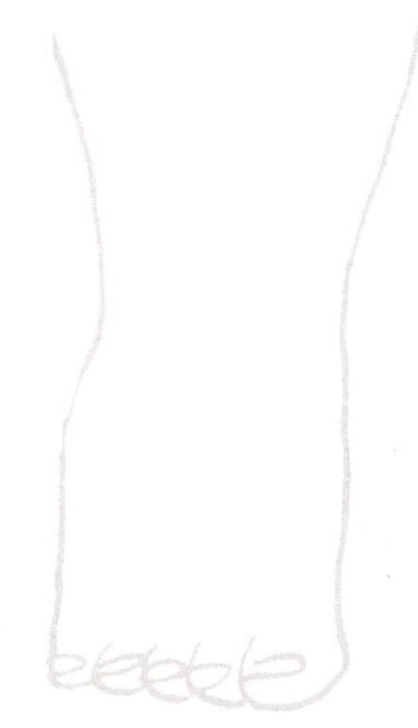

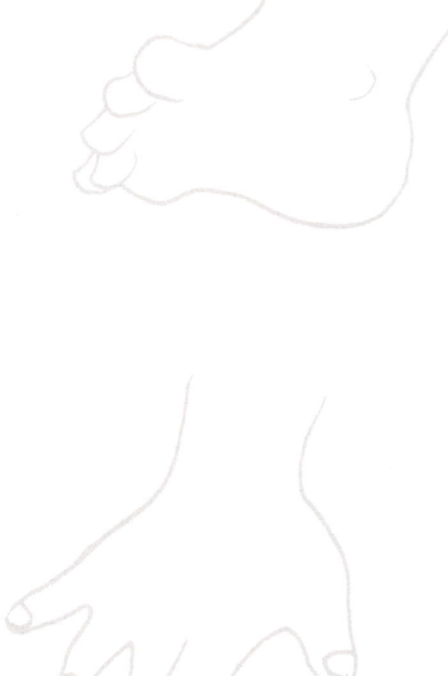

FIGURES AND PROPORTION

All of these studies are of the same male and female character shown at different ages. The ratios described are relative to the head length and width of the character, so this information is easily transferable to whatever size you wish to draw your characters. These simple ratios are a rough guide to real proportions. To help you with your observations, equally spaced lines (roughly one head length apart) have been drawn behind the characters.

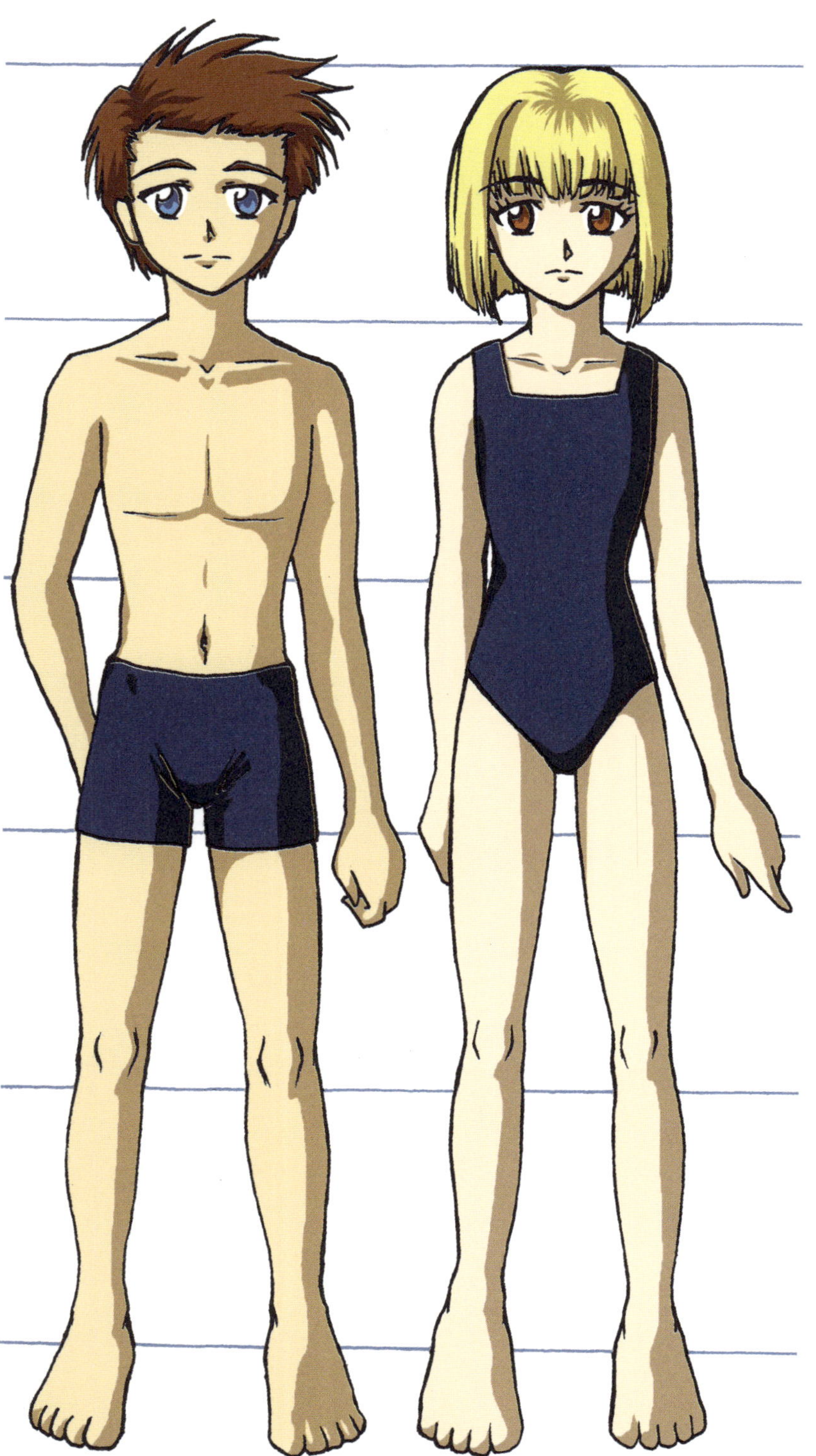

CHILDREN

These are children in the range of seven to twelve years of age, the most popular age group of children depicted in anime and manga.

- **Height: 4–5 head lengths**
- **Shoulder width: 2 head widths and under**
- **Torso length: 2 head lengths**
- **Waist width: 1–2 head widths**
- **Hip width: 1.5 head widths**
- **Leg length: 2–3 head lengths**

Children do not have greatly defined muscle tone. Their frames are not fully developed, so their shoulders are still quite narrow. Their faces are short and round, with large eyes. Note that there are already differences between the sexes – boys have longer torsos and a straight section at their waists; girls have higher, slightly pinched-in waists.

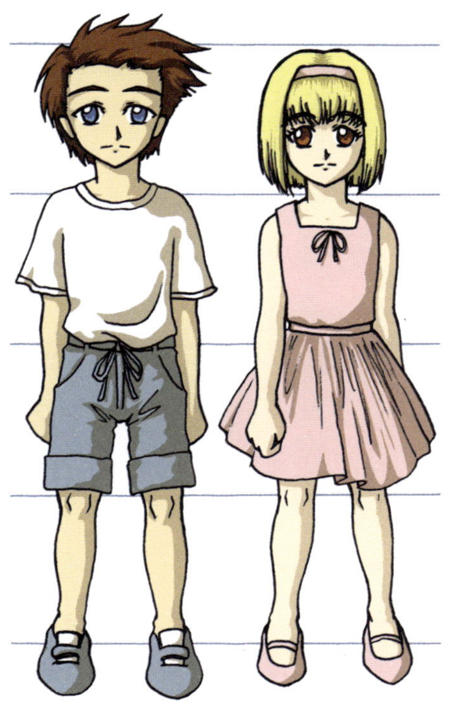

To draw children under seven years of age, bring their height down to 3–4 head lengths. Make their cheeks and limbs more chubby and rounded.

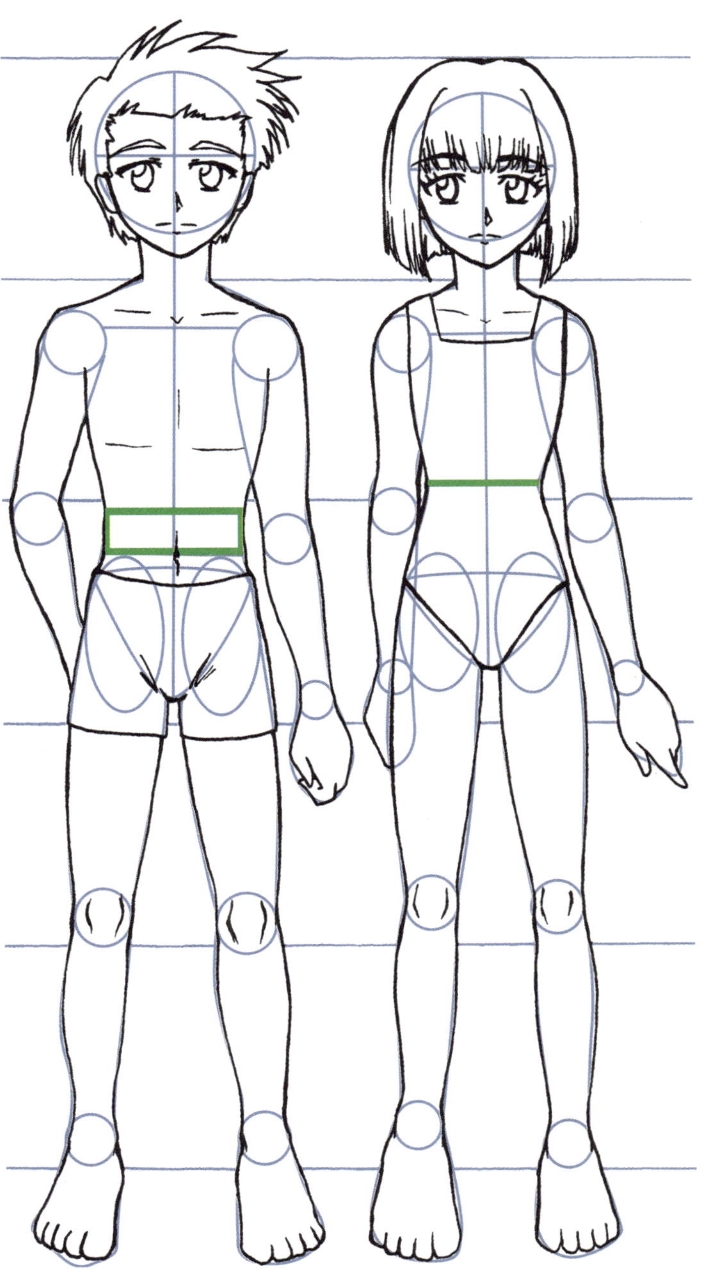

Once you have marked out the correct ratios with some rough lines, to build up the bulk of the body you may find it useful to use circles and ovals to remind you of the mechanics of the body and how joints work. Note the following observations:

- **The elbow joint is situated at waist level.**
- **The hand should reach halfway down the thigh.**
- **There is a small gap between the thighs where they join to the hips.**
- **A male waistline is a cylindrical band with straight sides.**
- **A female waistline is pinched in. The narrowest section can be defined by a simple line.**

YOU TRY!

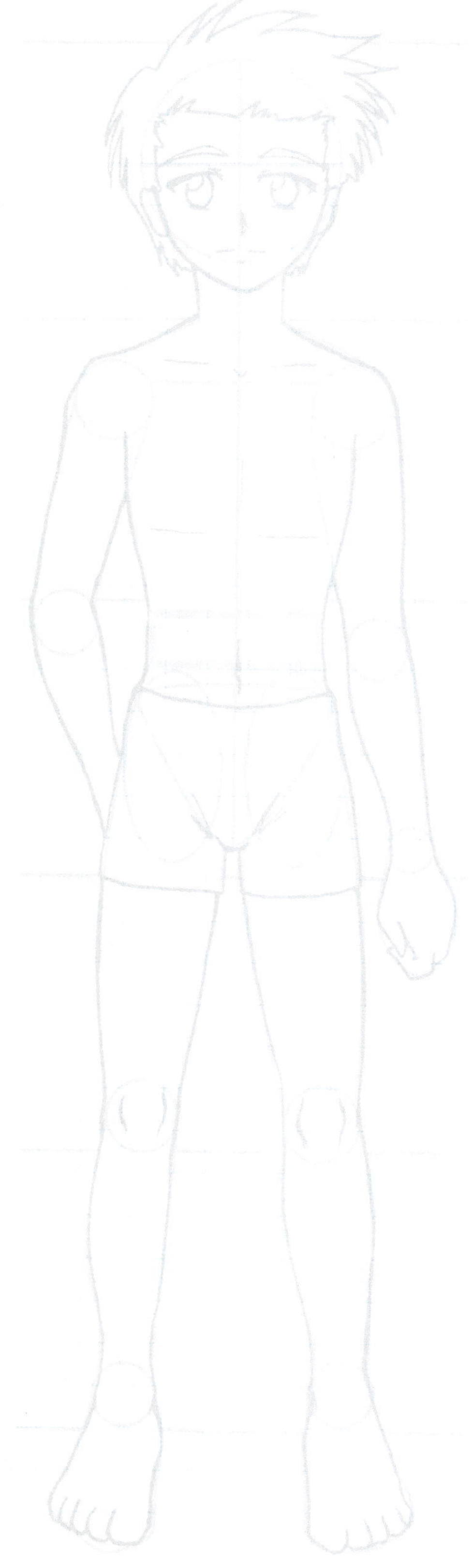

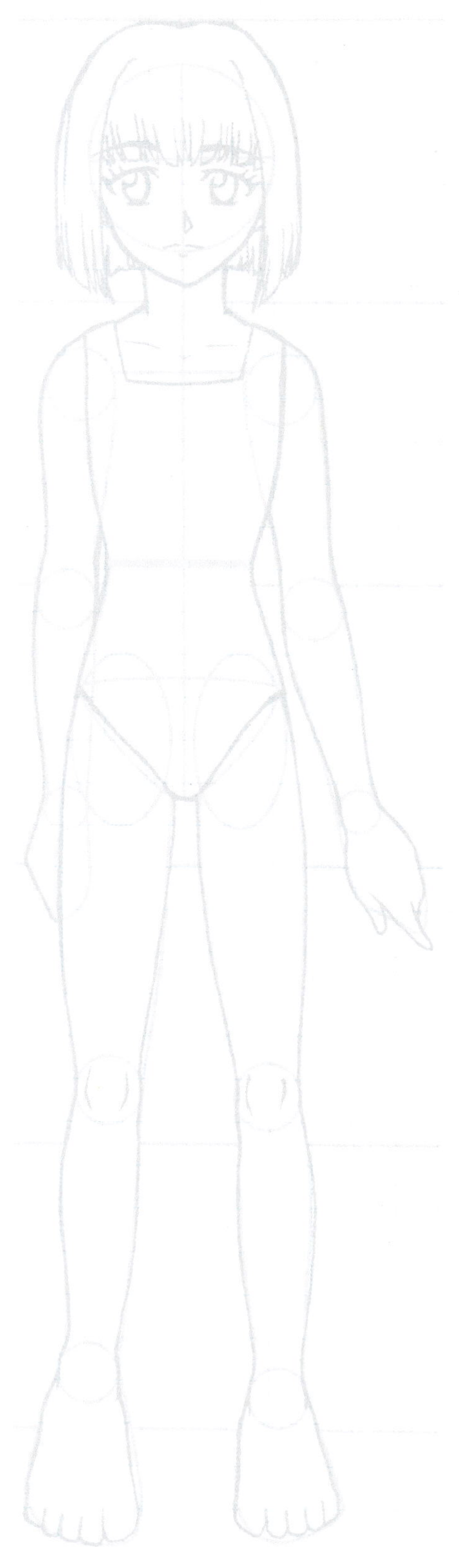

YOU TRY!

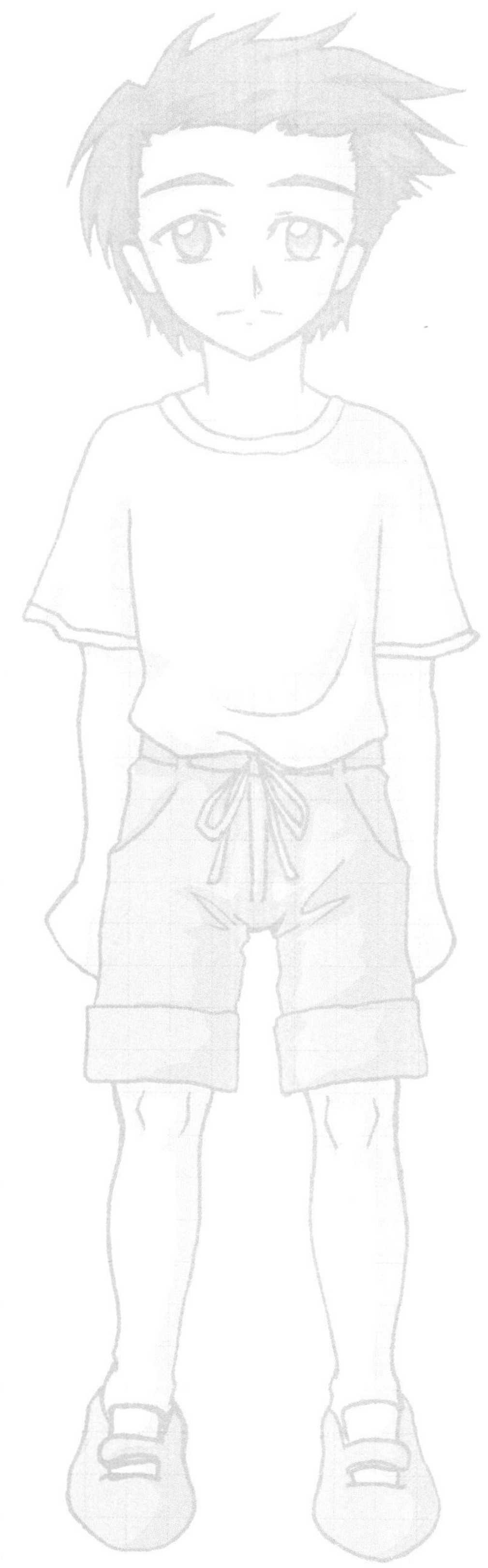

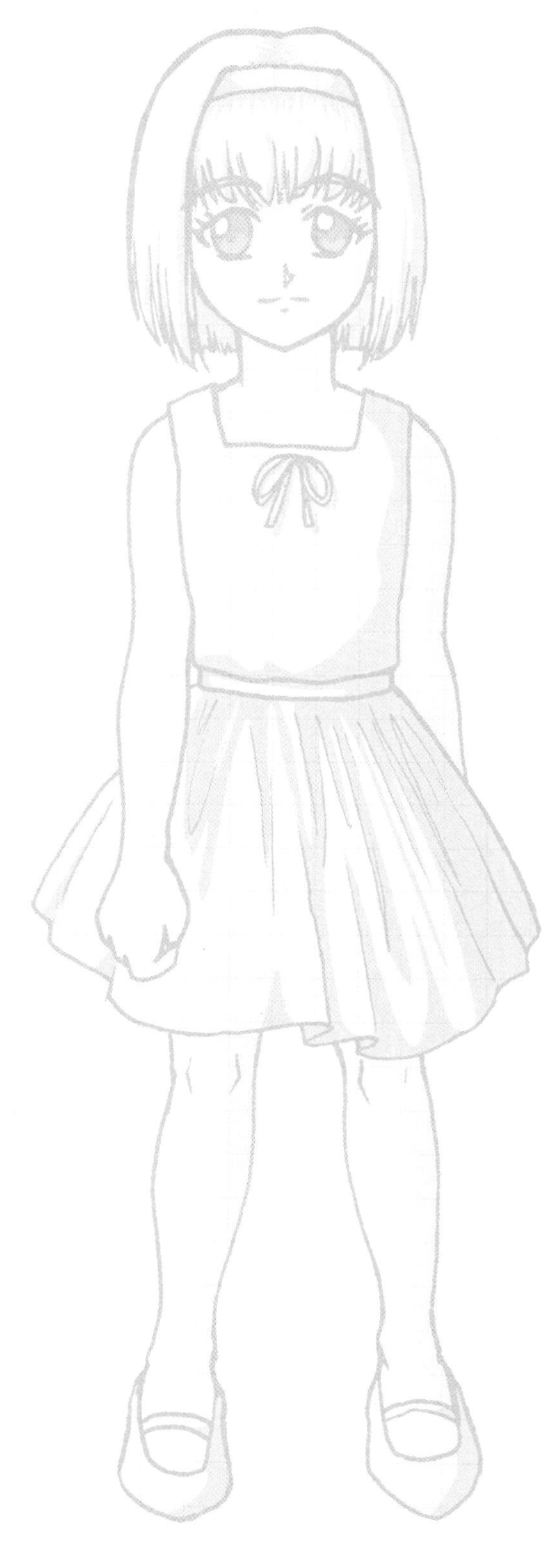

TEENAGERS

The characters are now between thirteen and seventeen years old. This age group can vary greatly in proportion set across different manga stories. This example could even be used for petite adults.

- **Height: 5–6 head lengths**
- **Shoulder width: 2 head widths**
- **Torso length: 2–3 head lengths**
- **Waist width: 1–2 head widths**
- **Hip width: 1.5 head widths**
- **Leg length: 3 head lengths**

Although this is dependent on whether your characters go through a gangly or chubby adolescence, in general more muscle and bone structure should be visible. This applies to both the face and figure. For males, shoulders are broader and the ribcage wider, which helps define the straight waist. For females, the hips are a little wider and breasts start to show.

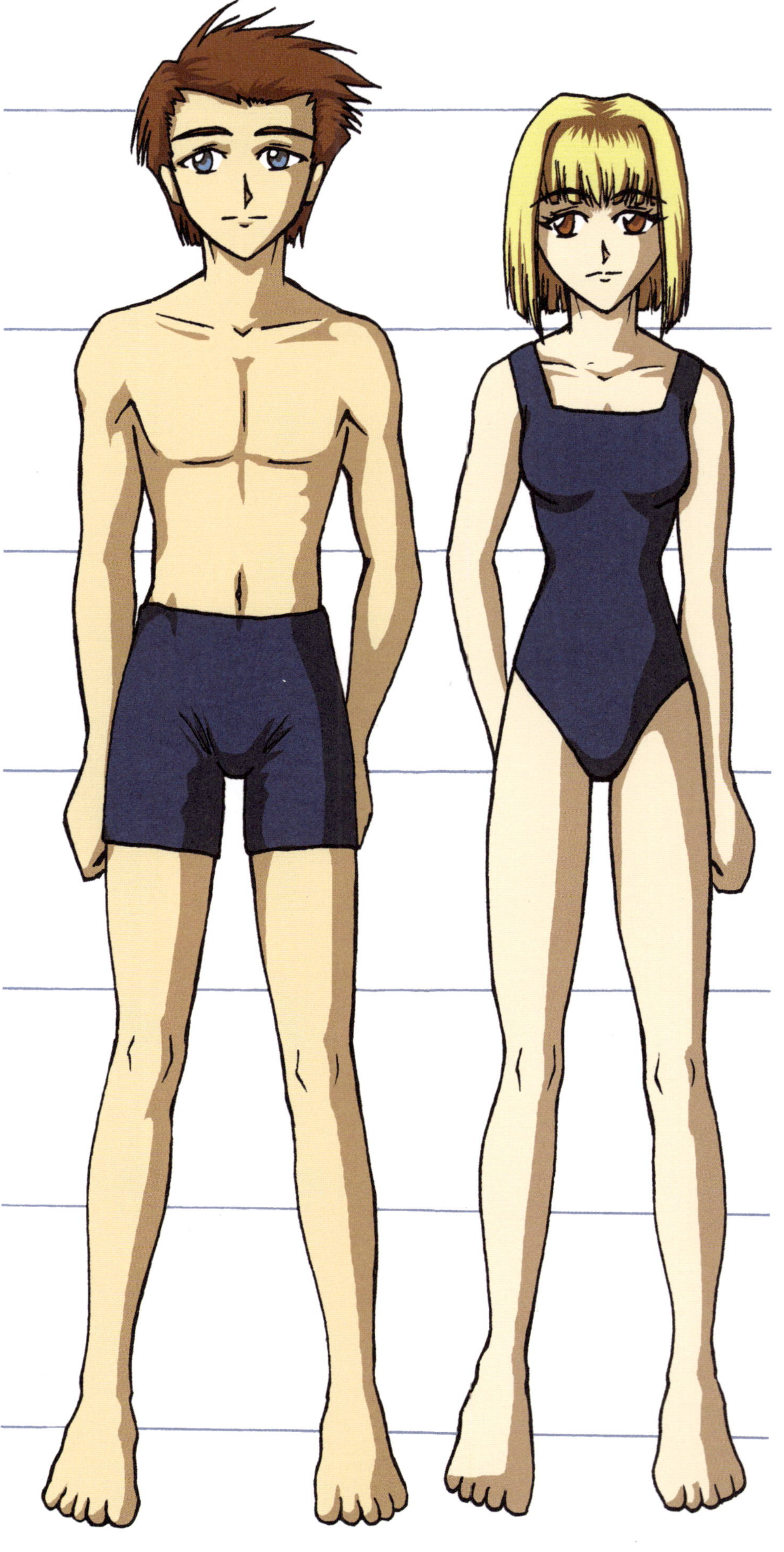

YOU TRY!

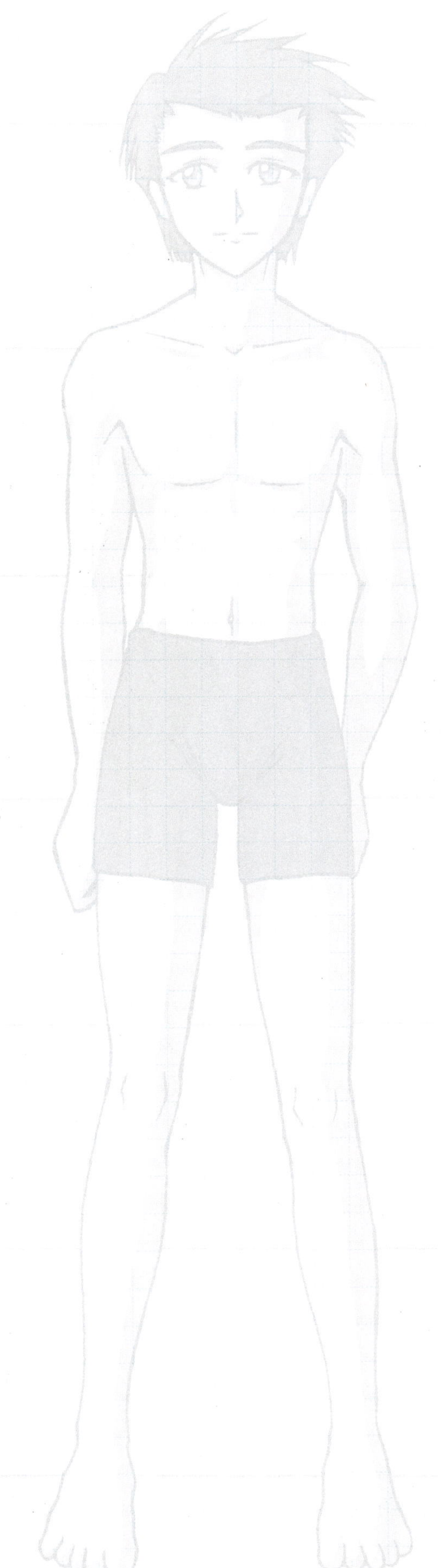

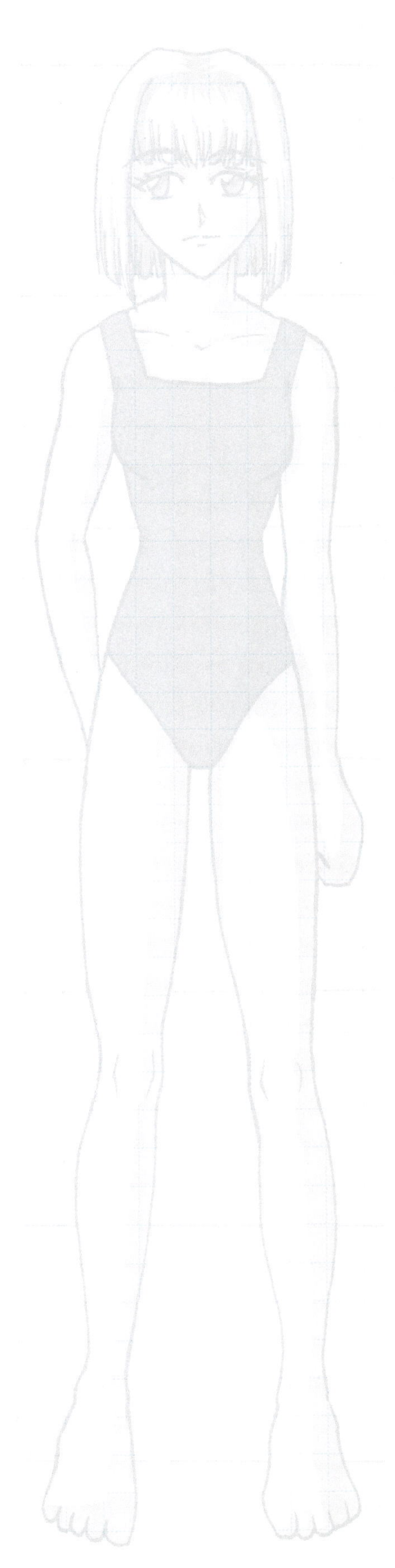

ADULTS

These are fully developed adults in their twenties to thirties. In this example the adults are quite tall and slim.

- **Height: 7–8 head lengths**
- **Shoulder width: 2–3 head widths**
- **Torso length: 2–3 head lengths**
- **Waist width: 1–2 head widths**
- **Hip width: 1.5–3 head widths**
- **Leg length: 4 head lengths**

Full muscle and bone structure have developed. Males have broad shoulders. The straight section of the waist is plainly visible now, leading into fairly slim hips, only slightly wider than the waist. Females have medium-width shoulders, full breasts, curving into a pinched-in waist, then widening into large hips, roughly the same width as the shoulders. Relatively speaking, men will have longer torsos and women will have longer legs.

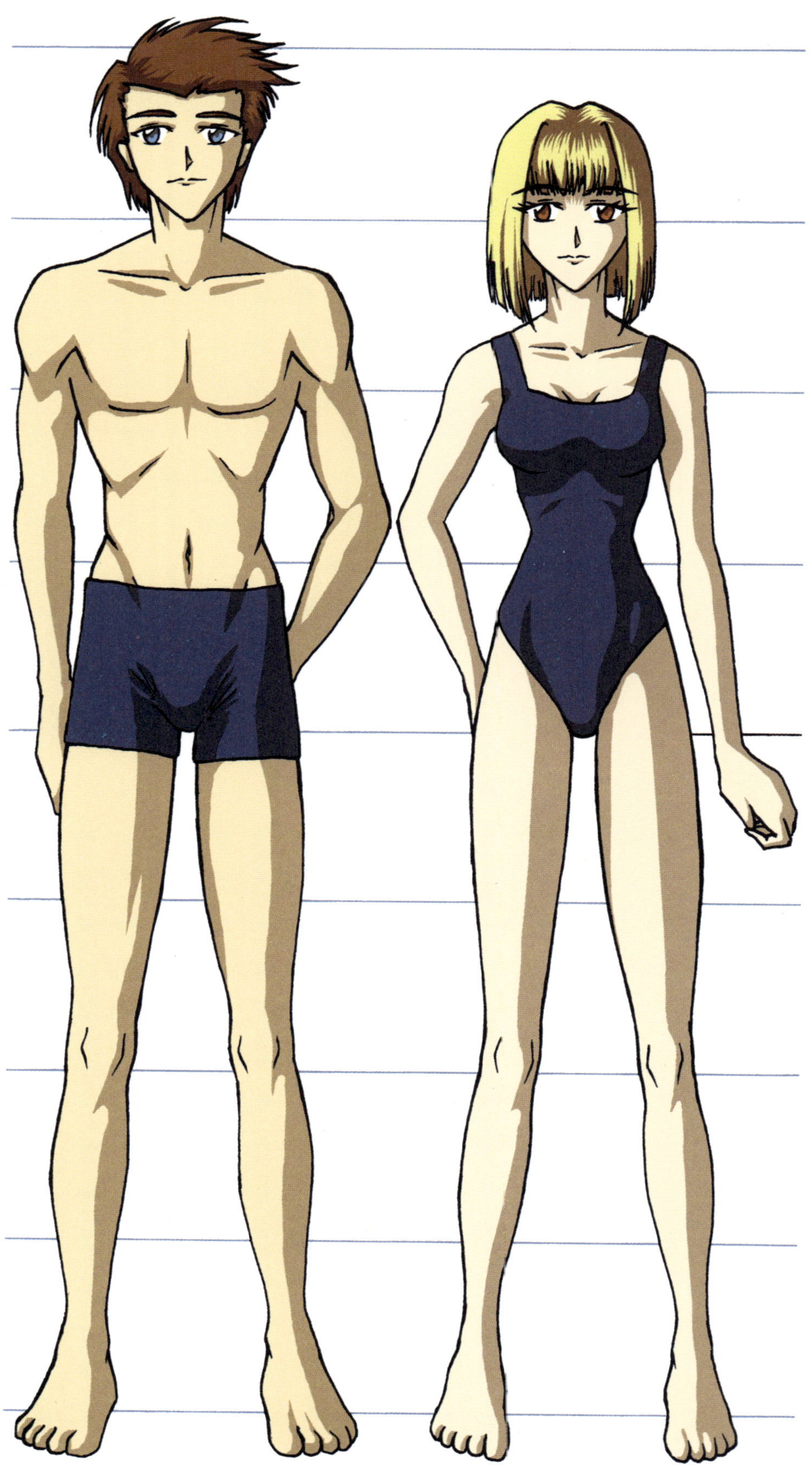

YOU TRY!

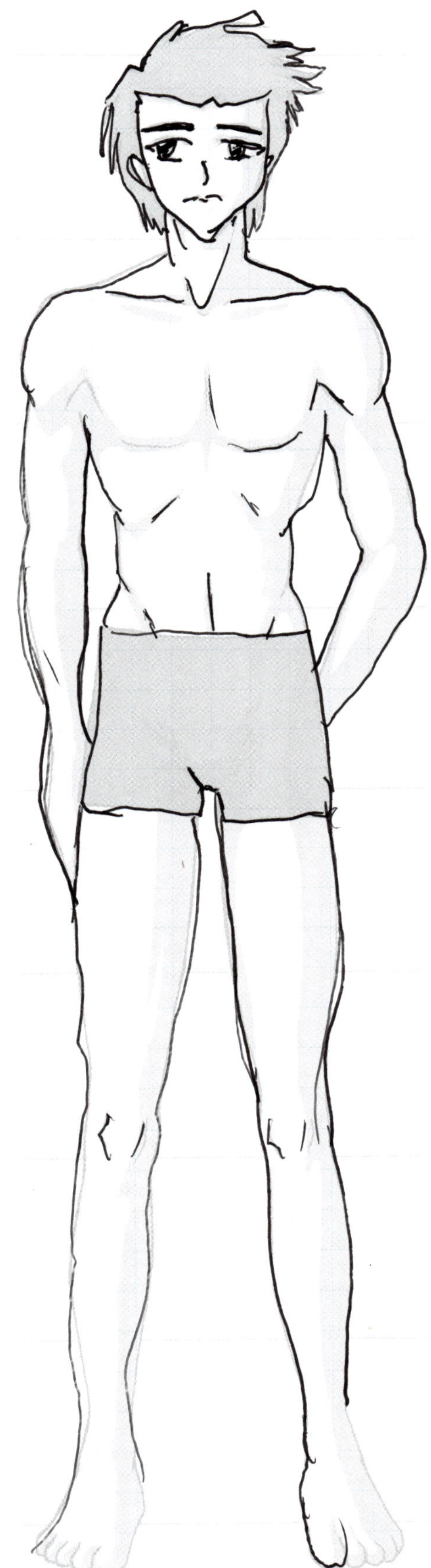

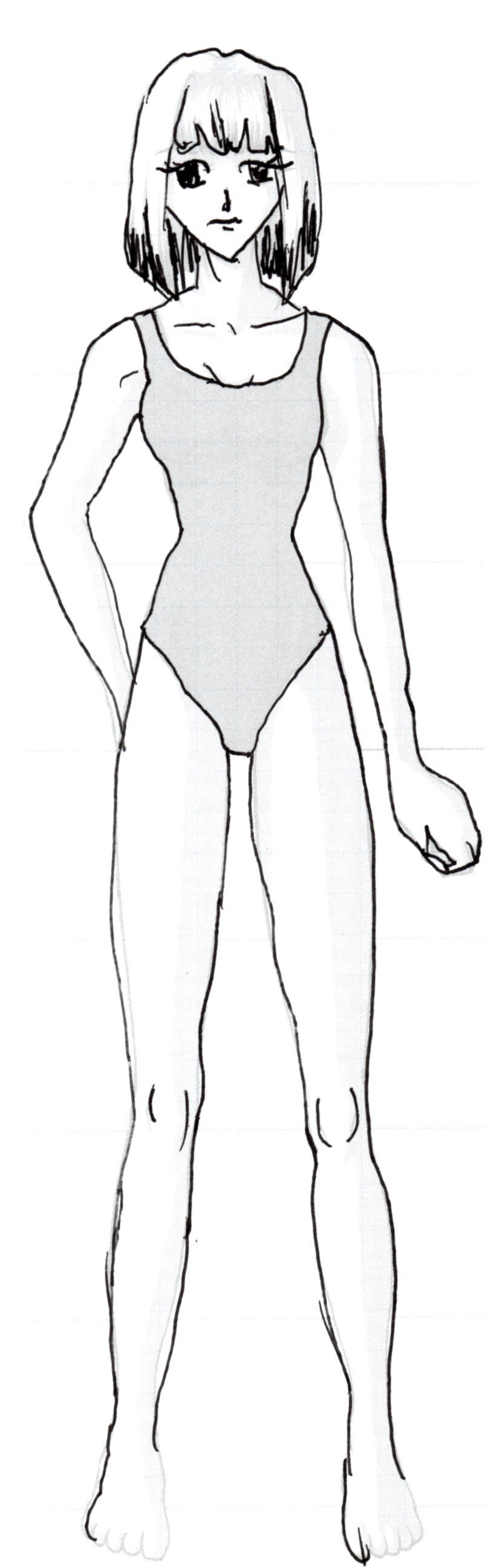

EXAGGERATED PROPORTION SETS

The world of manga art is filled with many genres, from gritty realism to lighthearted slapstick. Therefore, the style of drawing changes to match the atmosphere of the story. Once you have the foundations for correct human proportions, try out these different styles on your characters.

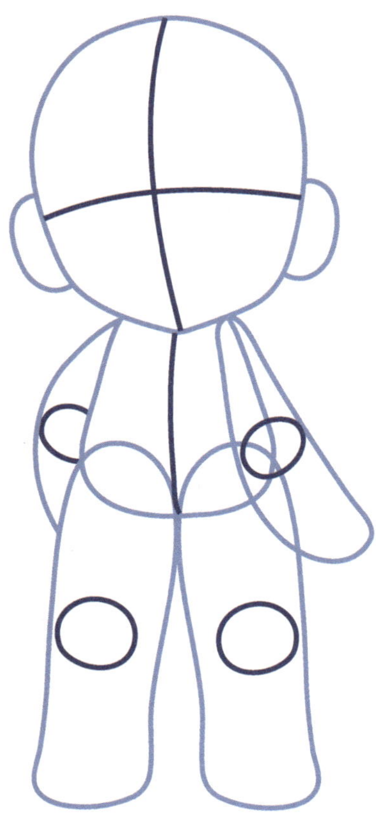

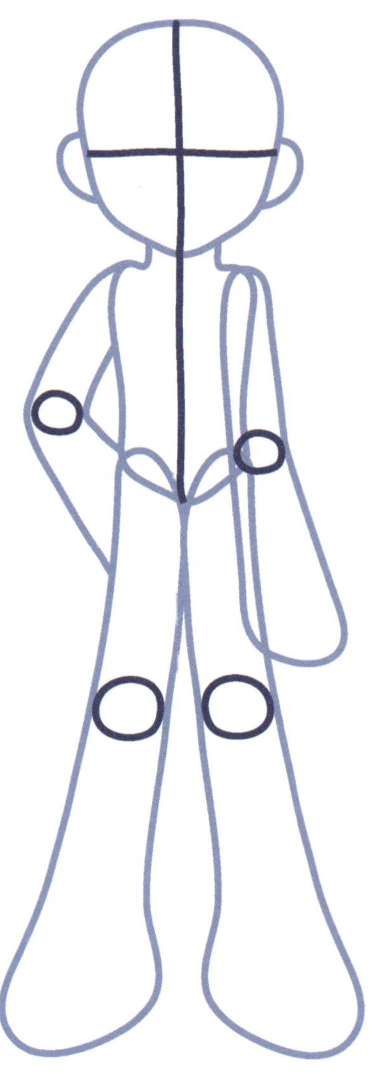

CHIBI

The most common form of exaggeration across all manga is to draw very cute, miniature versions of characters with very large heads (barely three head lengths tall) and squished, chubby bodies (in order to support the heads). This is "chibi," Japanese for "tiny," although the direct translation is slightly more like "little squirt." This style is not usually maintained throughout an entire comic book or animation because it is so extreme – characters tend to slip into this look at various points in the story when something funny happens. This style is so prevalent in manga that there is a section devoted entirely to it on pages 52-53.

CARTOON

This proportion set is used across many themes, but it all comes down to a general look of cuteness. This style has a chibi feel to it but is not as extreme. Often seen in manga aimed at younger readers, the characters look fun and funky, with fairly large heads so their features are clear to see, small torsos and limbs, but oversized hands and feet.

YOU TRY!

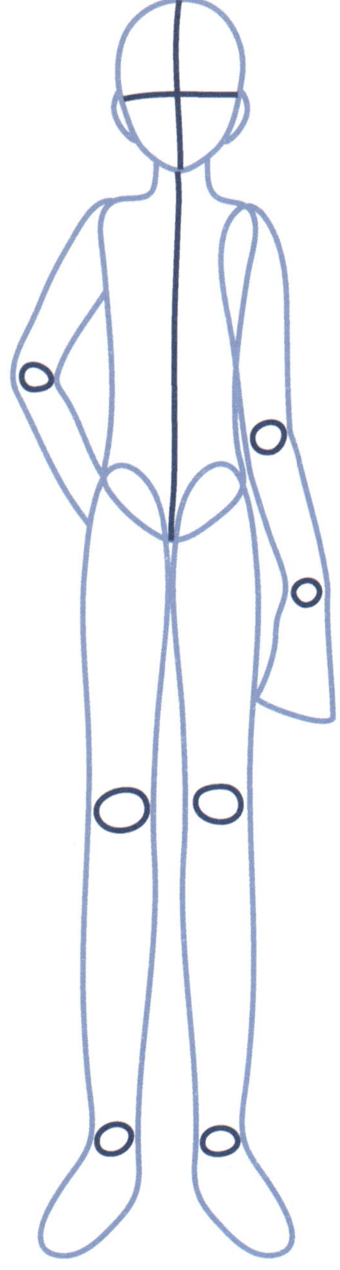

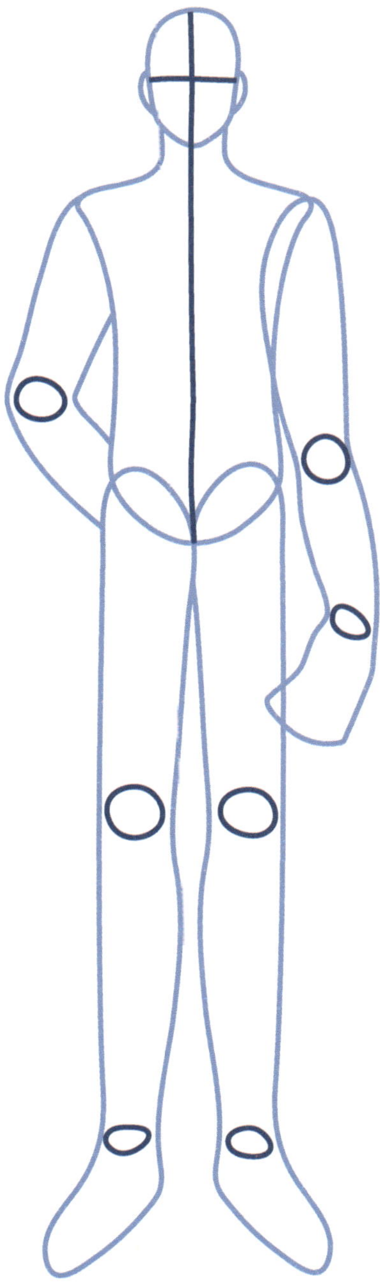

SHOUJO

Shoujo manga is aimed primarily at girls and young women. The characters are usually very beautiful and engaged in emotional storylines. Therefore the shoujo proportion set is very slim overall to complement the delicate characters, while the head remains its original size so it can hold expressive faces with large eyes.

SHONEN

Shonen manga is the opposite of shoujo – the target audience is men and boys – and it features action-packed stories with explosions, martial arts, or sexy women. Characters' proportions become heroic, very tall (around 10 head lengths) and strongly built. The most popular heroes of shonen manga tend to wear cool costumes and carry outrageous weapons, so the focus is taken away from the head and face.

YOU TRY!

CHIBIS/SUPER-DEFORMED CHARACTERS

Chibis are cute, pint-sized characters with small bodies, huge heads, and even huger personalities! Mostly these types of characters are used for comedic or lighthearted drawings or comics, or as cute mascots. While they may look simple to draw, it's much easier to create chibis if you already have a good understanding of how a standard manga character is pieced together.

ANATOMY OF A CHIBI

In contrast to regular-sized manga characters, chibi anatomy is very deformed and simplified. Chibis are a mere two-and-a-half heads tall, with rounded faces and enormous eyes. Their bodies are very simply drawn, with little or no muscle tone or definition.

- Shape of skull is very distorted. The facial features are very low compared to full-size characters' faces.
- Cheeks are small and low down. The chin is a very shallow "V" shape.
- Chibis very rarely have necks. Generally you will only see a small part of it at the back of the head.
- Chibi hands have tiny, pointed fingers.
- Legs usually take up at least 50 percent of the body. Shorter legs would make the chibi look even more squashed!
- Hair is one of the few parts of chibis that is drawn with as much detail as a regular-sized character.
- The eyes take up about as much height on the face as the nose and mouth.
- Chibi shoulders are nothing more than a gentle slope from the neck. Narrow shoulders help make the character look more childlike.
- Female chibis have very small breasts, and the waist or hips are not defined.
- Accessories and jewelry are clunky and oversized.
- Chibi feet are small, barely much bigger than the size of their ankles.

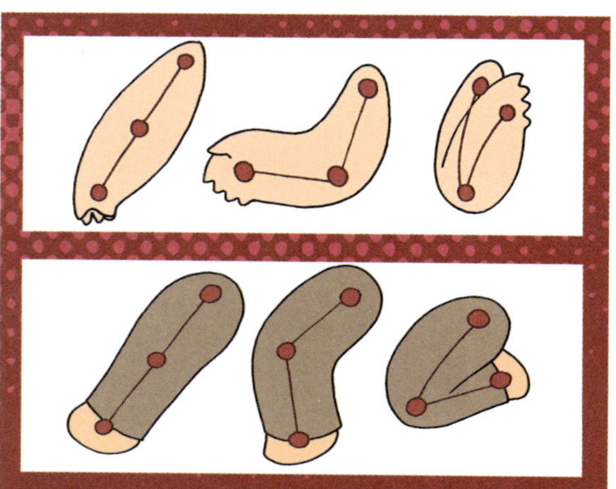

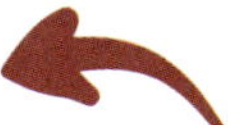

CHIBI LIMBS

Energetic and exaggerated, chibis are great for drawing in bouncy and bendy poses. The arms and legs of chibi characters should reflect this by being as curvy as possible. Also, because chibis are so compressed, a softer joint stops their limbs from looking too elongated for their bodies. Here are some examples of chibi arms and legs to show you how they bend and move.

CREATING A CHIBI OF A PRE-EXISTING CHARACTER

Drawing a chibi version of a full size character you've already created can be easier than starting a chibi from scratch. Also, it can draw attention to the particular features that make that character design so distinctive. The focus should be mostly on the facial features and expressions, and recreating the character's clothing and accessories in chibi versions. Try to put as much of your character's personality into the drawing as you possibly can.

The following 2 characters highlight points of the style to pay particular attention to.

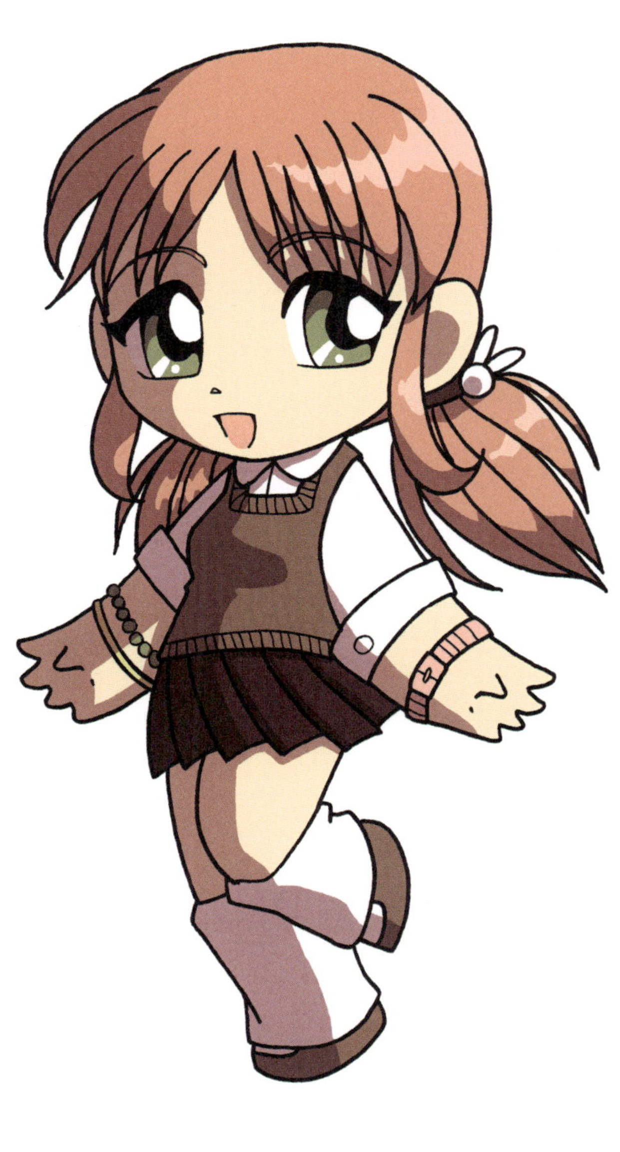

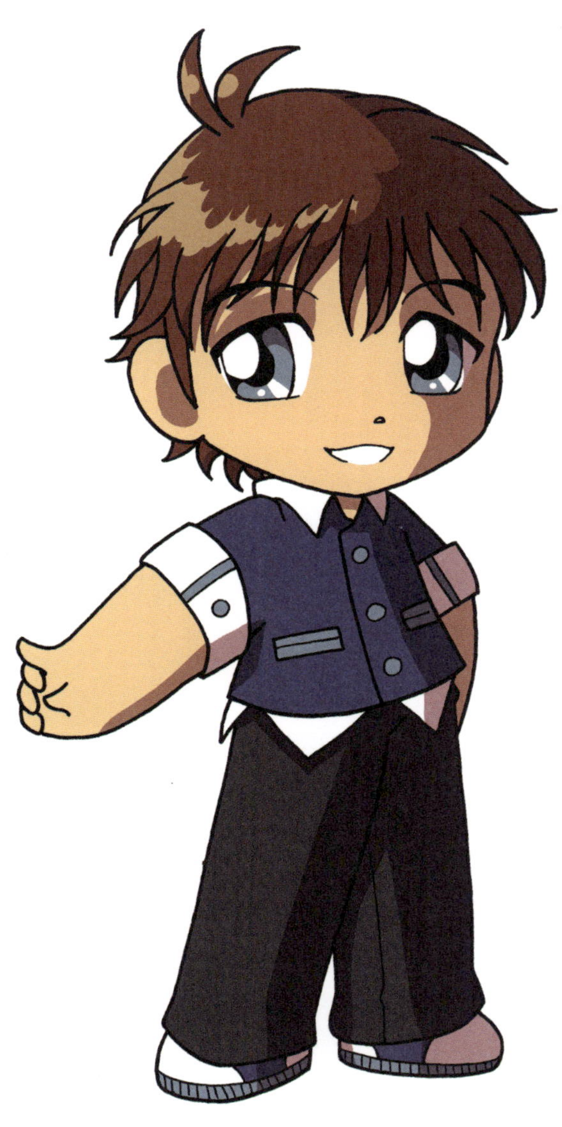

YOU TRY!

CLOTHING

Clothing your characters can be the most enjoyable part of creating manga. Costumes can range from cool, laid-back street style to futuristic, space opera suits – this is an area where you can let your imagination run riot. Clothing plays several important roles:

- It communicates to the reader the setting of your manga.
- It reinforces your character's personality.
- It is practical for the character's actions.

Clothing can be the most effective tool in portraying the setting of your manga. With just one look, readers can understand the location, time period, and genre of your story. If your character is wearing a full suit of armor, he is most probably a fantasy character of medieval lore.

What a character wears reveals much about their personality. For example, only a confident woman would wear a revealing bikini. When a character doesn't have so much choice over clothing or has to wear a uniform, it's not so much what they wear but how they wear it that gives away their attitude. Rolled-up sleeves, a messily tied tie, loose socks, a tightly tucked-in shirt – all of these are telltale signs.

Think about what your characters will be doing in your manga – they need clothing that is suitable for the story. So, if your character is a desert princess, she needs a thin, light, yet regal gown.

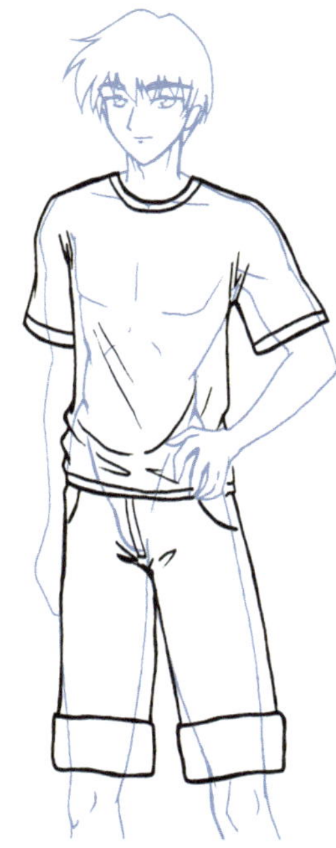

Here is an adult male character in casual clothing, wearing a T-shirt and shorts. Note how drawing out the nude body underneath the clothing helps you figure out where best to place key features – creases and folds, the appropriate way the cloth hangs off limbs, where to place the waistband.

USING THE BODY AS THE BASE

It is important to draw or bear in mind the human form before adding clothing. Clothing lies over the body but should not be used as an excuse to hide incorrect anatomy. If drawn without proper base work, clothes can distort the figure.

It is good practice to roughly sketch out the whole body in nude, particularly if the character is wearing very tight or revealing clothing. At the very least you should sketch the bulk of the body and limbs to match the clothing. For example, there is no need to sketch out full muscle definition if a man is wearing a thick sweater, or to draw the inside leg if a woman is wearing a long, bulky skirt.

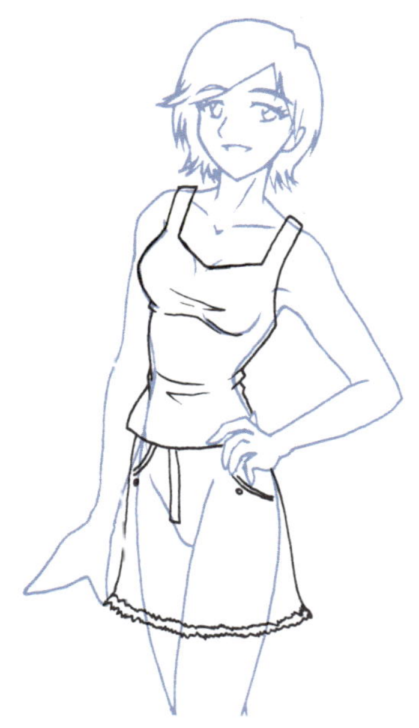

This woman is in very tight summer wear. It is vital to apply correct anatomy when drawing close-fitting clothing, particularly for her chest and waist areas.

EMPHASIZING THE HUMAN FORM

Now the man is wearing much more formal clothing, possibly for an office job. Here is where design features and differences between the sexes must be carefully observed – buttons are sewn on the right side; the cut of the shirt is wide for the shoulders; the position of the belt is quite low on the waist.

The woman is also dressed more smartly now, with stylish boots and a collared, tailored dress. See how feminine the dress looks. Her figure is emphasized in this design – her dress is tied at the small of her back, creating some folds and gathers at her bust and waistline.

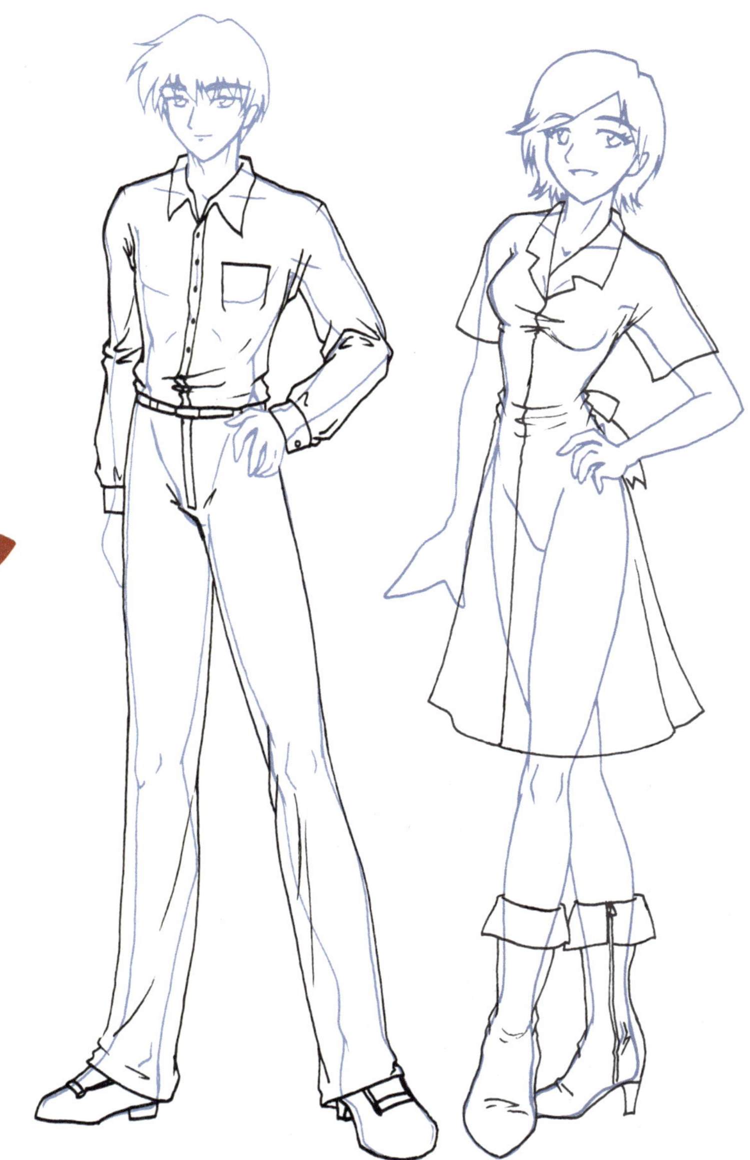

ENHANCING REALISM AND FINISHING TOUCHES

In manga, shading and coloring can add that final touch of realism that line art hints at. (Further examples are shown on page 58.) Folds, gathers, and creases should be depicted using minimal, fine lines to create the feeling that it is still the same piece of material – thick lines indicate an actual break between objects. Therefore, shading finishes the effect, enhancing folds. Use a mixture of curved shapes to bring out the roundness of the bust and sharp edges for thin creases.

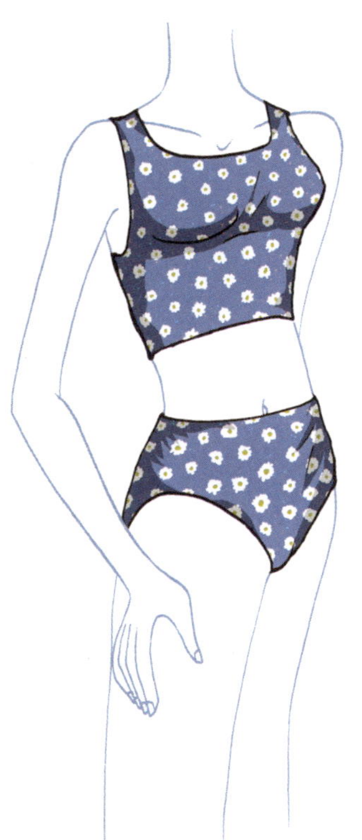

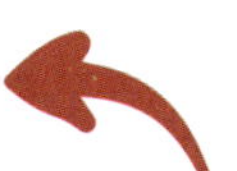

A tank-top bikini with a daisy pattern is a typical outfit for a teenage girl with a sweet nature to wear at the beach. Be sure to draw out the body in nude when dealing with such a tight outfit.

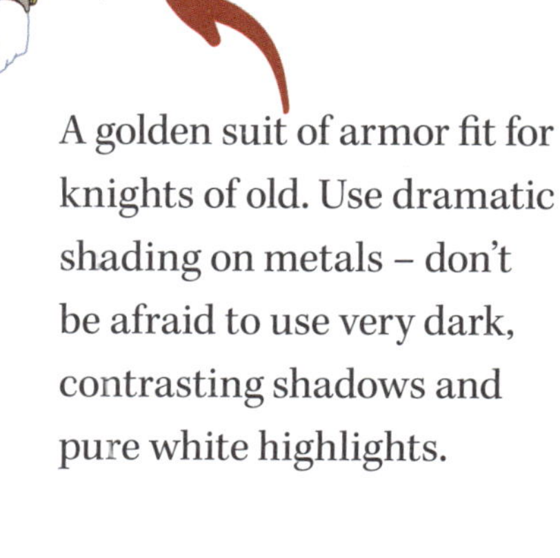

A golden suit of armor fit for knights of old. Use dramatic shading on metals – don't be afraid to use very dark, contrasting shadows and pure white highlights.

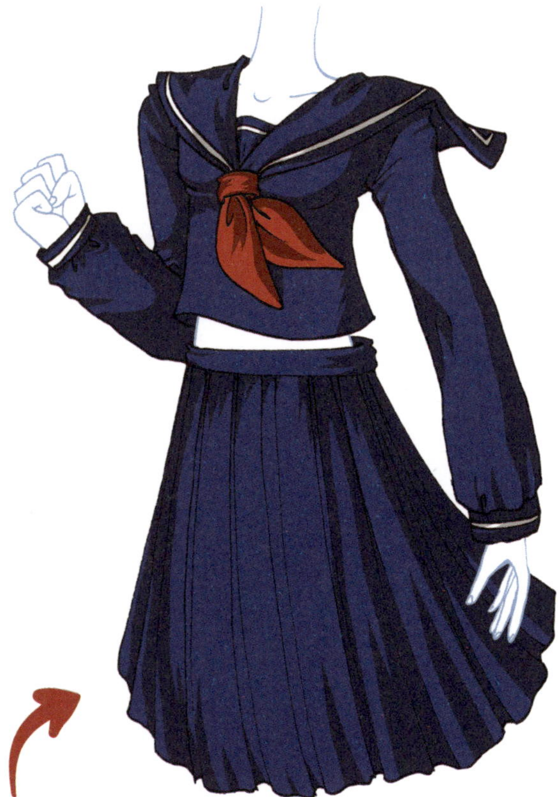

A distinguished gentleman in period dress with Baroque- and Regency-influenced embellishments. Make an effort to draw in the small details of his cravat and brooch.

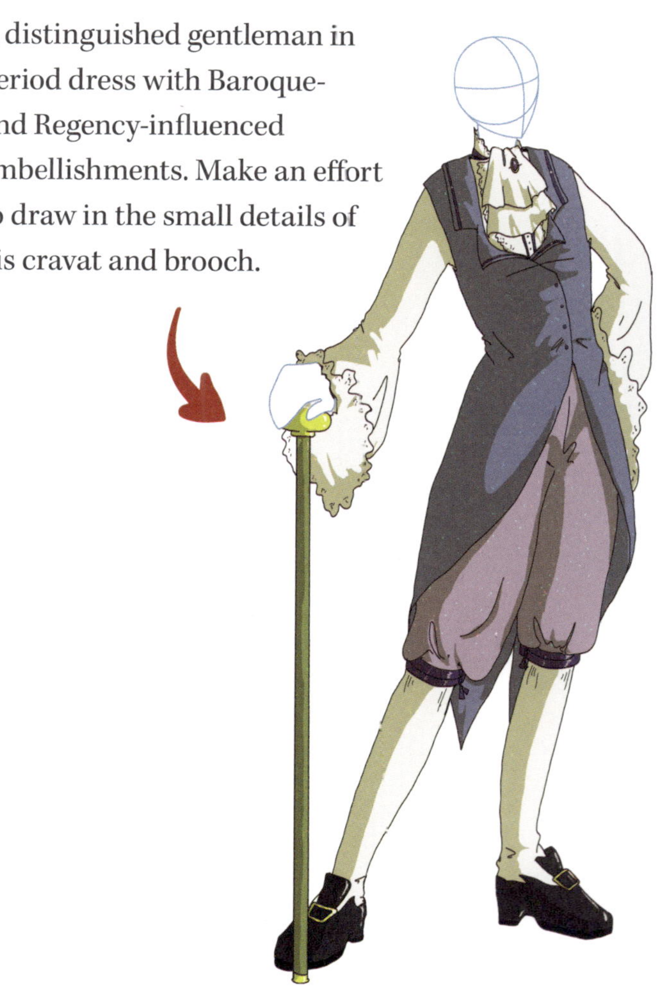

This school uniform is often seen in manga and anime – this is a Japanese schoolgirl uniform for the winter season. Draw in the details of the famous "sailor" collar carefully and add a brightly colored necktie.

ADDING ACCESSORIES TO SHOW A CHARACTER'S CIRCUMSTANCE

Even a generic character can be transformed by a clever choice of accessories. Look at the examples below. See how she changes from a dull schoolgirl to a confident fashionable character, to a sci-fi adventurer, to a fantasy heroine.

Even though the fantasy and sci-fi characters here are quite an unusual combination of contemporary dress and fantasy accessories, they work within context. If the character is in a whole school of sci-fi or fantasy students, then the uniform is completely acceptable. However, if they are surrounded by regular students in a regular school, their outfit would look out of place.

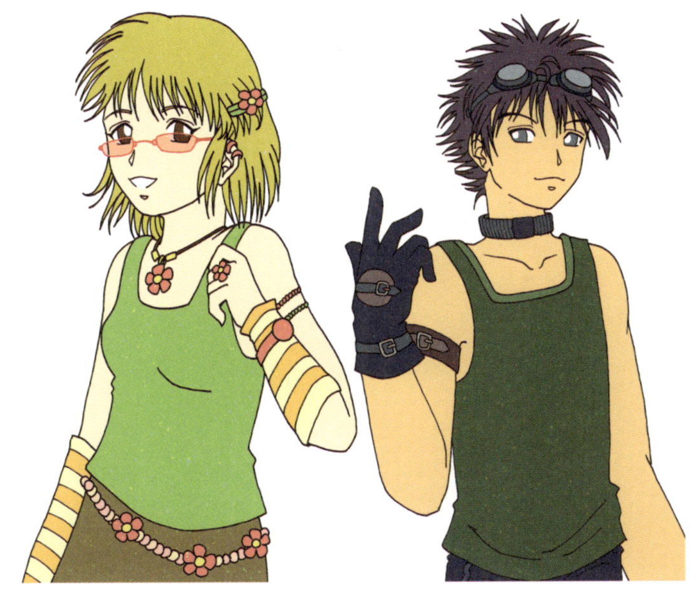

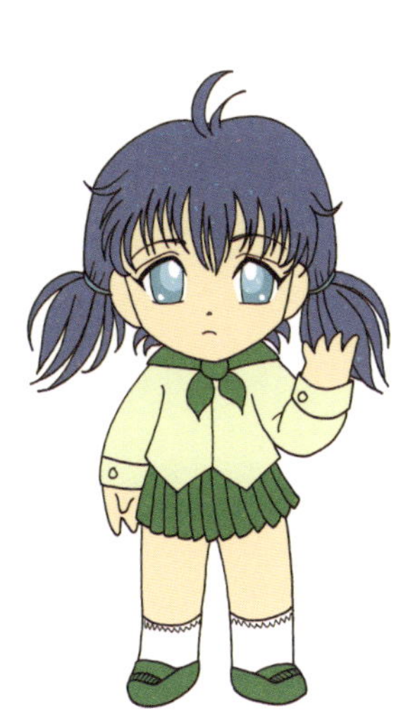

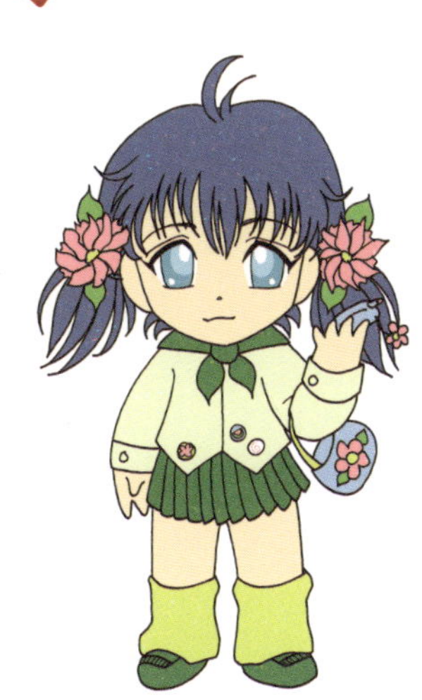

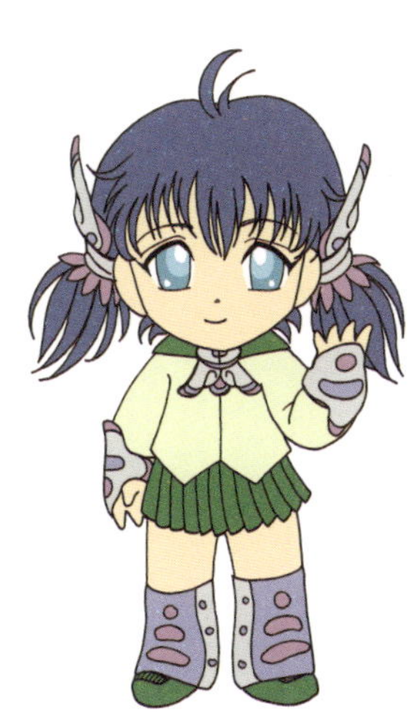

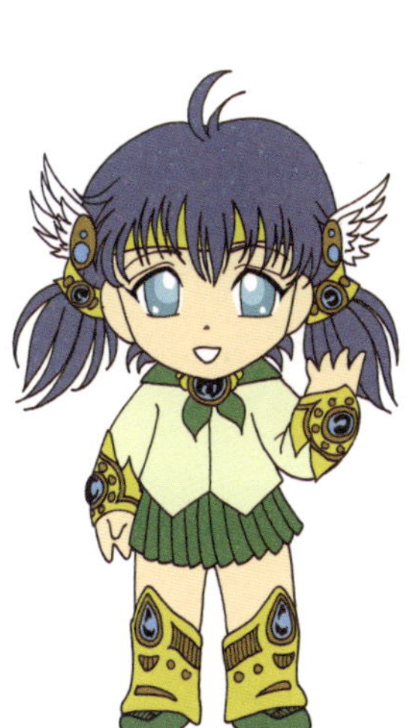

CREATING MEANINGFUL ACCESSORIES

Many accessories work best when they have a function or a reason to be there. If your character has a lot of belts strapped around its waist, why are they there? Could they hold something, for example a weapon or tools? Does your character have a job that requires any specific accessories, like gloves, hats, or goggles? Accessories could even be part of a uniform, like a bandana specific to a gang or friendship bracelets shared between groups of schoolgirls. Consider these points and try to incorporate accessories into your design that are useful to the character.

YOU TRY!

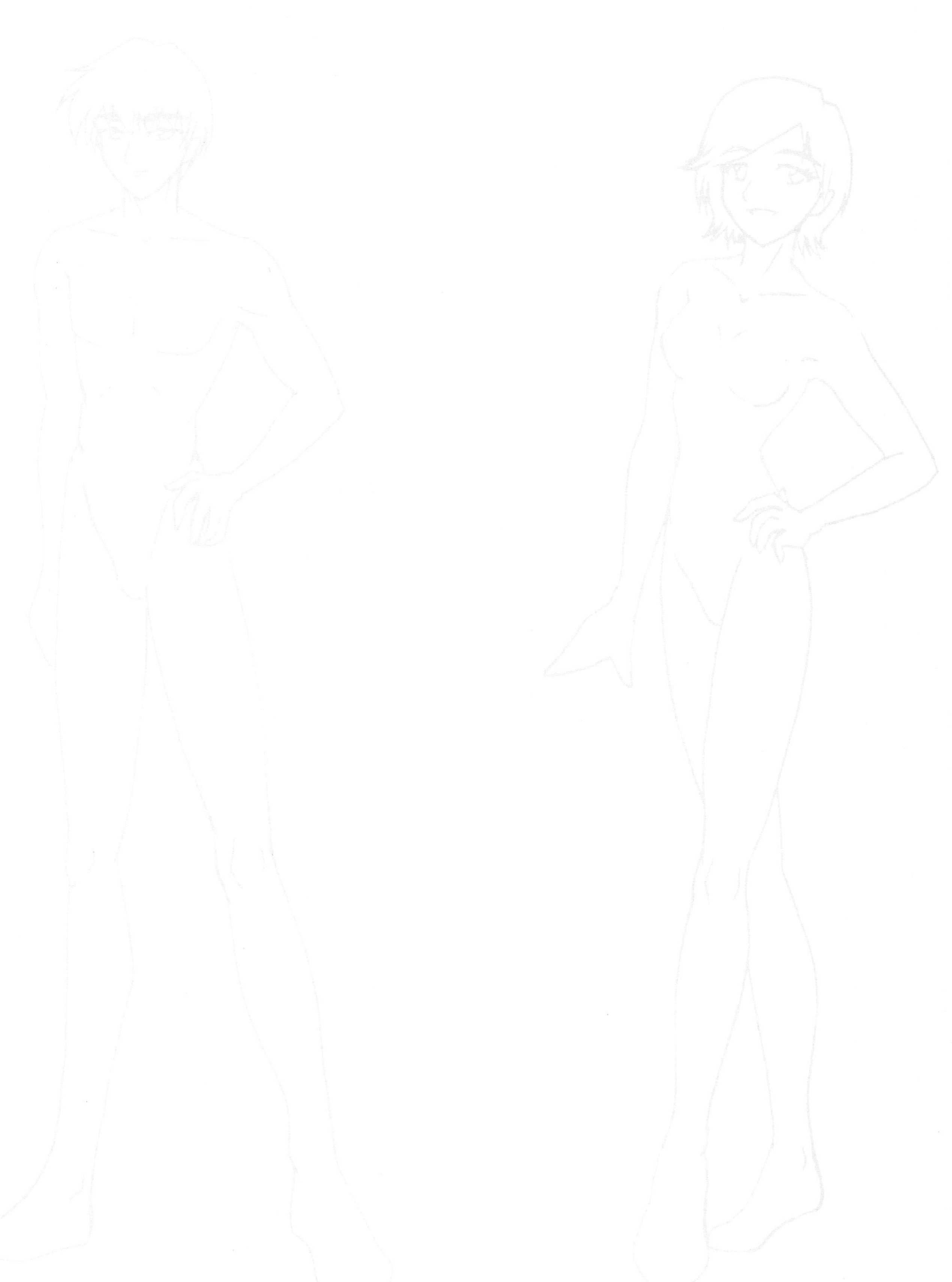

TOOLS AND EQUIPMENT

Every artist has to start somewhere, and that somewhere is usually choosing the right tools and materials to draw with. No matter what your experience level, selecting the appropriate media and good-quality tools is essential to achieving the best results.

DRAWING TOOLS

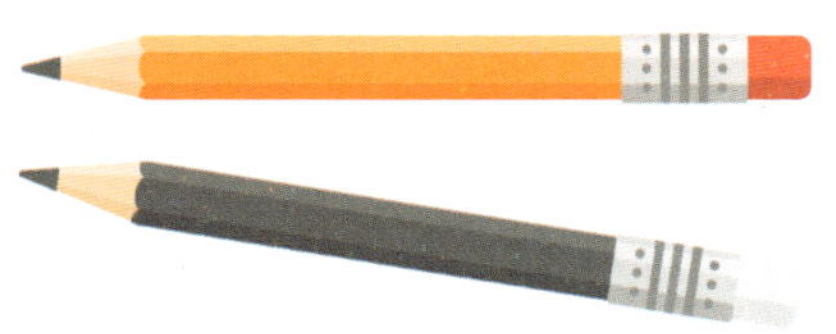

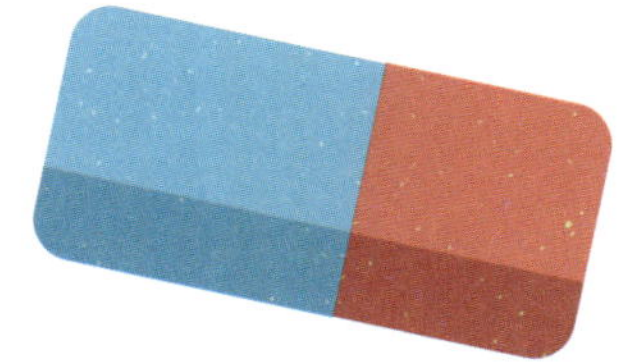

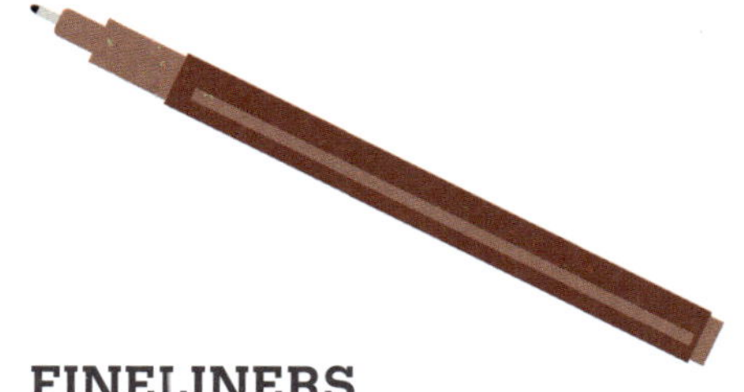

PENCIL

A pencil is the most essential tool for drawing. For illustration, hard leads (H onward) are best as they don't smudge under the normal hand movements you make while drawing. Many artists use mechanical pencils, enabling them to draw constantly without having to stop to sharpen the pencil.

ERASERS

There are two types of eraser: plastic and putty/kneaded. Plastic erasers come in a variety of shapes and sizes and are best for general use. Putty erasers are soft and can be kneaded into different shapes, making them great for erasing small mistakes or adding detailed highlights to pencil drawings.

FINELINERS

Fineliners are pens with small plastic tips, used for technical drawing or illustration. They give a flat, consistent line and come in a variety of nib sizes. Most fineliners are disposable, but there are some more expensive brands available that are refillable and give you more choice over the ink you use in them. Fineliners are the easiest pens to ink with.

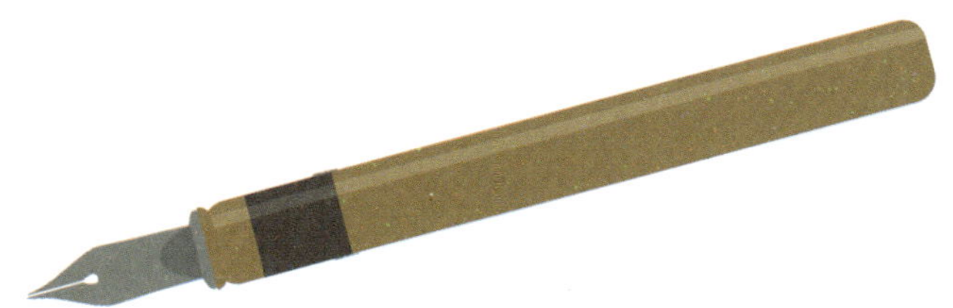

BRUSH PENS

A modern alternative to inking with a brush, brush pens are easy and clean to use. Fiber-tipped brush pens are cheap, firm, and easy to control, but are disposable. If you want something almost exactly like a brush, there are more expensive types with bristle tips. These usually take refill cartridges, but will still wear out eventually as the bristles can split or fray.

DIP PENS

Dip pens are the traditional tool for inking. They have great flexibility and variation in the lines they produce, and you can use a huge range of different inks with them. However, they are messy and not easily portable, and it takes a bit of practice to learn to control the pressure on the nib properly. Nibs need frequent cleaning while working and need replacing regularly.

COLORING TOOLS

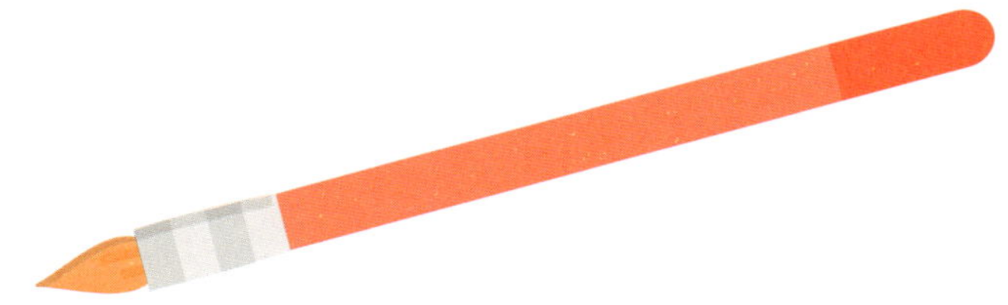

BRUSHES

When choosing brushes, make sure they're suitable for the medium you're using. Soft brushes are best for inks and watercolors, coarse brushes for acrylic and oil paints. Avoid really cheap brushes and brushes that have split tips.

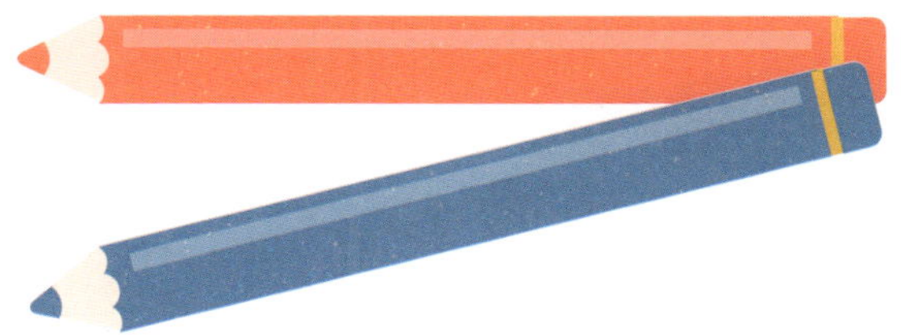

COLORED PENCILS

Colored pencils are cheap and come in a wide range of colors and types (such as watercolor pencils or chalk pastel pencils). They are easy to use but can be time consuming when working on large drawings. Often they work best when used to supplement other media.

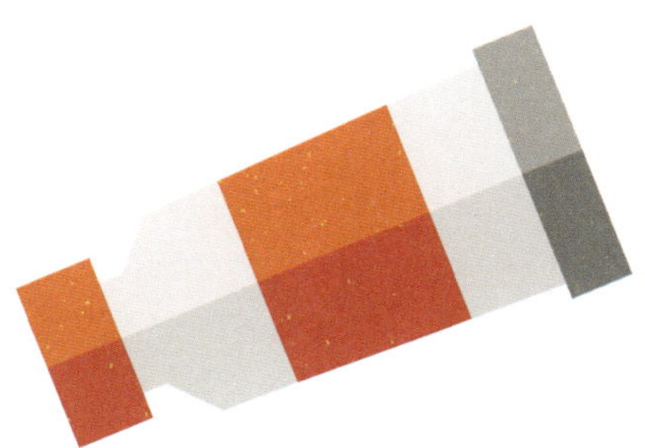

WATERCOLORS

Watercolor is a water-soluble paint that comes in tubes or solid in pans. It can produce a range of effects but needs time and practice to master. It is a cheap, easily obtainable medium used by many illustrators.

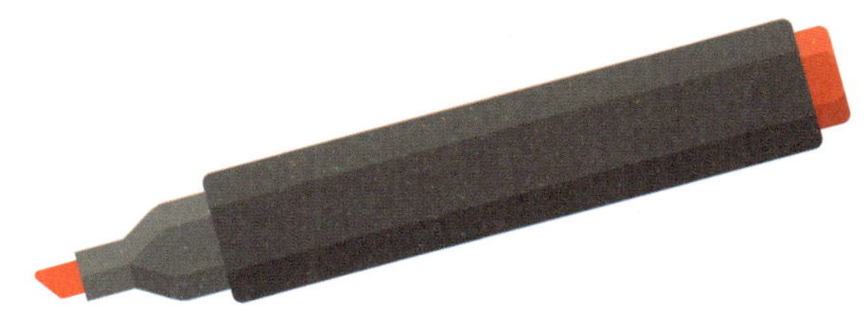

MARKERS

Favored by many manga artists, markers offer great permanence and consistency of color. Alcohol-based markers are easier to use and give better results than water-based ones, but they are also more expensive. Markers are portable and quick to color with, but it requires a huge investment to get a large enough range of colors to make the most of your work.

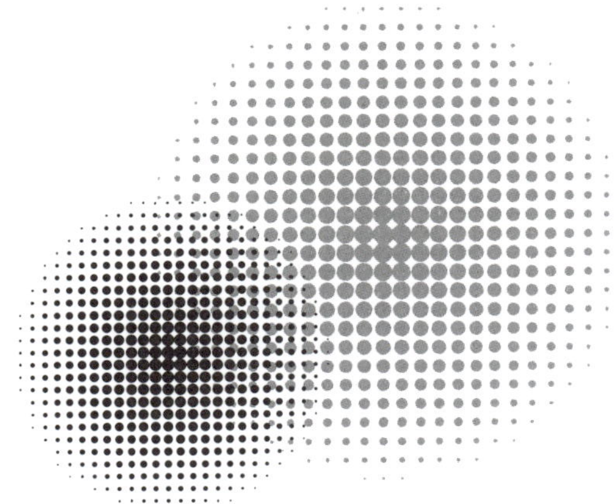

SCREENTONE

Screentone is used to add shading to comic pages and black and white illustrations. The majority of tones available are simple "halftone" dot patterns, but there are many more abstract patterns available, and even colored tones. Screentones are self-adhesive and are applied by cutting out the shapes required with a knife and pressing them firmly onto the illustration.

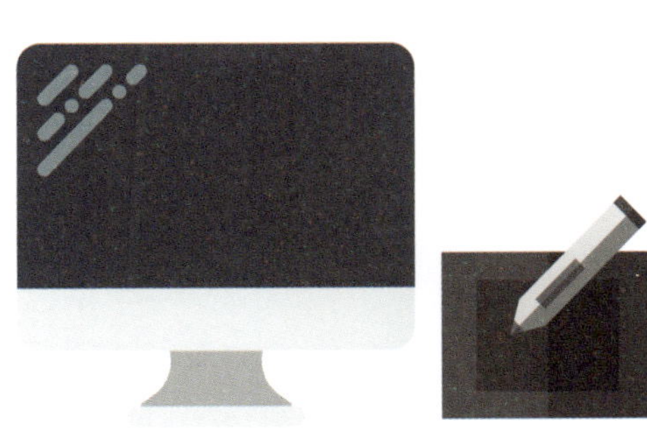

COMPUTERS

Computers are used by both professionals and amateurs to create pristine-looking illustrations. Many people work with a graphics tablet: a pressure-sensitive digital pen you use on a special location-sensitive tablet. This gives artists great control despite working with an intangible digital medium. There are many types of software that give different results.

LIGHTING

Lighting helps to define the three-dimensional shape of an object and makes the drawing much more believable. It can communicate the relative position of a character within a world and explain its surroundings. It can also be used as a method to express emotions and dramatic atmosphere, completely changing the way a picture is perceived by the viewer. By understanding and applying some simple lighting methods to your artwork, you'll be able to vastly improve the look of any illustration you do in the future.

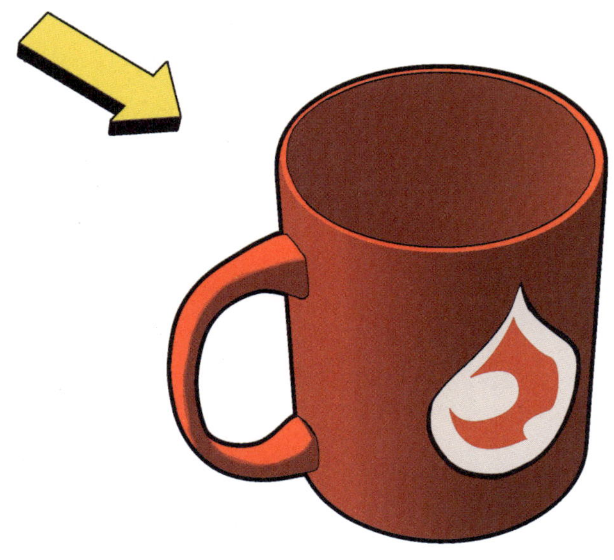

BASICS

The most basic and important principle of lighting is that the object is lightest on the parts that face the light source, and darkest in parts that face away from the light source (as illustrated with the yellow arrow in the diagram).

If a light source has a small area of influence, like a dim light bulb or a candle flame, then the object will be visibly brighter in areas closer to the light, becoming darker further away. However, most light sources continue for a long distance until they hit an object.

SHADOWS

When an object intercepts a light source, it will cast a shadow on other objects. The presence of shadows is one of the most important aspects of establishing the shape and location of an object, so it's worth spending time on drawing them. In this diagram, you can see the shape of the mug has been cast onto the white surface.

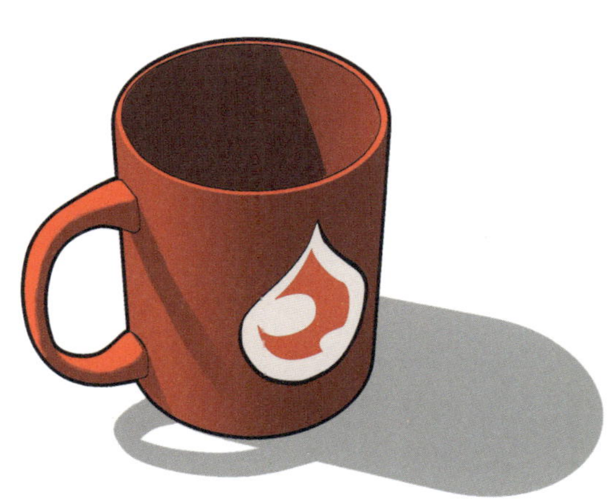

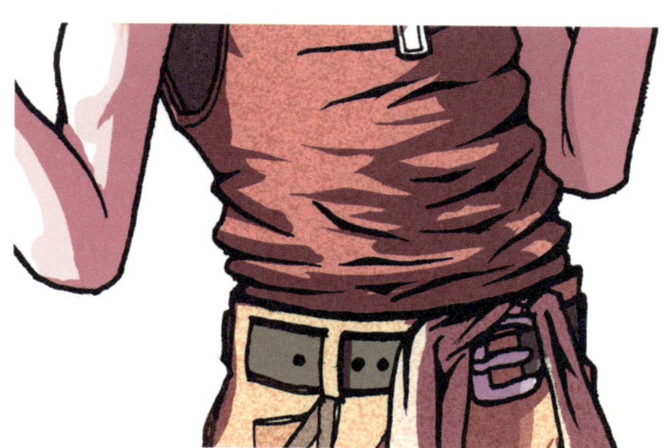

Items with detailed surfaces, such as folded fabric or heavily carved armor, will often cast shadows on themselves, and this can act as an effective way to vividly define detail.

Also, semitransparent objects, such as plastic bottles, cast colored or translucent shadows, which can lead to some dynamic visual effects.

SHINY AND REFLECTIVE OBJECTS

Some materials are more reflective or shiny than others, so they tend to catch much more light than matte or dull objects. Dark and light objects are seen in the surface, and this leads to the item having a shiny look with heavy contrast. Strong backlighting at the darkest part of the shadow is often employed to define volume and imply an especially shiny material.

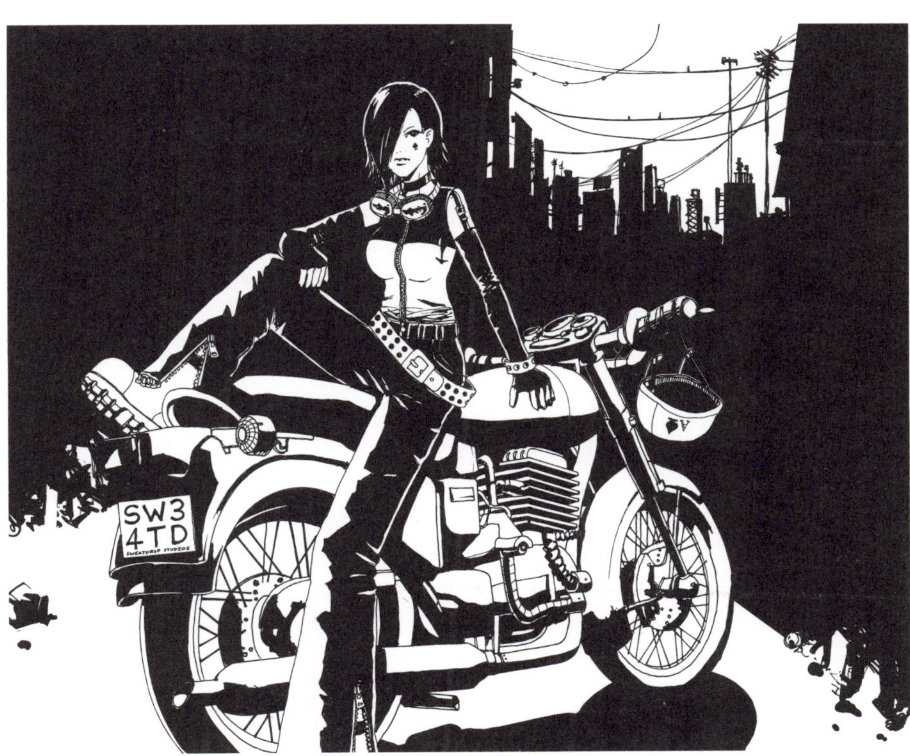

Many artists tend to ignore realism to some extent when dealing with shiny objects, preferring to render them to a learned method. Fake glints and highlights are used to emphasize the type of material. For cylindrical objects, such as poles or even legs, it can be effective to draw a thin line of highlight. This technique is often used on hair to make it shine brightly.

The way shiny materials are drawn in manga style varies heavily depending upon the artist's preference. Pay attention to artwork and look for styles that suit you.

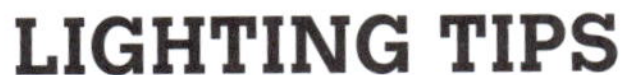

LIGHTING TIPS

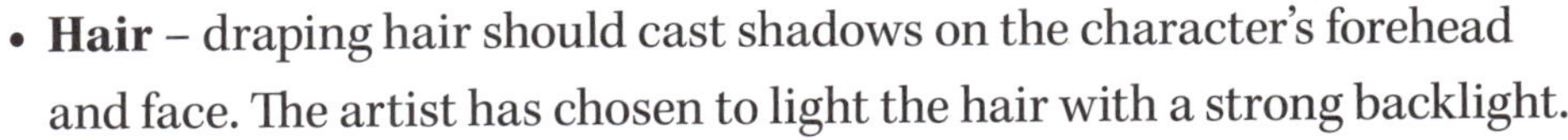

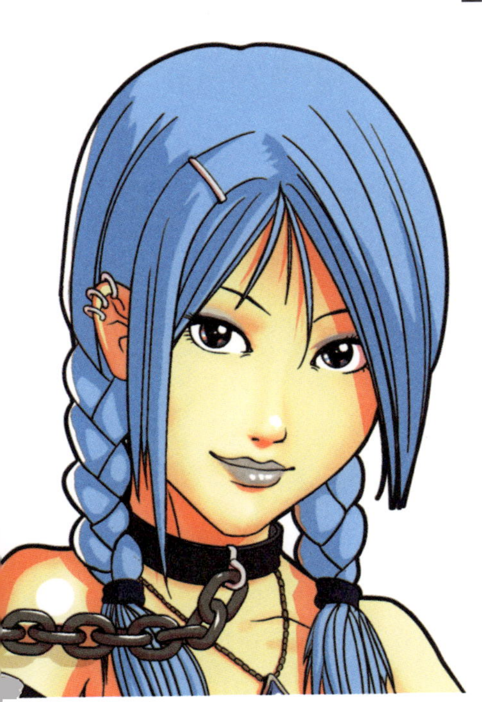

- **Hair** – draping hair should cast shadows on the character's forehead and face. The artist has chosen to light the hair with a strong backlight.
- **Nose** – a subtle shadow beneath the nose helps show its shape.
- **Lips** – the lips have been given extra highlights to show their shine. The bottom lip casts a small shadow also, giving the lips a sense of shape.
- **Eyes** – the glossy eyes are reflective of many different colors; in this case blue and pink shades have been chosen to complement the colors used, finished off with bold white reflections. The eye sockets are defined with a subtle suggestion of shadow, setting the eyes back slightly from the brow.
- **Neck and shoulders** – shadows are cast from the chin onto the neck, and the hair braids cast a shadow onto the body. Be sure to include all objects and overlaps when drawing shadows on a character.

COLOR THEORY

Choosing the right colors for an image can often be just as significant as the illustration itself, and can sometimes be just as difficult. Not only can the mood of an image be changed by the use of color, but the focus and general effectiveness of the composition hangs entirely upon the colors chosen.

BASICS OF COLOR

So, how do you go about choosing the right color? Should you choose the color that is technically correct, or choose one because you personally prefer it? Whatever your motive, it's important to understand the generally accepted associative values of color and how it can be most effectively complemented and emphasized. Color theory will allow you to be more confident with your color choices and make the most of the look you want to capture.

The color wheel organizes and explains the basics of color. It is also a valuable tool to help you choose your colors and to judge the relationship between different hues.

PRIMARY COLORS

Yellow Red Blue

Every color in the color spectrum can be achieved by mixing one or more of these colors together in varying quantities.

SECONDARY COLORS

Each of these three colors is made by mixing two of the primary colors together.

TERTIARY COLORS

Yellow & orange, Red & orange, Red & purple

Blue & purple, Blue & green, Yellow & green

Tertiary colors are mixed from one primary and one secondary color.

COLOR PALETTES

Using the color wheel, it's possible to make informed decisions about which colors you use for your manga characters.

ANALOGOUS/ RELATED COLORS

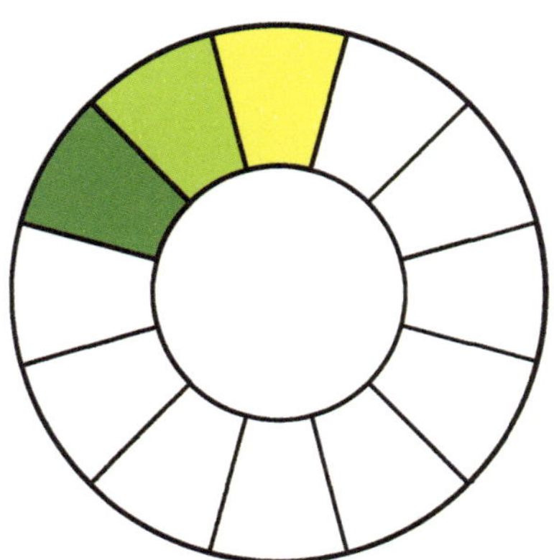

Analogous colors are close together on the color wheel but far enough away to introduce variety to the hue of the image and keep things interesting. Three or four neighboring shades may be chosen to achieve this effect.

COMPLEMENTARY COLORS

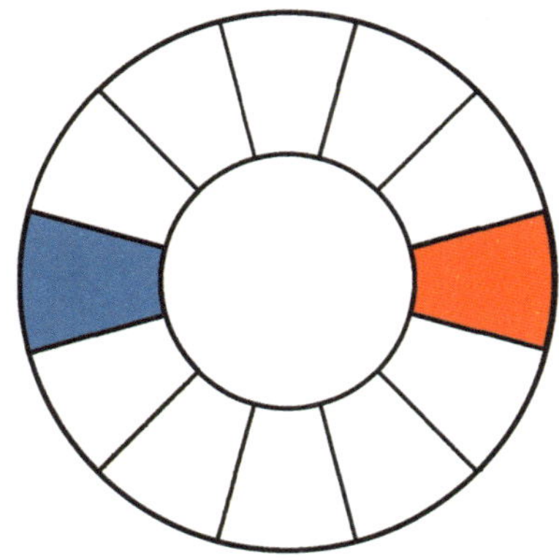

Colors from opposite sides of the color wheel have the greatest contrast with one another, but the effect can often be garish. When one of the colors is duller, then the complementary shade can function as a striking accent color.

TRIADIC COLORS

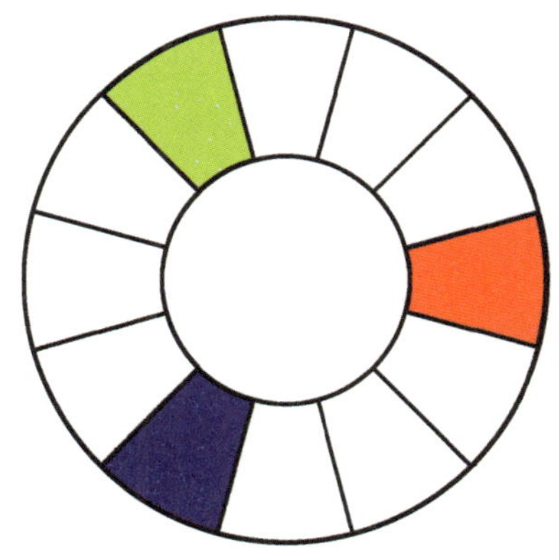

A triadic palette comes from choosing three colors from the wheel that are evenly spaced from one another. Typically, two of these colors are used as the basis of a color scheme, with the third being used occasionally for highlights and accents, as it is equally contrasted to each of the other two tones.

CREATE YOUR OWN ANALOGOUS COLORS

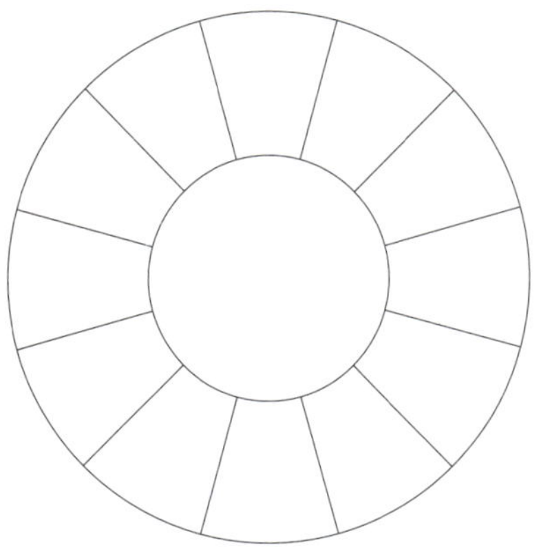

CREATE YOUR OWN COMPLEMENTARY COLORS

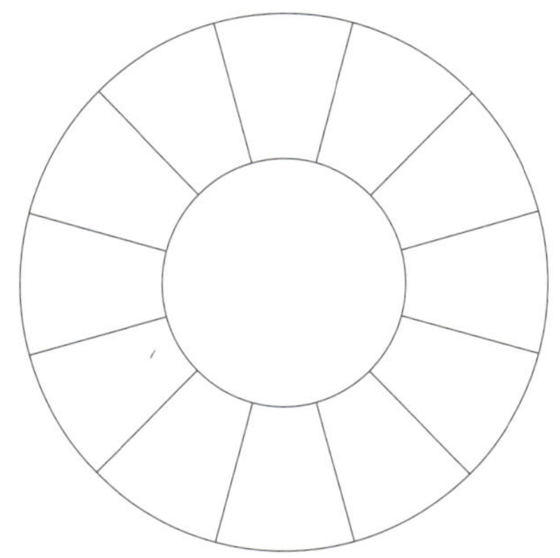

CREATE YOUR OWN TRIADIC COLORS

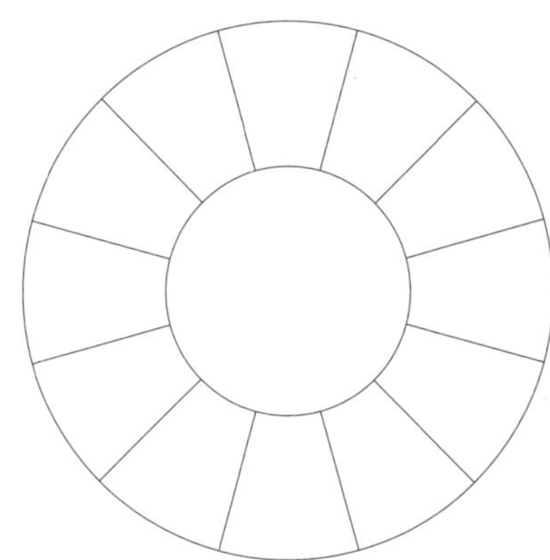

SIGNIFICANCE OF COLOR

Different ranges of colors tend to evoke different emotional responses, so it's important to pay attention to the way colors can be interpreted. The use of color applies not only to the palette you choose but also to the tints and shades of any lighting in the scene.

WARM COLORS

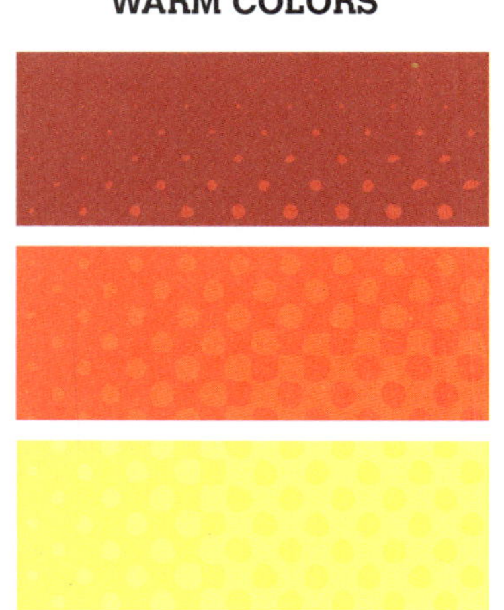

Red, orange, and yellow – these colors give the impression of warmth because of their association with fire and sunlight. While yellow is the most visually bright color in the spectrum, it is red that is the most striking and alarming.

COOL COLORS

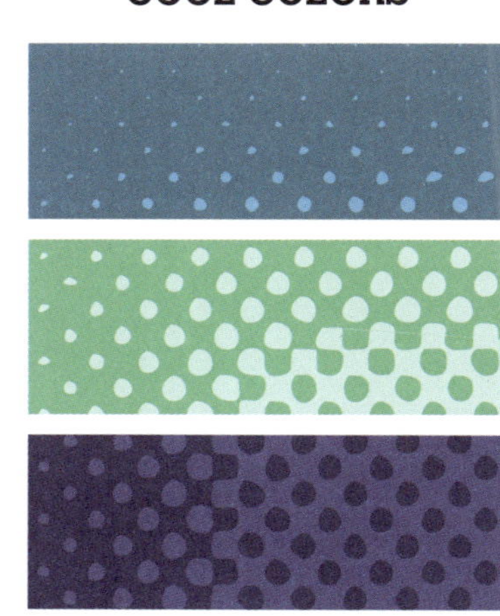

Blue, green, and purple – these colors suggest a cool sensation because they remind us of water and grass. They typically attract less attention than warm colors and are more relaxing, even in their richer variants.

NEUTRAL COLORS

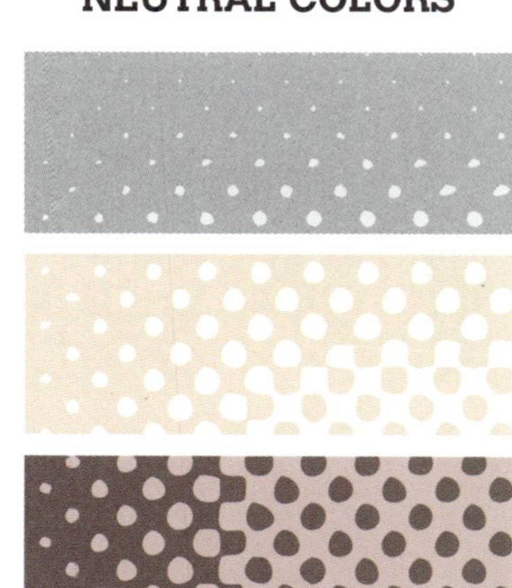

Gray, beige, and dull brown – gray is the most neutral of all colors. Therefore it does not contrast with other colors and removes focus from objects in this color. The use of neutral colors can be especially effective with bright or rich colors.

COLOR COORDINATION

Simply coordinating the colors within a character's outfit and accessories is often enough to create a strong visual look. Whether you choose similar neighboring colors or outlandish and bright hues, it's important to retain a persistent palette. Try to choose tones of similar saturation or intensity, and be sure to echo colors throughout the design. For instance, if a character has rainbow-colored arm warmers, then consider giving her rainbow-striped shoes to match.

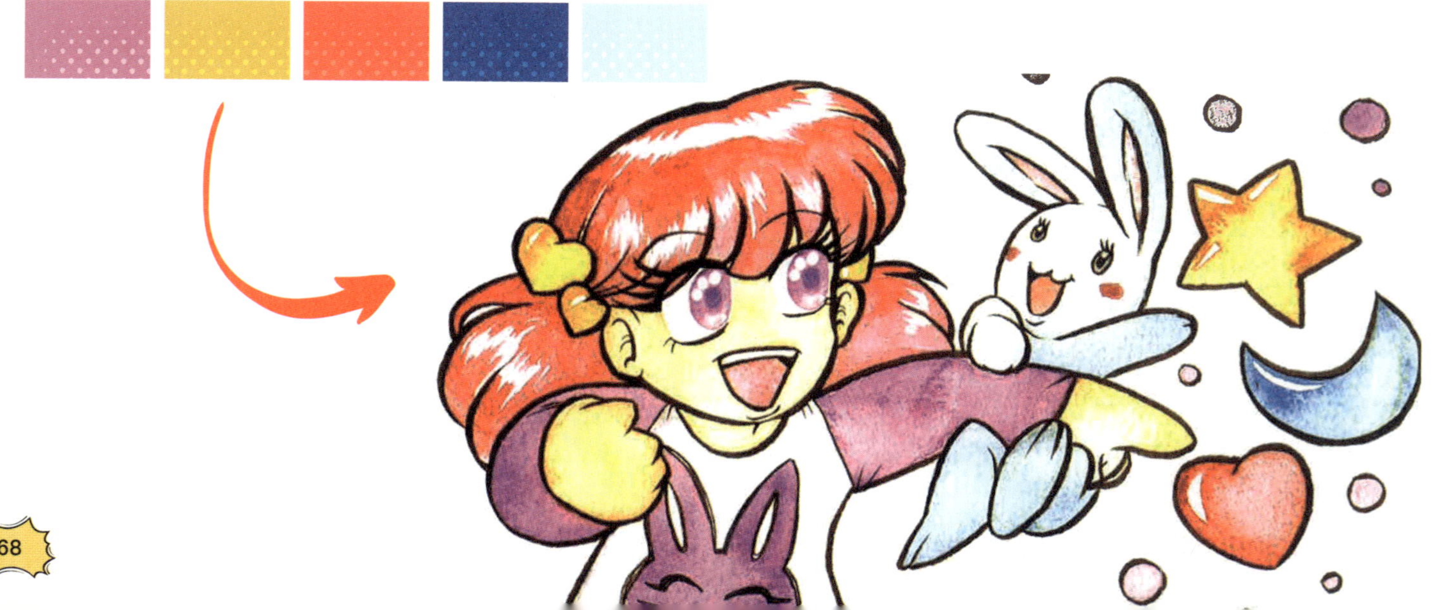

CREATE YOUR OWN PALETTES

Try putting together your own color groupings to see what visual effects they create.

MY CUSTOM PALETTE #1

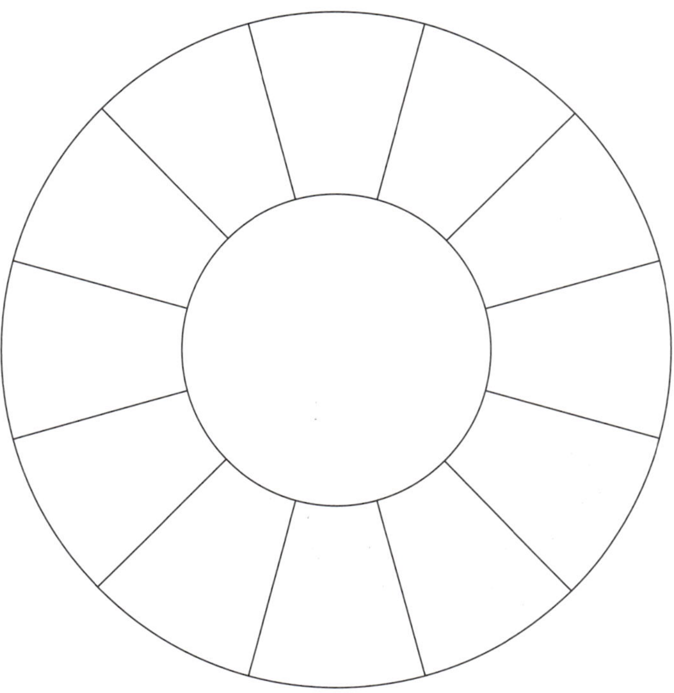

MY CUSTOM PALETTE #2

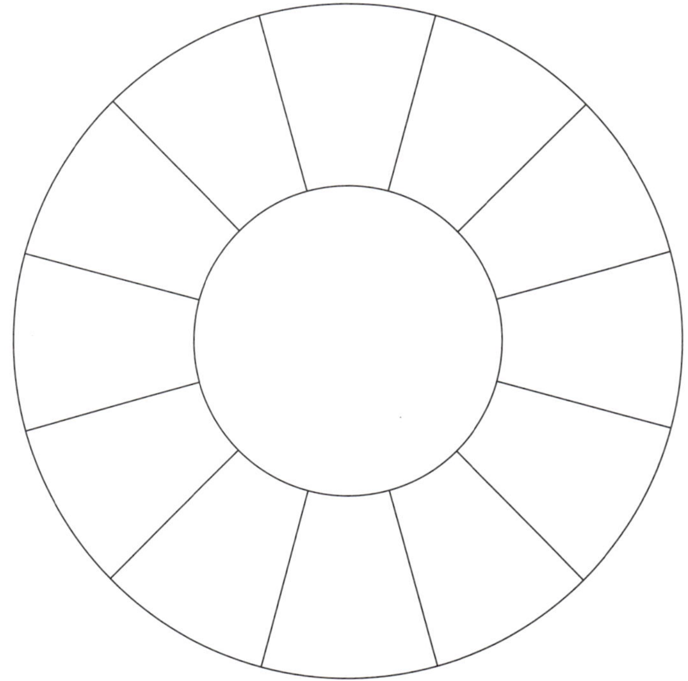

MY CUSTOM PALETTE #3

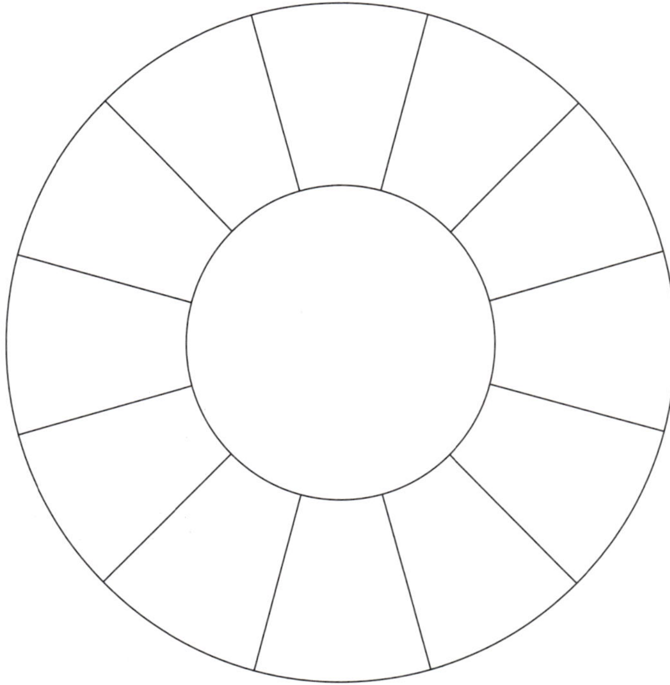

MALE CHILD

It is important to remember that while the design should reflect a character of roughly twelve years of age, the standard manga child tends to be far more mature than they would be in reality. Often in stories aimed at the preteen market, these characters are given central roles, with a great weight on their shoulders and skills far beyond their age. Their true age makes them accessible to a younger audience, while their maturity opens them up to older readers.

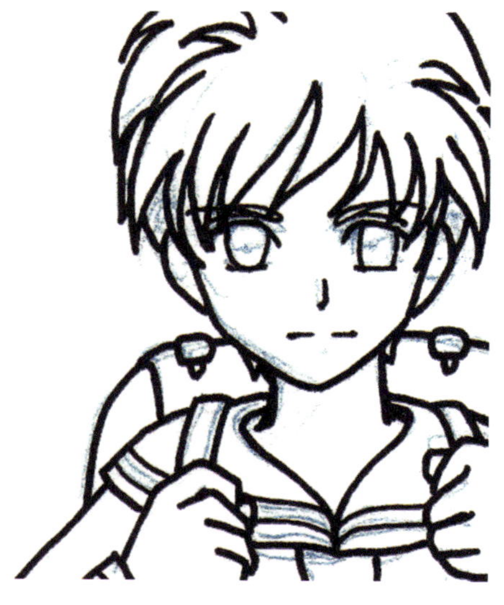

ROUGH SKETCH

As the image shows, this design was originally marked out in blue pencil before inking. This means that when adding the inks it should be very hard to miss any lines and the sketch work can be easily removed at a later stage.

The personality and demeanor of the character will drastically affect how it's drawn. Here, the standard young boy is confident and so his head is held high, shoulders squared and loose. However, he is still of an age to be slightly wary of the world around him. He has a fixed expression that suggests he is happy, but he's being a little cagey about it. His hair is untidy, not something he's too worried about at his age.

He is obviously still attending school, and so in this image the character sports a school uniform and regulation backpack. As with the body features, clothing can be drawn as slightly oversized to emphasize the smallness of the frame. The outfit shown is loose and comfortable. There are minimal creases in the top, but they are enough to show how much movement there is in the material. For young male characters especially, the style of long shorts used can really show their age. These boys are too old for shorts, but not yet old enough to feel comfortable in full trousers. This character's true personality is shown in his accessories.

Here are some alternative looks the standard young boy might sport.

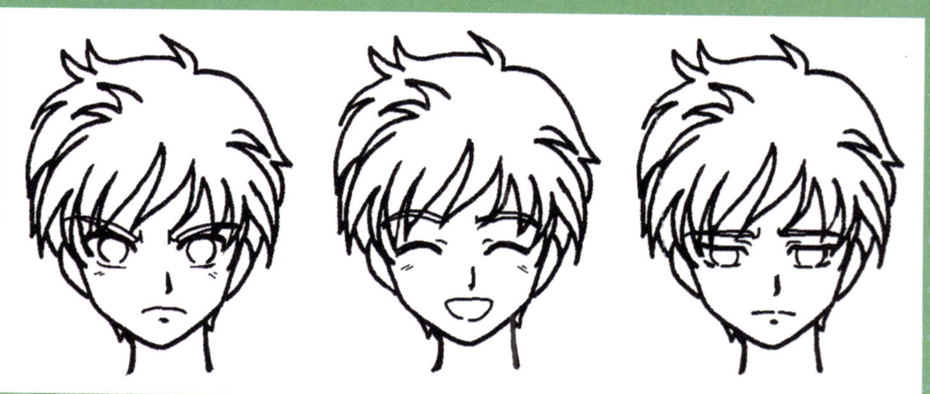

FIGURE

The standard young boy has not yet matured. He measures in at around five heads high and his frame is small, without any of the tone or features developed in the teen years. Often, younger characters can be drawn with slightly oversized hands and feet to emphasize the smallness of their frame. This same effect can be achieved with the ears. As the character is young, the eyes are large and are set slightly below the center of the head.

His pose here suggests he is moving forward. Be sure that at least one foot is planted firmly on the ground to give the character balance.

BASIC COLORS

As far as clothing goes, in this design he is wearing a Japanese sailor-style school uniform. Regulation colors dictate blue and white as the chief color scheme. However, you can complement or contradict this scheme with other details. The character sports a large red backpack. On a design level this adds a splash of color; on a character level this suggests that there is an element of the rebel in him!

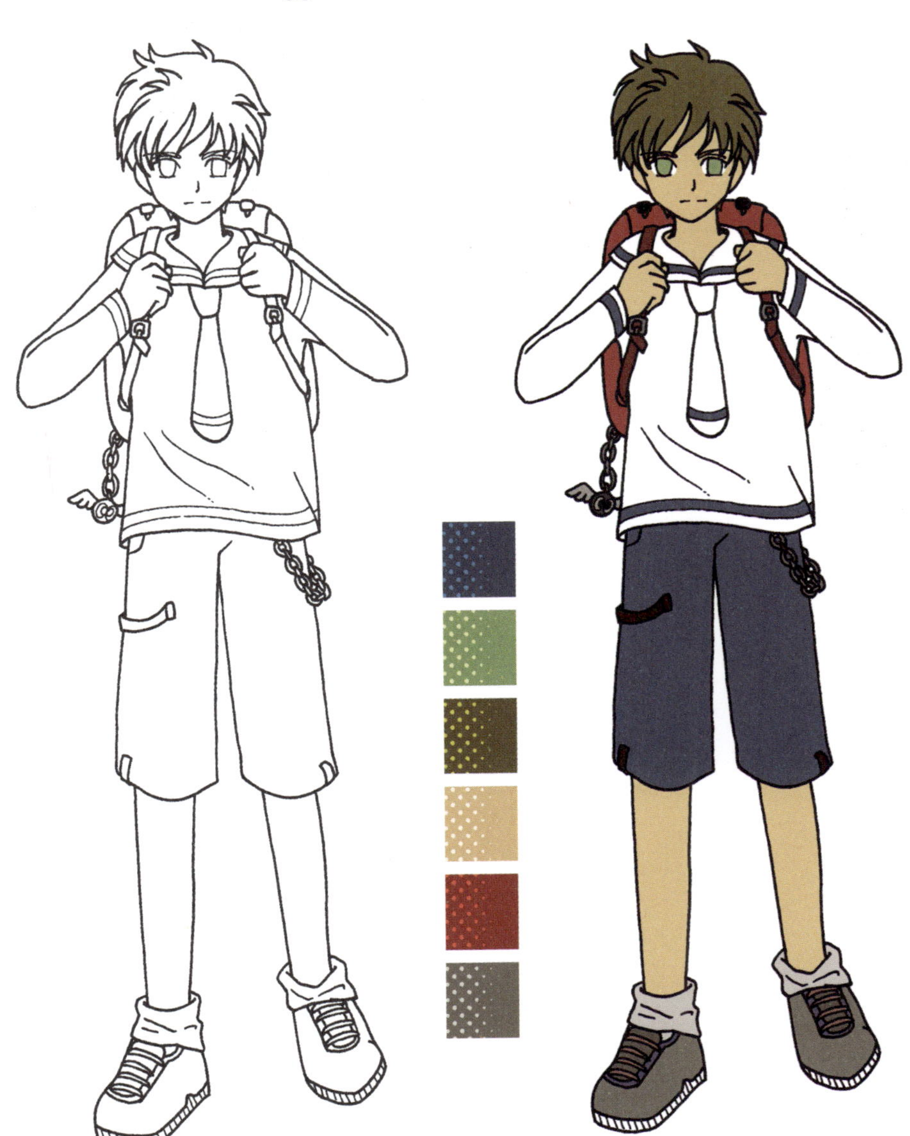

His skin tone is slightly tanned. This is a character that probably spends a lot of time outdoors, and so pale, white skin wouldn't suit him.

As the character is a realistic one, his hair couldn't really be a very unusual color without changing the design radically, so a fairly natural hair color has been chosen. His eyes, though again a fairly normal color, have been colored in a way that increases their wideness. There is no pupil, only a darker shadow of the same green. This lends the character an almost catlike appearance and suggests that he is the inquisitive sort.

MALE CHILD

SHADE AND HIGHLIGHTS

The style of shading used in this image is simple to match the clean lines of the design. One layer of shade has been used throughout, rather than building up any kind of gradient. As with any picture, care must be taken to ensure that the shade is coherent. In this image you can see that the light source would be somewhere to the left and above the figure, as all of the shade falls to the right and below.

Highlights are kept simple and are only used on key areas: the hair, eyes, and metallic buckles. In each case, rather than a pure white highlight, a lighter shade of the same color has been used.

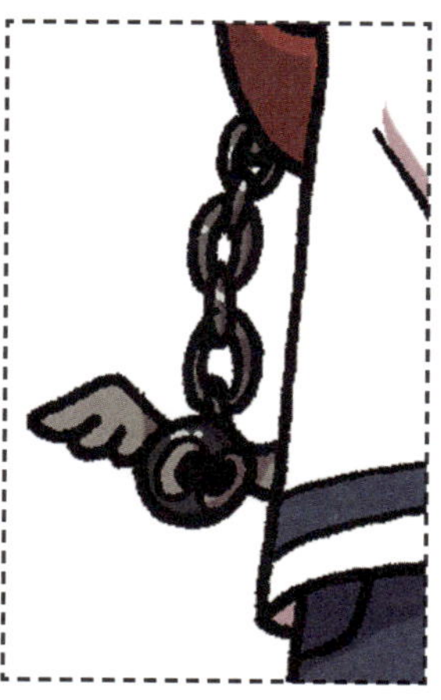

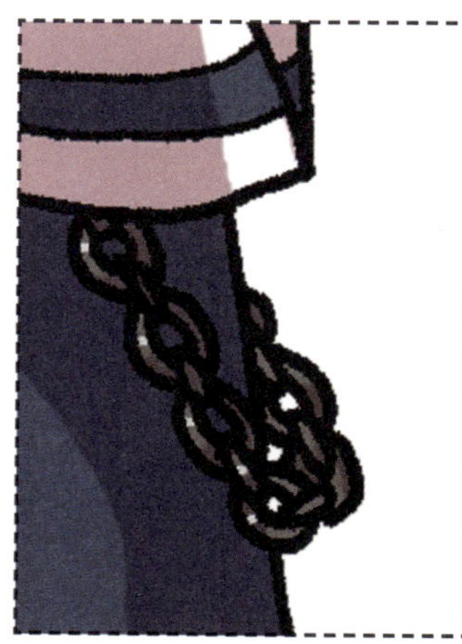

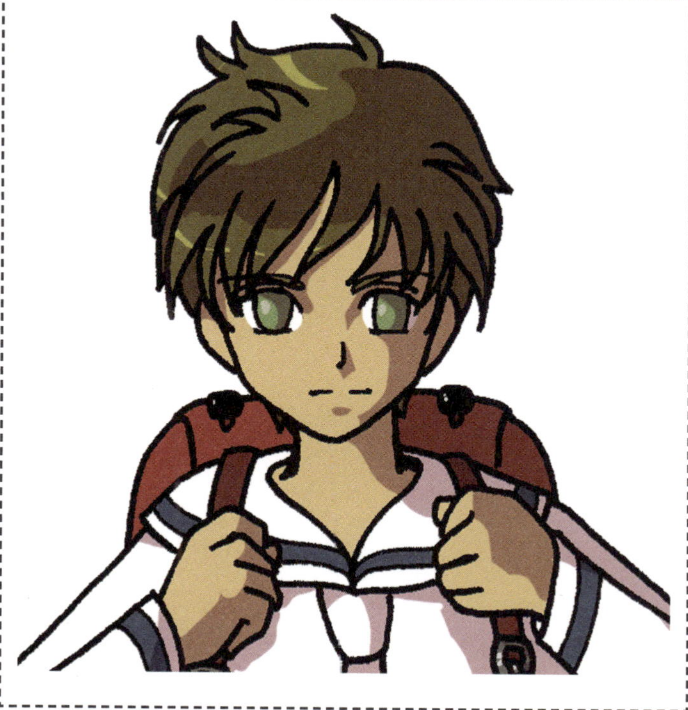

The boy has attached a chain to his shorts and also wears an unusual key chain on his bag. These items show a desire in him to be a little bit different and not to conform. The key chain is a cute mascot figure, which suggests he has a playful nature. Small features like these can make all the difference in a character design. Even when you are limited by the confines of a set uniform, there is nothing to stop you from adding details that can illustrate a character's true personality.

PERSONALITY

- Confident
- Inquisitive
- Rebellious
- Playful

SETTING

- School
- Modern Day

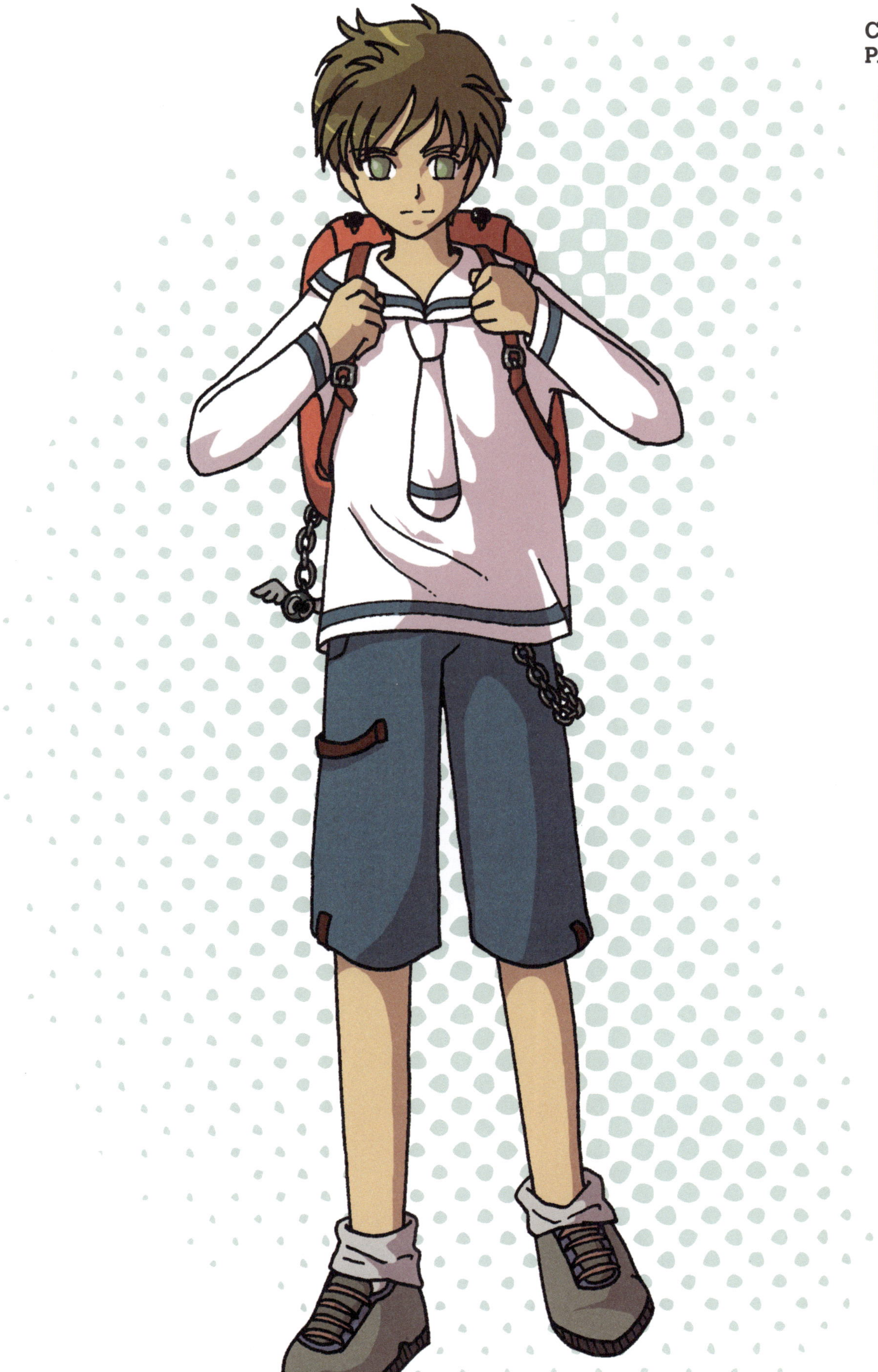

COLOR PALETTE

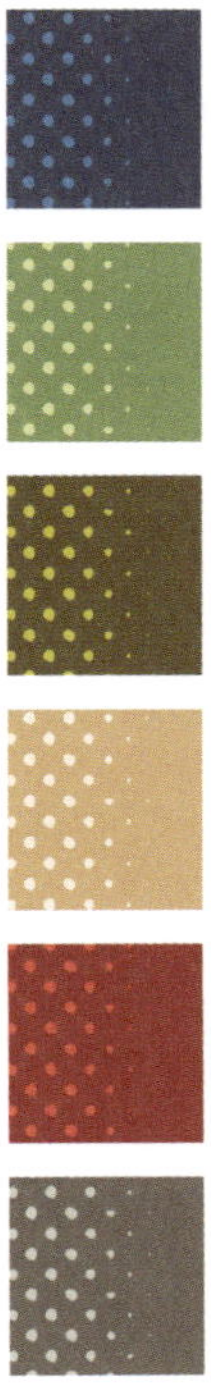

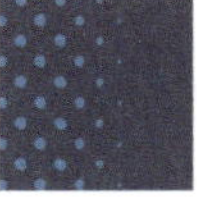
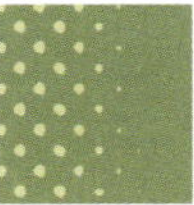
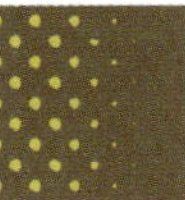

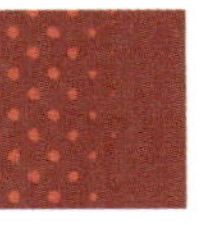
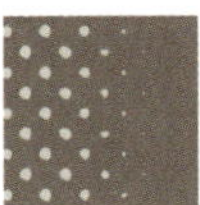

YOU TRY!

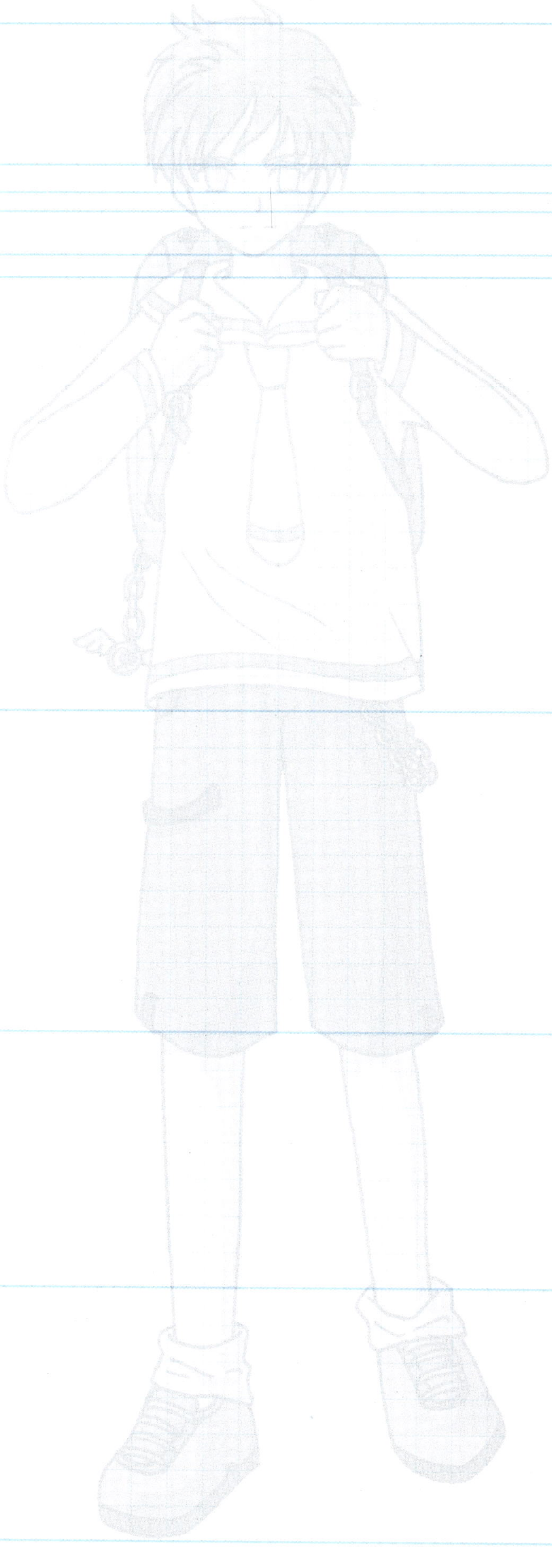

MALE CHILD ALTERNATIVE 1

This boy is from a different, harsher world – his torn clothing yet technological accessories hint at an apocalyptic future.

Someone used to hardship and fending for himself, he is defensive and stubborn. He reacts heatedly to criticism, shaking his right fist, yet he still shows signs of naivety, his left hand at a petulant angle as if throwing a childish tantrum. He's set his feet apart and they are firmly planted – this is a strong and resilient pose. When drawing him, it is important to use a vertical action line to ensure he is correctly balanced.

To further distance him from our world, he has unusual coloring – violet eyes and purple hair. His dark skin and flashing eyes, almost red, complement his hot temper. His ripped, white shirt and the aqua-toned vest offset and enhance the reds and dark skin tones.

His outfit contains a blend of high-tech gadgets and torn, pauperlike clothing. While this may not make sense at first, it completely fits the setting of a science fiction story – a futuristic world in the aftermath of a global disaster leading to sparse resources, a race struggling to survive in a hostile environment.

Chunky, fingerless gloves suggest a tough character – lots of wires, buttons, and metal plating have been added to give them an electronic look. Metal is a recurrent theme throughout the outfit, used in his pendant, on his shoes, and as his belt. When trying to depict metal, use a mixture of soft blends, fades, and gradients interspersed with thin, white, streaky highlights. The more concentrated the transition from dark to light, the more reflective the metal is.

PERSONALITY

- Stubborn
- Defensive
- Honest
- Tough
- Determined

SETTING

- Science Fiction
- Future
- Wastelands

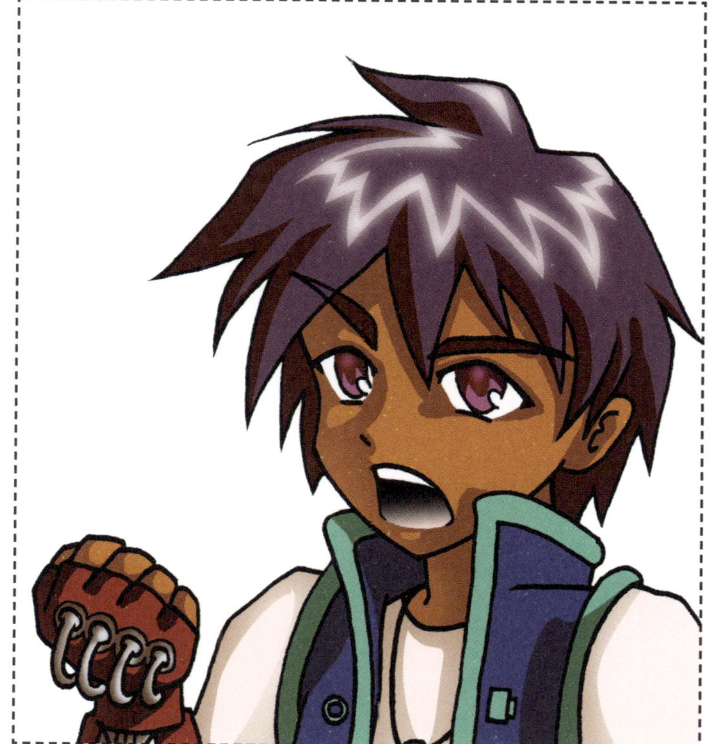

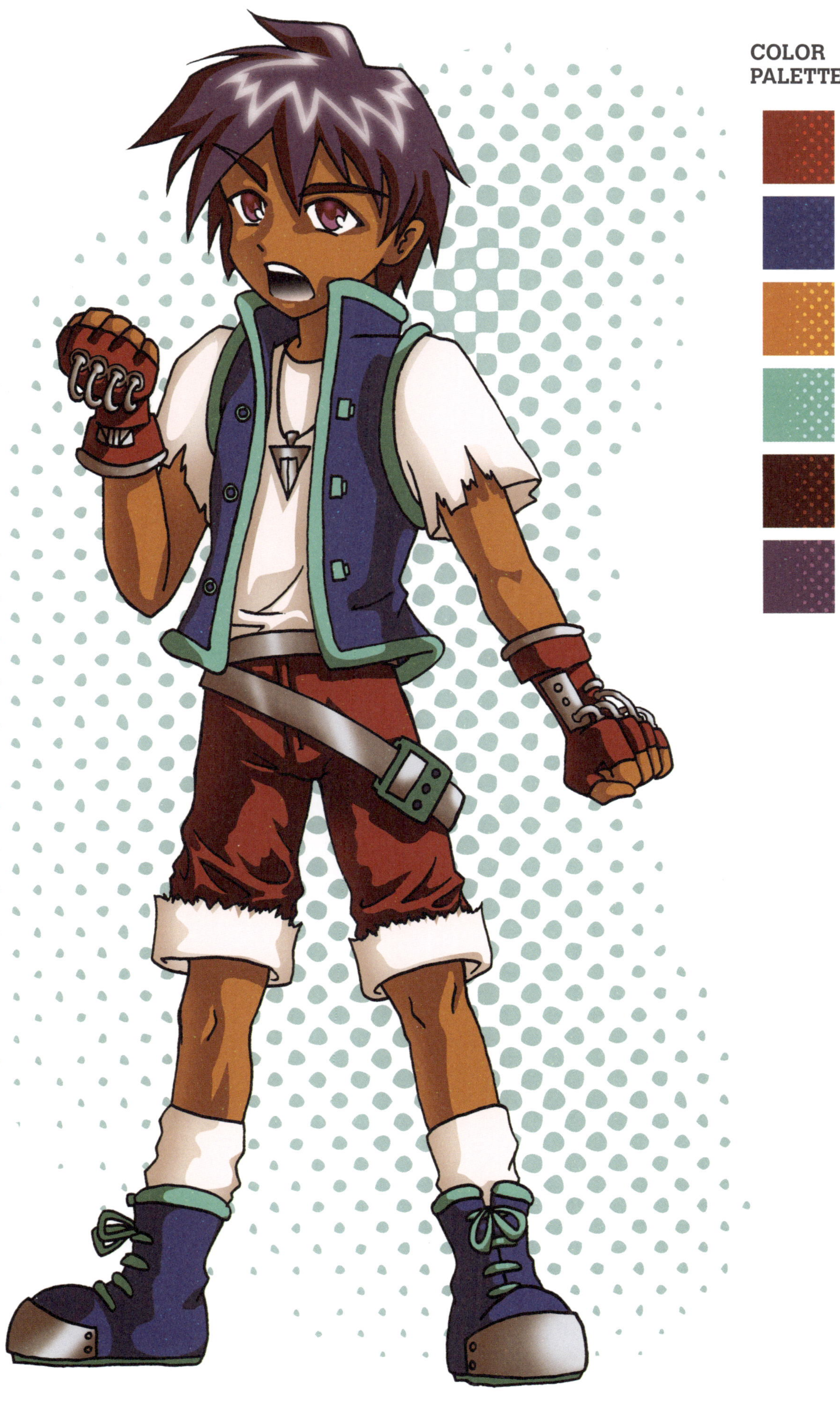

COLOR
PALETTE

YOU TRY!

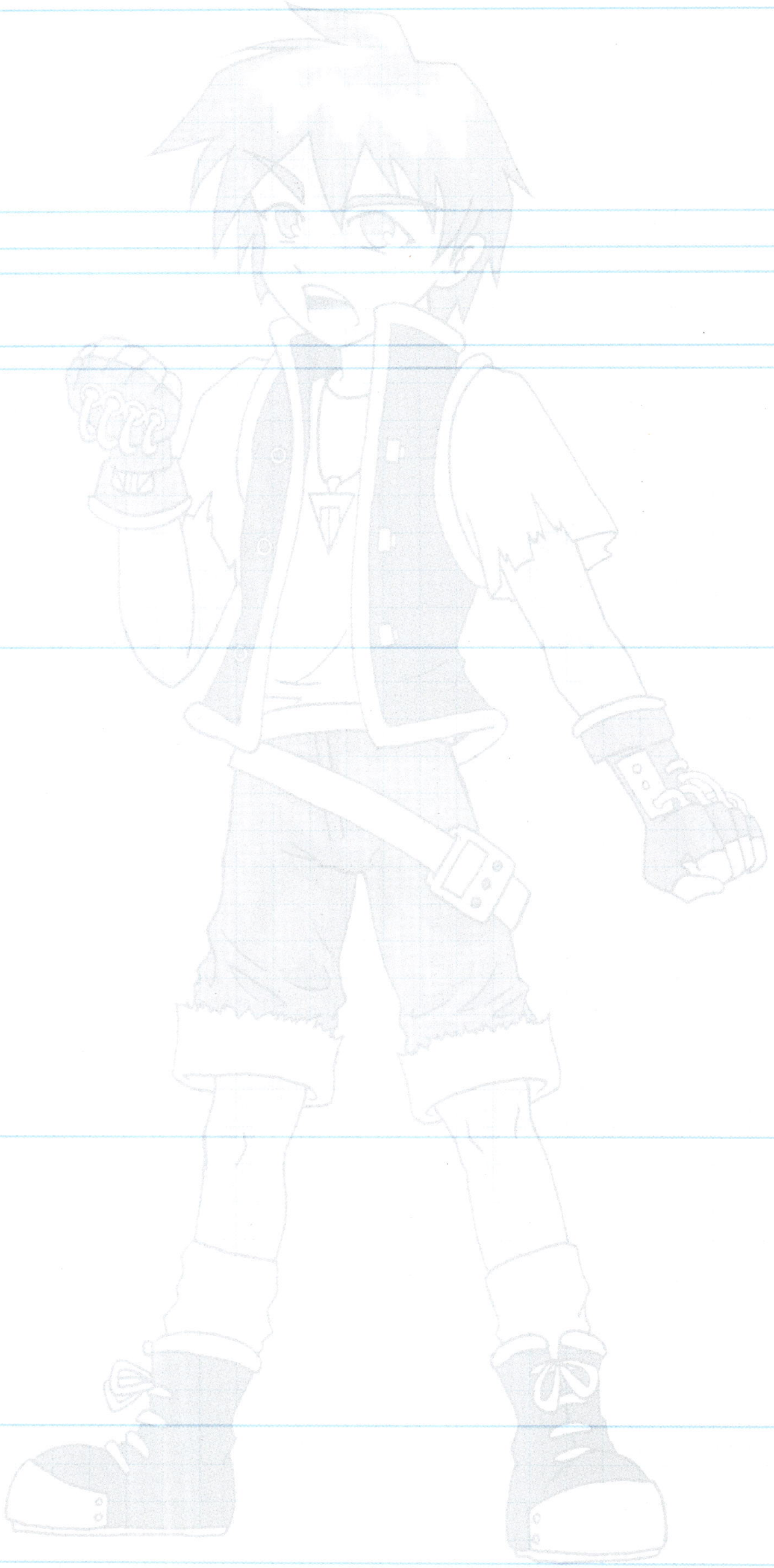

MALE CHILD ALTERNATIVE 2

This young boy aspires to be a skilled magician one day. He is a student training in the arts of magic and wizardry, practicing whenever he can so that he may gain valuable experience. He is holding a grimoire of spells in one hand while casting a spell with the other.

His stance and mellow facial expression suggest that he is confident in his abilities. He's enjoying the craft of magic and wants to improve. With a calm, relaxed smile and overall peaceful expression, it's obvious this boy is someone who dislikes violence and conflicts.

The light colors, such as his shiny blonde hair and bright blue eyes, reflect the boy's laid-back attitude and gentle personality. However, it hints that he can also be naïve and overconfident at times.

You can tell he is from another world from the design of his clothes and the presence of magic fire. A long cloak and fancy-looking shawl decorated with a silver trim and held together by clips with golden buckles give the character the appearance that he is from a role-playing-game fantasy world.

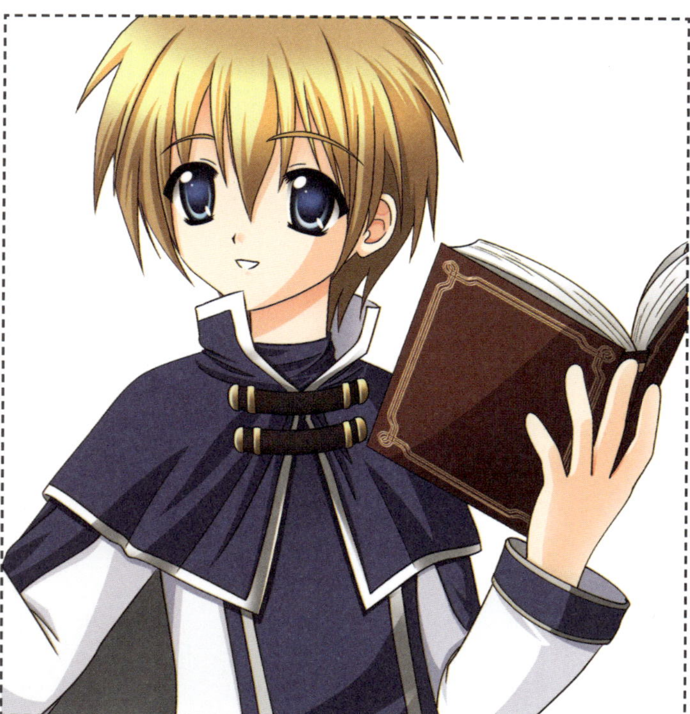

The colors of his outfit also help to identify that he is a fantasy-type character. Brown leather is commonly used in fantasy designs, therefore the use of brown for the book, his belt, and the clips on his shawl and shoes make his setting more recognizable, as well as adding a common accent throughout the image.

This is complemented with the main color combination of indigo and white for the whole outfit, which is dark in comparison to the boy's hair, eyes, and magic fire. The purple and grays used in the outfit give him an air of mystery without making him look aloof. Use long streaks of highlights and shading to bring out the folds in his cloak.

PERSONALITY

- Optimistic
- Confident
- Thoughtful
- Trustworthy
- Hardworking
- Naïve

SETTING

- Fantasy
- Magic
- School
- Academy
- Laboratory
- Castle
- Adventure

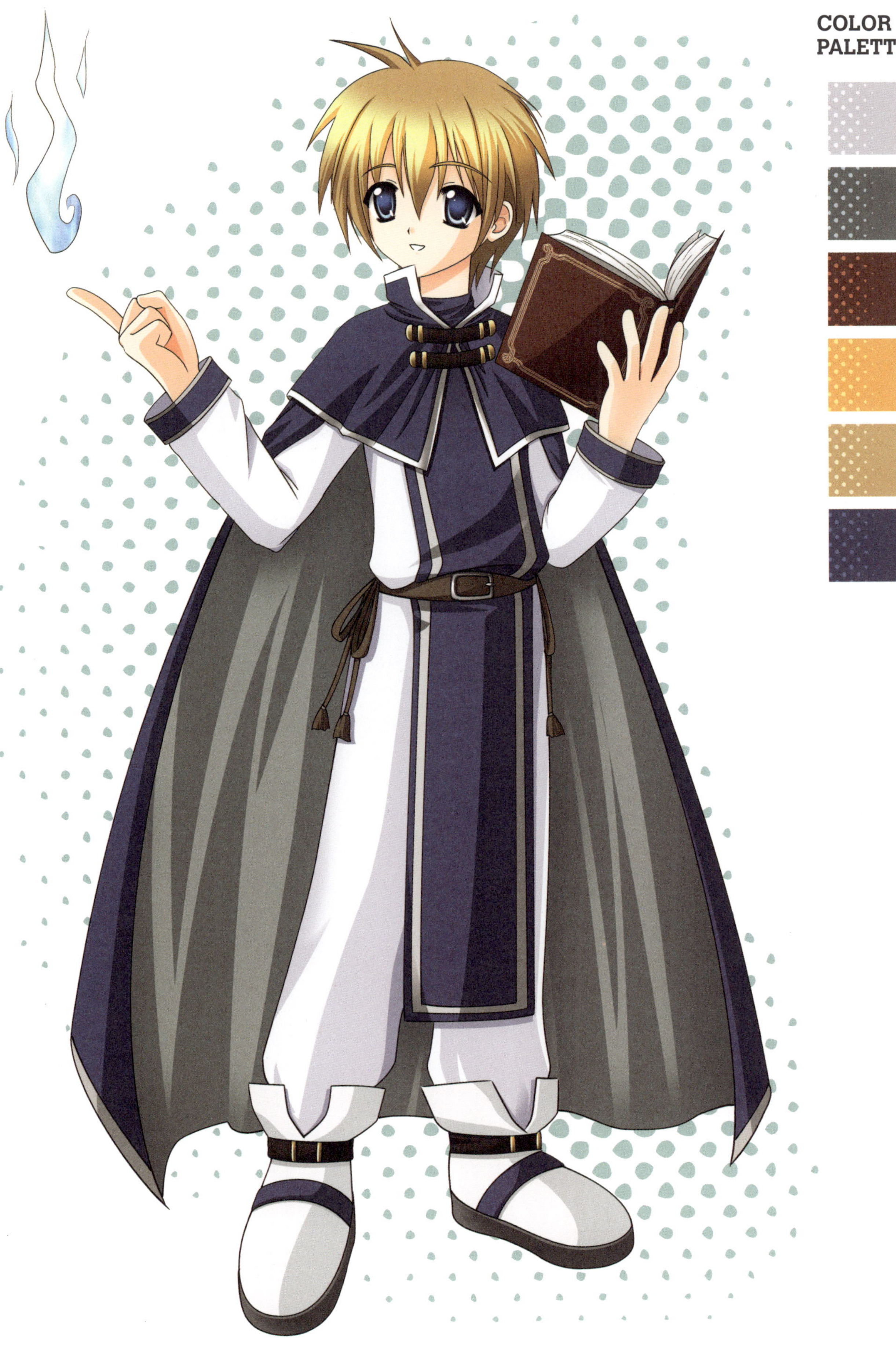

COLOR PALETTE

YOU TRY!

FEMALE CHILD

At first, very young characters may seem to have very limited roles in manga; maybe they're an annoying younger brother or sister to the cooler teenage protagonist, or just in the plot to be rescued by an older, stronger character time and time again. However, there is a whole wealth of stories out there aimed at young children with protagonists they can relate to. Often, in comics aimed at young girls, the protagonist has some sort of magical power or special talent that sets them apart from their peers. These kinds of stories reflect the fantasy and innocence of childhood and are hugely popular with children in both Japan and the United States.

ROUGH SKETCH

The figure is built up lightly in pencil. The lines are quite loose and will be tightened at the inking stage. If you are confident, you can sketch quite quickly and freely and leave the neatening up and details until the inking stage.

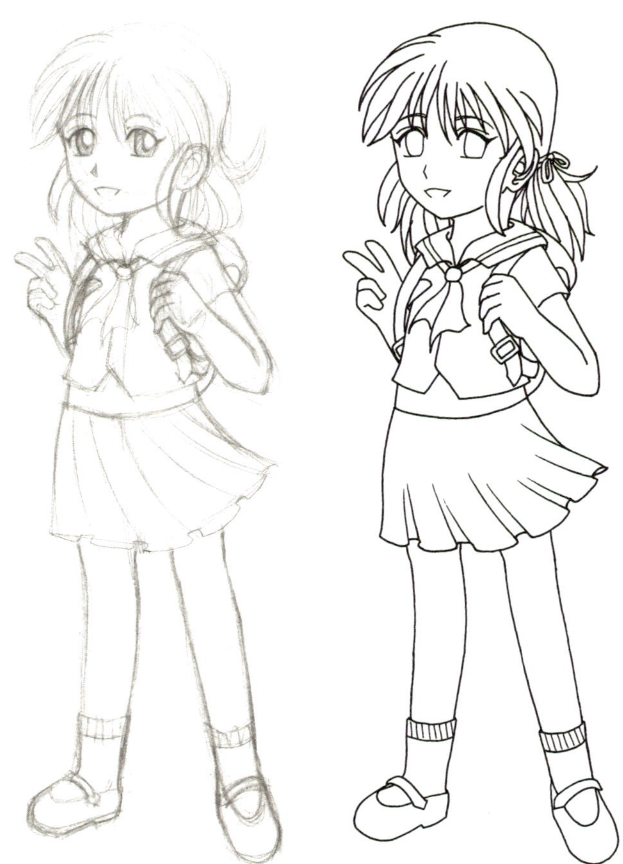

FIGURE

Young characters, similar to this girl, have almost exaggerated looking proportions. This character is a mere four and a half head heights tall and has a large head with huge eyes and a small nose and mouth, which make her look younger and more innocent.

She also has narrow shoulders, which add to her young appearance. As young children have barely developed, their anatomy is very immature. The character here is around six years old, so she still has small, dainty hands and feet. Her fingers are small and round, but without looking too fat. Also, she has no definition around the waist and hips.

This character is wearing a school uniform, a modified version of the traditional "sailor fuku" (sailor suit). The collar on her shirt is more square than it would be typically, and the pleats on her skirt are less rigid and flow more freely. Her shoes are "Mary Janes," which are quite typical of the simple shoes children wear.

Even though she is wearing a uniform, her personality can be shown through small details in the design. Her ribbon-tied bunches show she is quite girly, and her neat short socks show she is quite prim (as opposed to a more tomboyish character, who would have messier hair and socks that were falling down). She appears very tidy and is probably a good student.

Take particular care when inking details like her hair ribbons, the stripes on her collar, and the buckles on her bag straps – don't be afraid to switch to a finer-tipped pen to make things easier.

POINTS OF DESIGN

Very young children have not yet developed much of an interest in fashion. As such, it would be inappropriate to give them too many trendy accessories, or too daring an outfit. But that's not to say they should be completely unfashionable. Try to make young characters' clothes look contemporary but not too over the top. Cute, stylish logos and other simple designs work well in place of fashionable accessories – for example, a school bag with a cute animal mascot logo.

BASIC COLORS

The character's uniform is an unusual color (the standard palette for sailor suits is blue and white). When relying on traditional design elements, don't hesitate to make them more unique by experimenting with color schemes. Even though she is a child and should be quite active, her skin is a pale tone, showing that perhaps she spends too much time studying indoors instead of playing outside. Her hair is shaded in a cute, girly shade of pink.

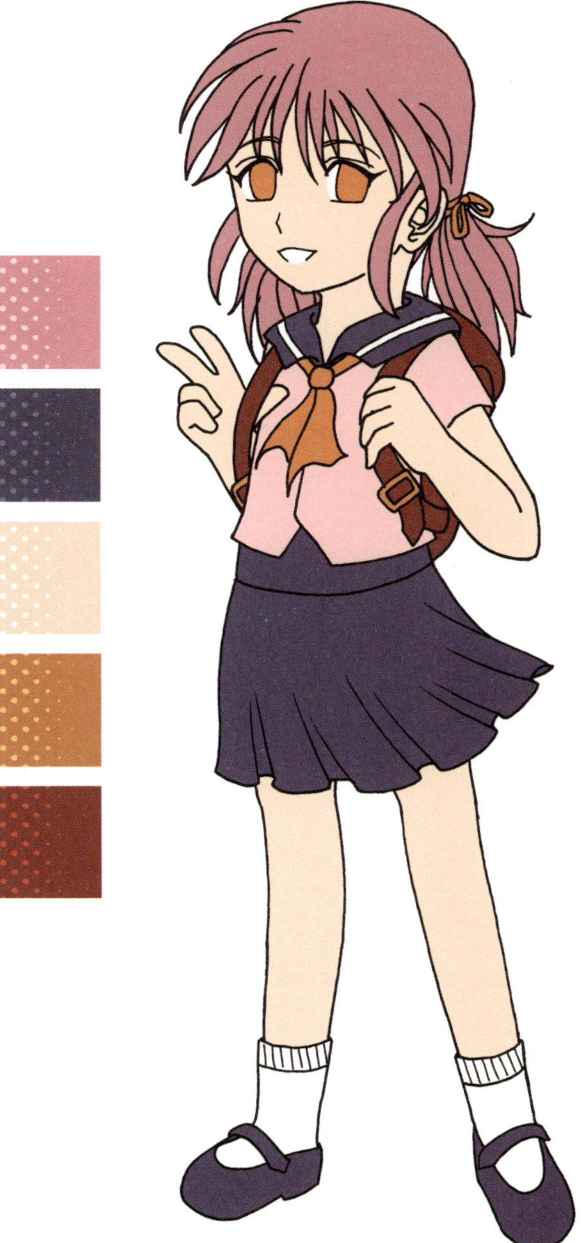

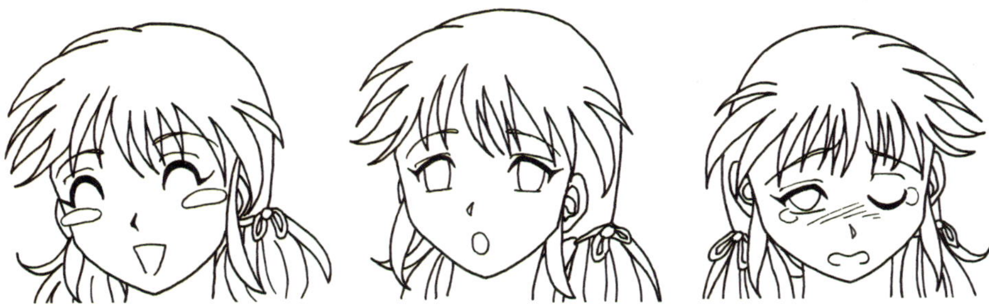

Here are some expressions you might use on characters of this type. Children are often very happy and bouncy, or curious and confused, so those types of expressions suit them best. More adult expressions, like sarcastic ones, could look inappropriate on a young character.

SHADOWS AND HIGHLIGHTS

The shadows are added in warm shades to complement the pink colors used in the image. Remember to add shadows in between the pleats of her skirt. To bring out the shine and texture of her hair, light pink highlights are added in jagged streaks. Her eyes also have bright white highlights in circles and ovals to emphasize their roundness.

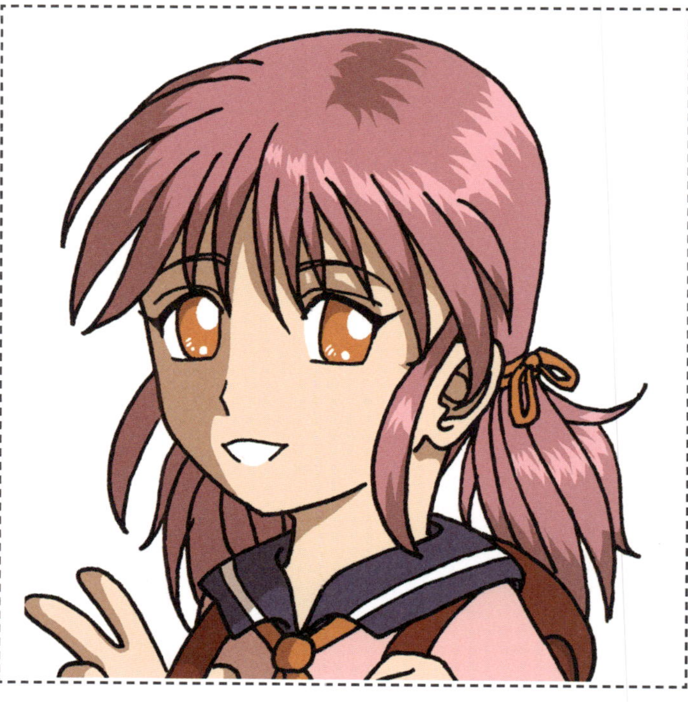

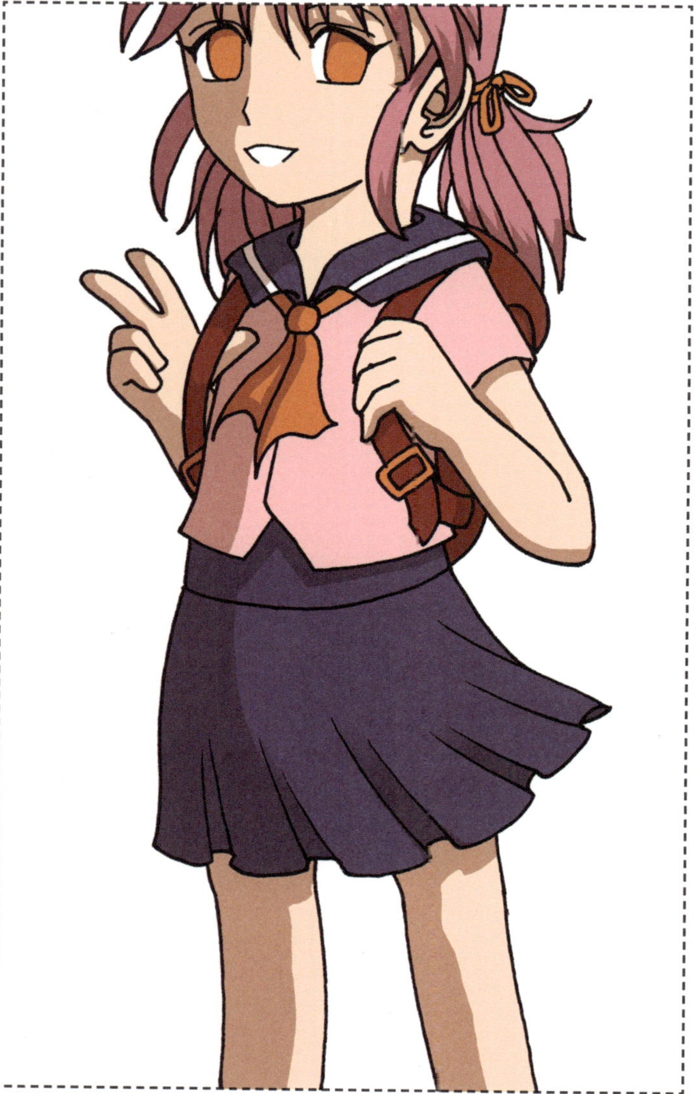

PERSONALITY

- Cheerful
- Shy
- Gentle
- Kind
- Neat

SETTING

- Contemporary
- School
- After-School Clubs
- Home

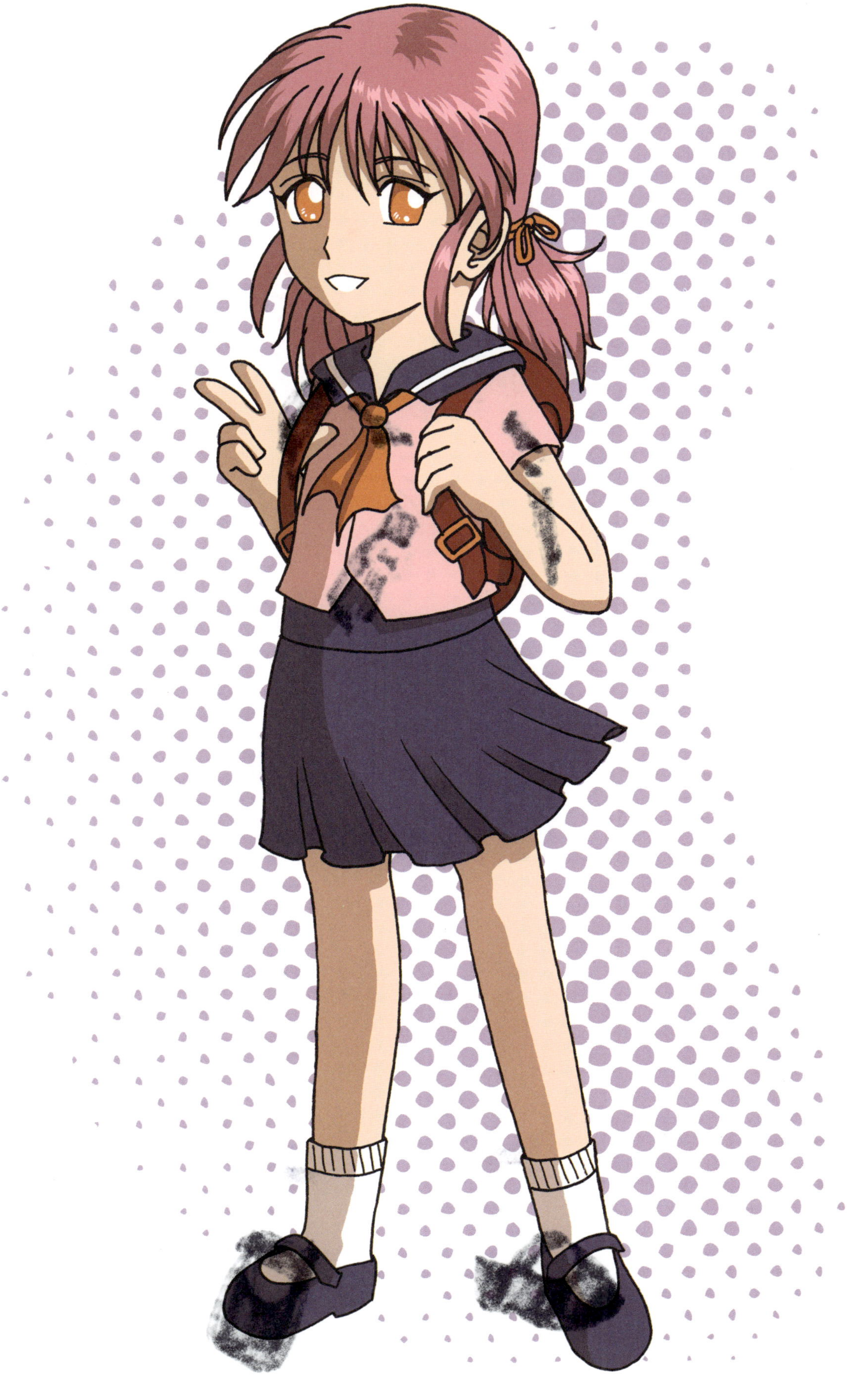

COLOR PALETTE

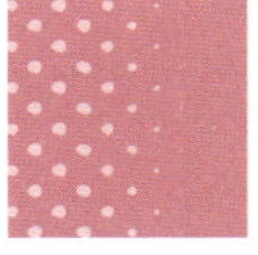

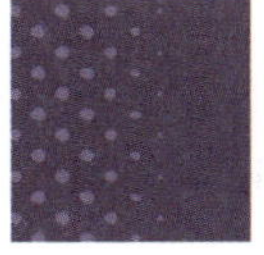

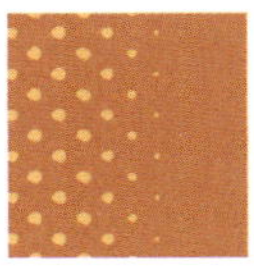

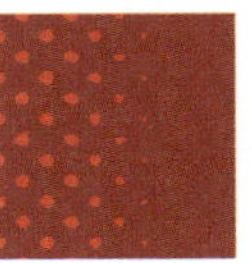

YOU TRY!

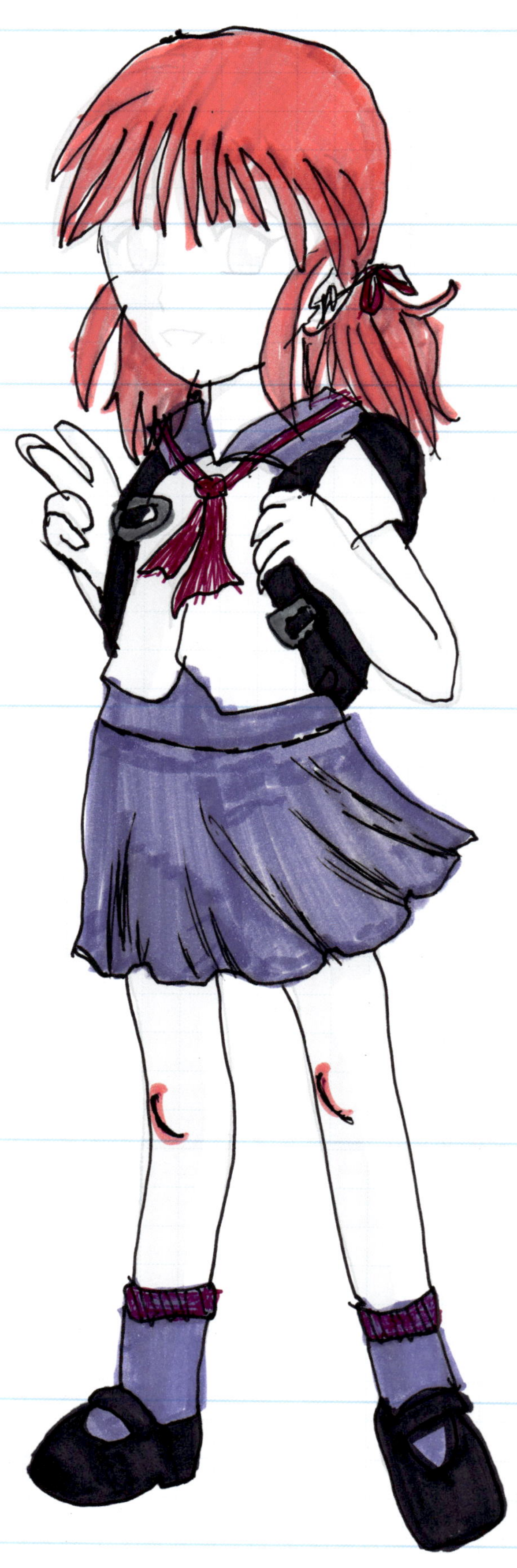

FEMALE CHILD ALTERNATIVE 1

This character is very commonly seen in anime and manga – the magical girl! She's a bright, happy, outgoing little girl who magically transforms into a fairy princess to save the day, with a magic wand and a cute little animal sidekick.

She is drawn in a fairly realistic proportion set of four to five head lengths, but she has very large, expressive eyes with very little white showing – this makes her look cute and trustworthy. Her stance is confident, leaning forward with feet firmly placed. She holds her wand in a cute, girlish way, arms fully extended and both hands close together. Her exaggerated hair is very long, wavy, and softly luminous in a magical blue. It's tied into a ponytail with a ribbon, in line with her active nature. The ringlets framing her face also add to her prettiness.

The velvety blue of her hair inspired the rest of the color scheme in the picture – cool, pastel, and smoky shades of blue, purple, and green. Her dress is very pretty, with puffy sleeves, ruffles, and many skirt layers. Don't be tempted to let the costume hide incorrect anatomy – draw the body outline first before experimenting with an elaborate costume.

Note the coloring on her wings and on her mascot – the shading and patterns were actually inspired by the natural world. Her wings are colored like a seagull's, white with a short fade into black tips. Her mascot has bat wings as a design contrast, but is colored entirely in shades of green. It still looks very realistic, due to soft, natural shading – the stripes are based on a normal tabby cat.

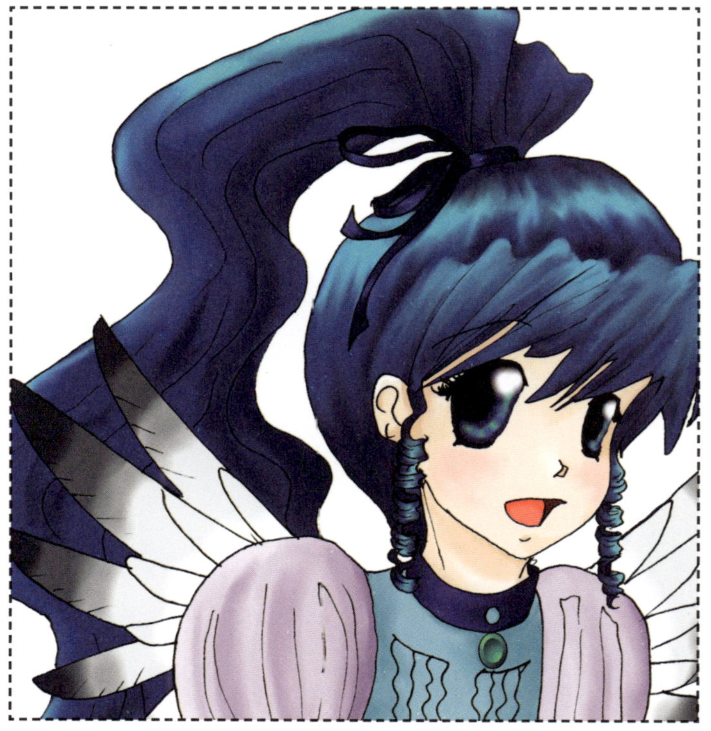

PERSONALITY

- Bright
- Cheerful
- Energetic
- Good

SETTING

- Modern
- Fantasy
- Romance
- Action

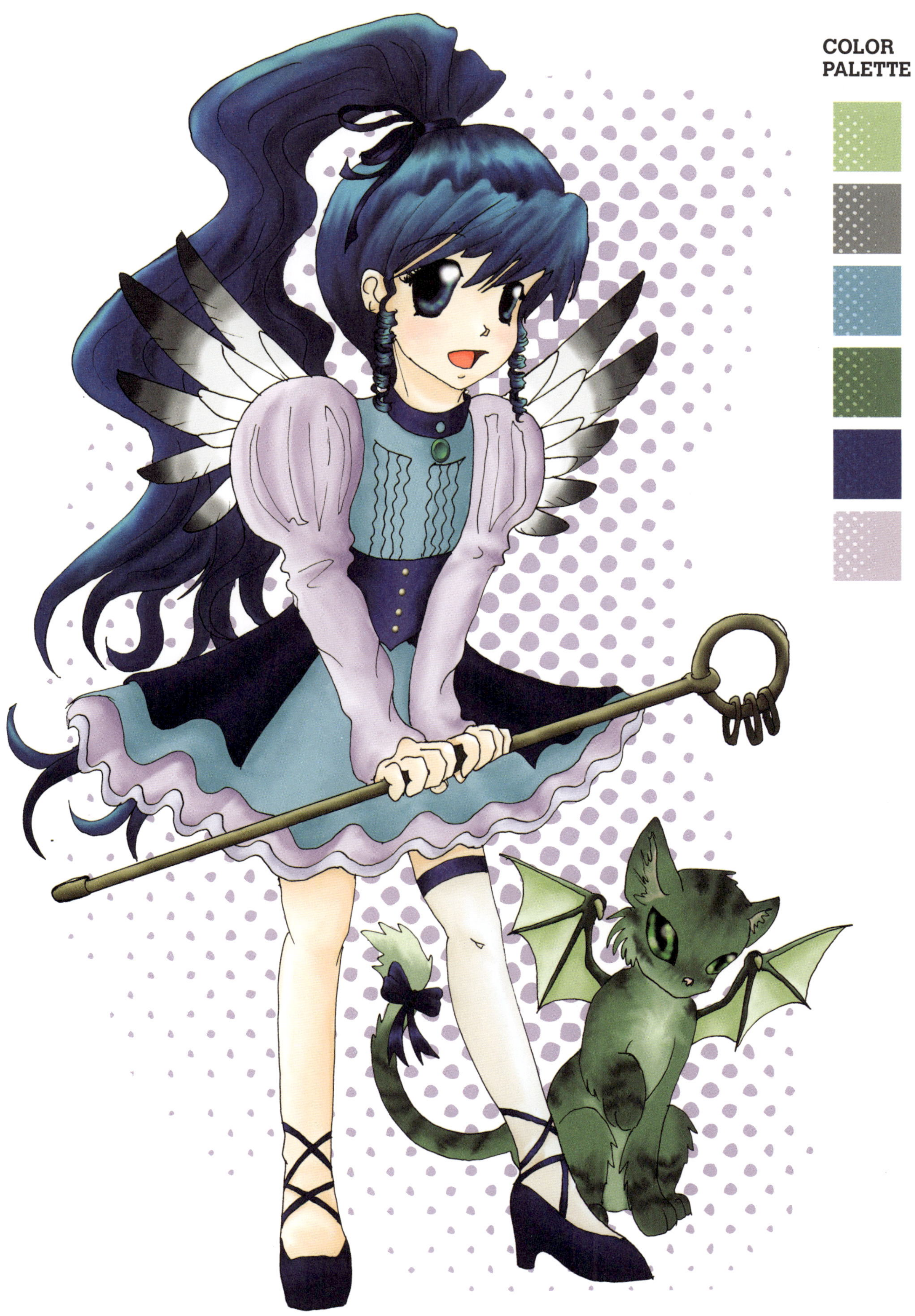

COLOR PALETTE

YOU TRY!

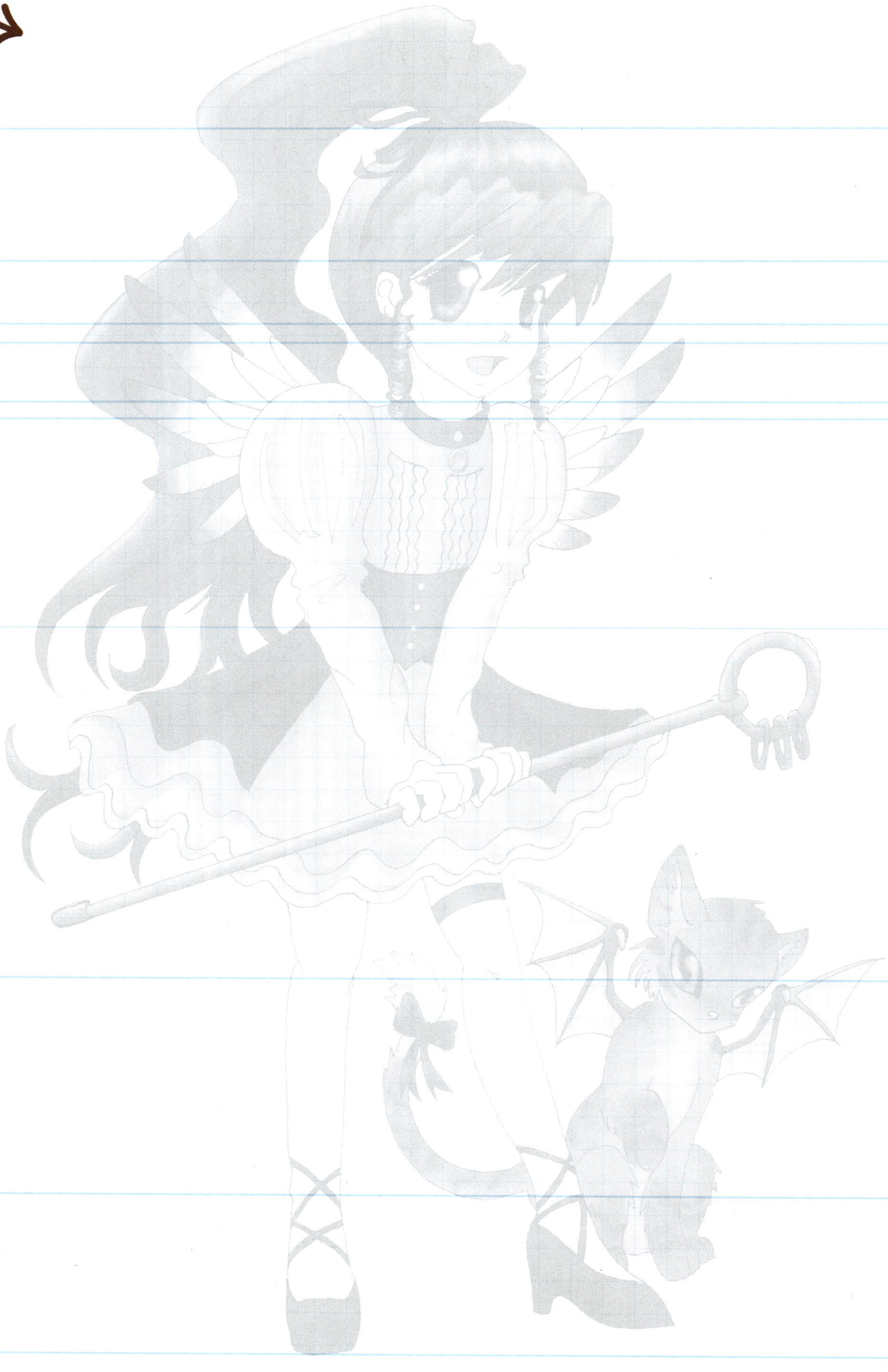

FEMALE CHILD ALTERNATIVE 2

This little zombie girl has elements about her that mix up pop culture themes from both east and west; gothic Lolita elements of Japanese street fashion, mixed with Frankenstein zombie horror themes, drawn in a cute "super-deformed" manga style.

The proportions may seem strange at first; make sure her head is no wider than her body. Her body should be chubby so it, theoretically, can support her head. Her wings must be equal and symmetrical. The pupils in her eyes are slightly pointy, which would imply a vampirish nature. Her legs and arms can be quite chubby; her feet should be rounded and chunky.

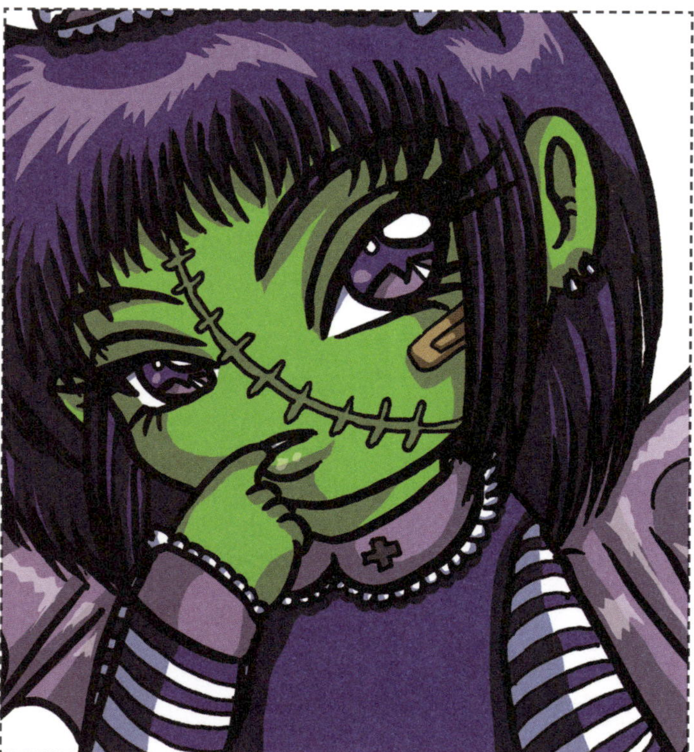

She is dressed in typical little girl fashion but shows a dark side to her girlishness with her medical kit and awkwardly stitched-up plush toy (which is ironically falling apart). Stickers and adhesive bandages reveal her clumsiness, and her earrings and skull fashion motifs give her an appealing, contemporary edge. Her green skin tones complement her purple dress and match her setting. The cross on her lapel and lunchbox suggest she is following some kind of surreal nursing course.

Her eyes are large, suggesting innocence, but their shape hints that she knows more than she should! Her hair is bobbed sensibly but has smallish strands that require attention to detail when reproducing.

Her stance is a very innocent one, emphasized more by how her feet are pointing inward and by the insecure finger held near her mouth as if she is nervously chewing on it. Has she done something wrong? Is she prepared to admit it?

PERSONALITY

- Subdued
- Suspicious
- Shy
- Clumsy
- Eager to Help but Things Always Turn Out Wrong

SETTING

- Fantasy
- Horror
- School
- Gothic

COLOR
PALETTE

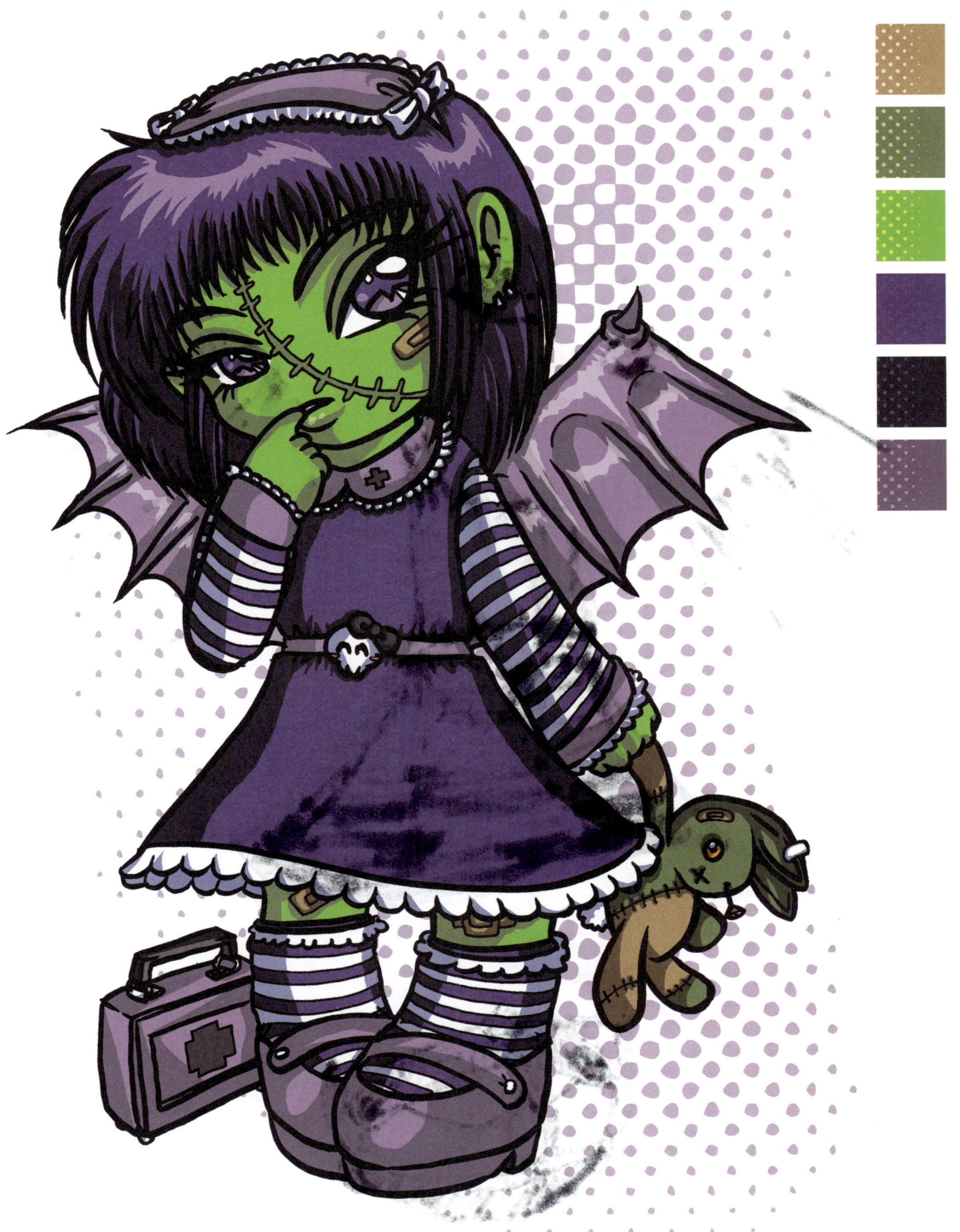

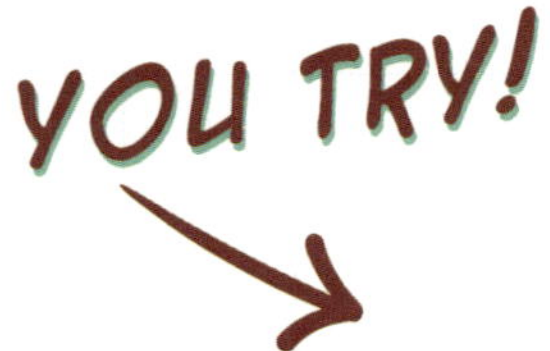
YOU TRY!

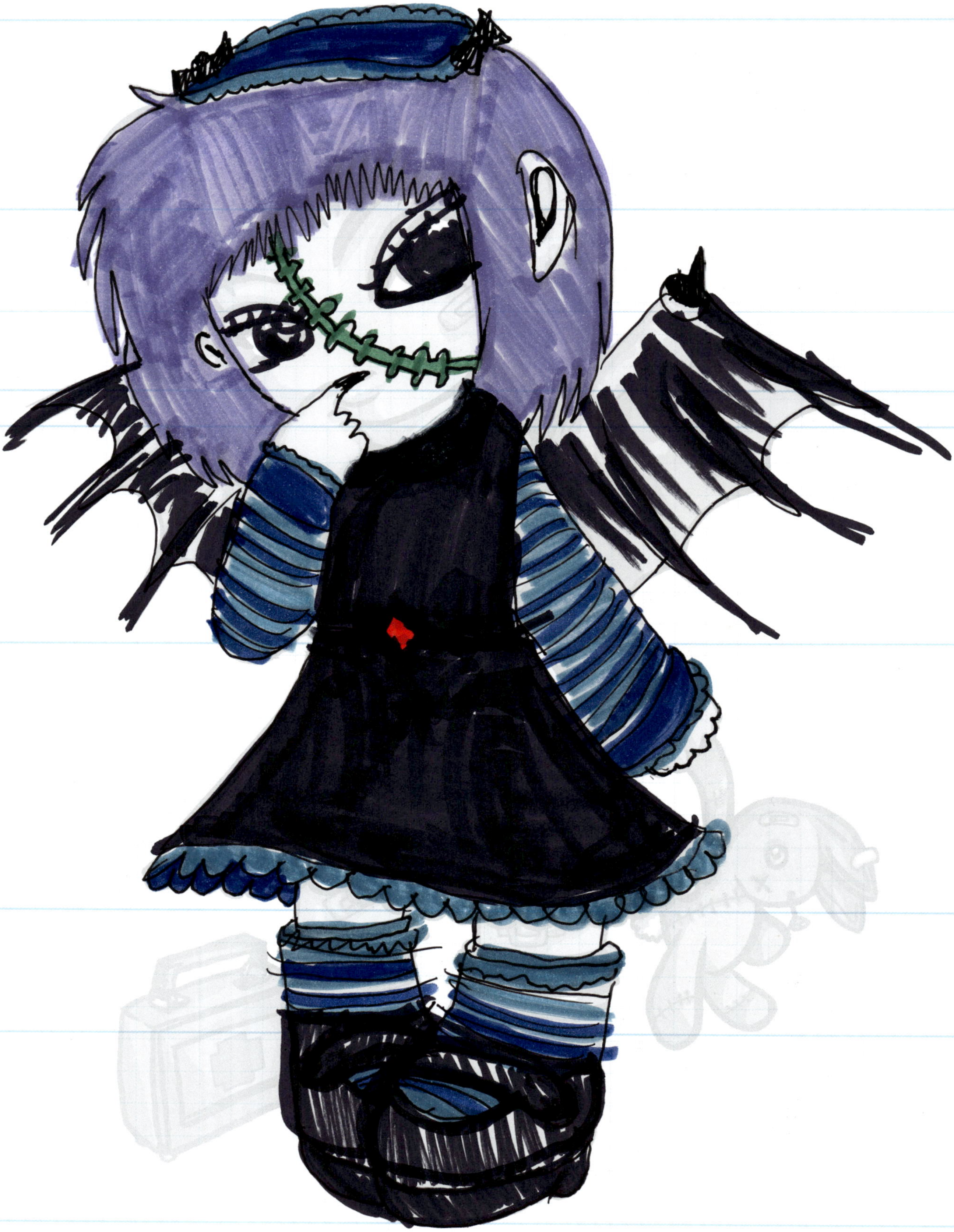

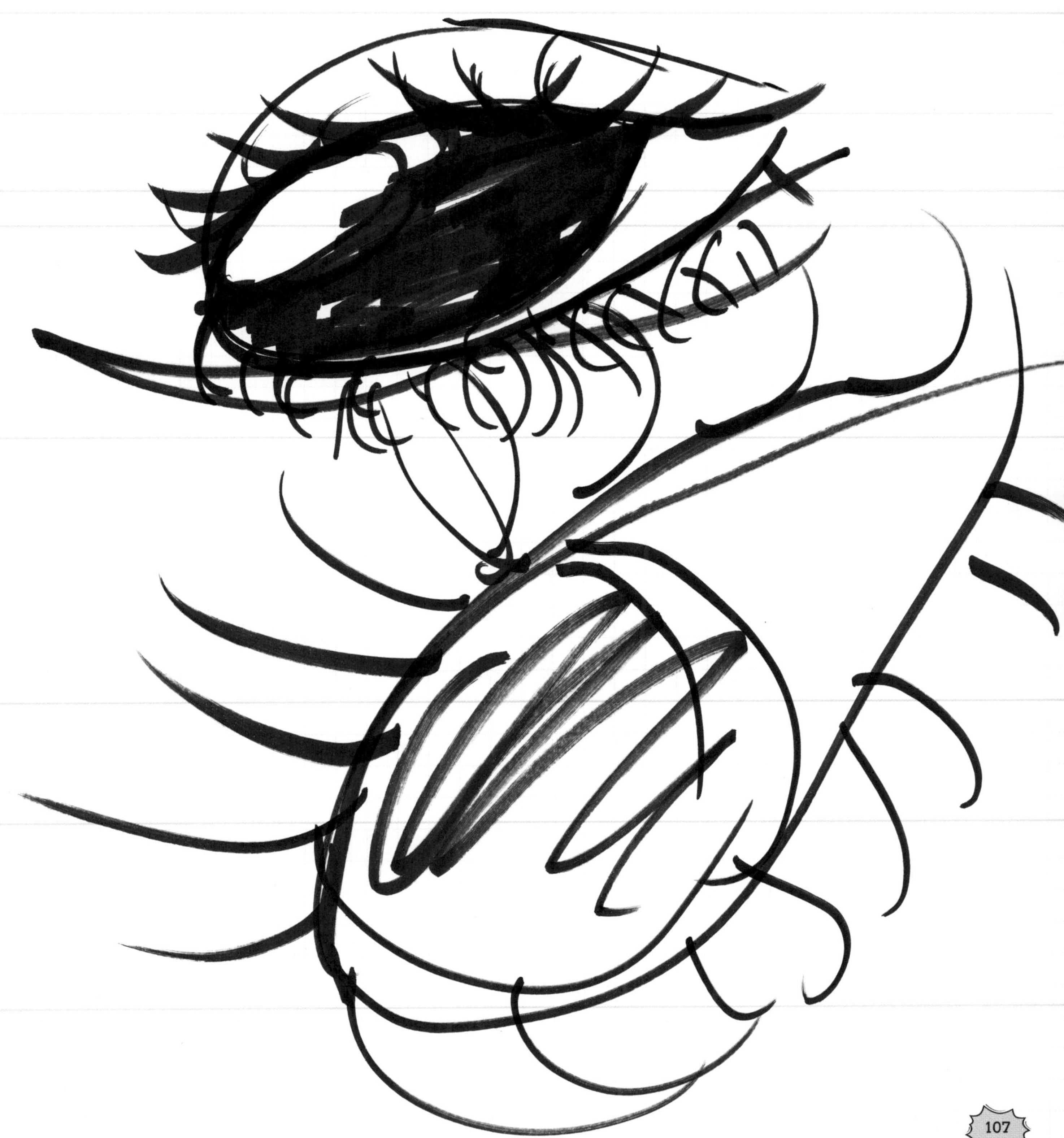

108

TEENAGE MALE

Teenage males are possibly the most common of all manga protagonists. Offering a perfect compromise between youthful enthusiasm and freedom of youth combined with the strength and opportunity of an adult character, the teenage male is in a perfect position to have conflict, battles, adventures, and romance. The passage into manhood for a teenage male also represents a certain acquisition of power, both socially and physically, introducing a new circumstance and opportunity for a character to compete against other people in the world but without the experience that can make behavior predictable or withdrawn. Most of all, the role for a teenage character is far more fun than any other age group because their actions are deemed less finite, with plenty of opportunity for reconciliation.

ROUGH SKETCH

The body has been built up gradually, first with faint lines and then with increasingly dark line work. Details in the clothing are included at this stage so that they can be properly interpreted when it comes to inking. Suggestion of shading and fabric folds are also sketched in. Although these details may not be fully defined until the coloring and shading are added at the very end, it allows the choice of whether or not inking detail is necessary in this area and gives a better approximation of how the overall image will look. Certain details, such as the chains, are not defined clearly at this stage but will be rendered properly during inking.

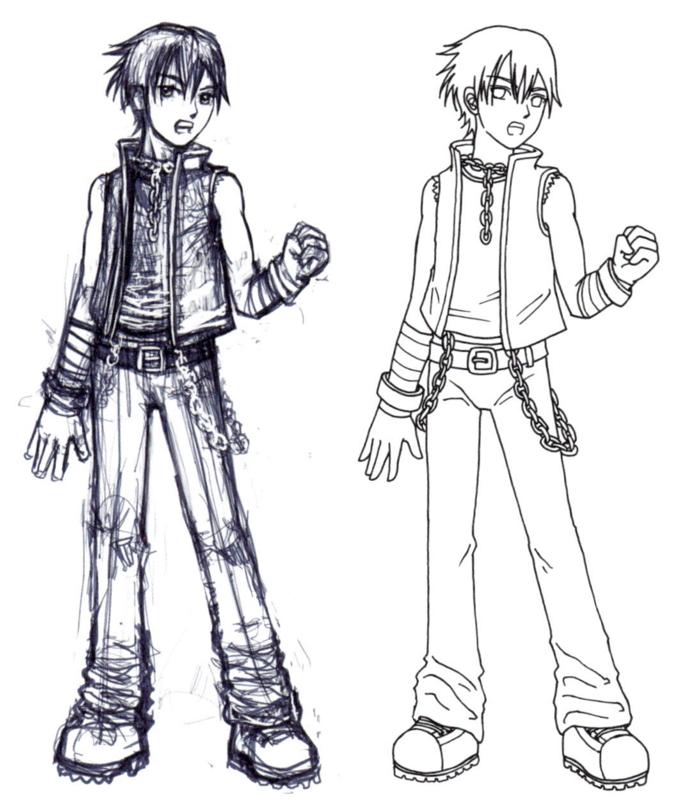

FIGURE

Teenage males have very little definition in their body shape. Although they have matured past puberty, they have not yet developed muscle tone or a full male physique. As a result, the torso, hips, and waist of male characters at this age are almost shapeless with only slight variation. Loose-fitting clothing help to define the volume of the limbs, with emphasis on the slight folds on the base of the vest and the way it hangs stiffly from the sides. Detail is introduced to the center of the image in the form of chains, wrapping around the back of the character and helping to express the volume of the figure.

POINTS OF DESIGN

Teenagers have the opportunity to express themselves quite freely with the way they dress. Fashionable or trendy choices of clothes are commonplace, with little regard for practicalities or long-term wear. This character has obviously dressed with a specific look in mind, trying to come across as a fighter or tough character, perhaps to compensate for his meager physical stature. Chains are worn around the neck to complement those hanging off his waistband, introducing areas of detail to some of the plainer areas of the image, as well as drawing something distinctive. Arm bandages are worn entirely for cosmetic purposes, combined with heavy bracelets, tying the design elements together perfectly.

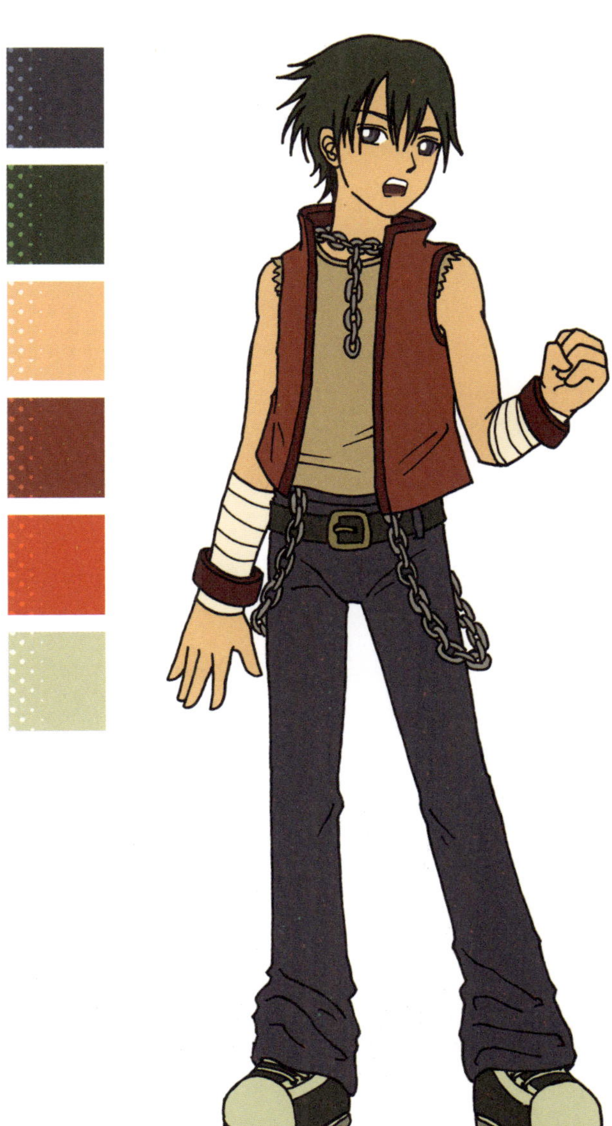

BASIC COLORS

This character's choice of clothing is obviously well considered, so it's likely the colors would be appropriately coordinated. Opting for more autumnal shades, the choice of palette is less flamboyant and garish than some teenage characters, but possibly reflects the impression of the character being tough and not someone to mess with. The hair on this character is a deep shade of green, with details of his belt and shoes chosen to complement this. A neutral tone for the vest and bandages allow greater focal emphasis on the brown vest and burgundy bracelets.

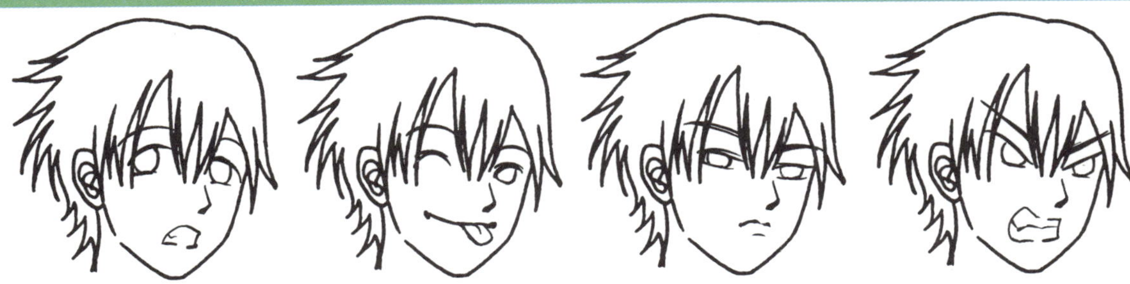

Teenagers are especially malleable when it comes to expressions and can be more expressive than any other character type. Although teenagers often have emotions of brooding and anguish, they're also playful and joking a lot of the time, so both extremes are commonplace. Conversely, teenage characters, especially male characters, often suffer from a lack of subtlety – characters won't have developed such a defensive front or methods of hiding the way they feel at this stage, and this should come across in the way you present them.

SHADING AND FINISHING TOUCHES

His clothing is not overly tight or loose, nor is his figure well developed, so some block shading with a few instances of folds and creases will suffice. Particular areas of importance are his head and the details of his chains. His head is tilted a fair distance away from the light, so most of the left side of his face is in shadow, but a tiny bit of light spills onto his left cheek. The chains are metallic, so they require at least three levels of shading – base colors, shadows, and light highlights. Each chain link needs attention, so take care!

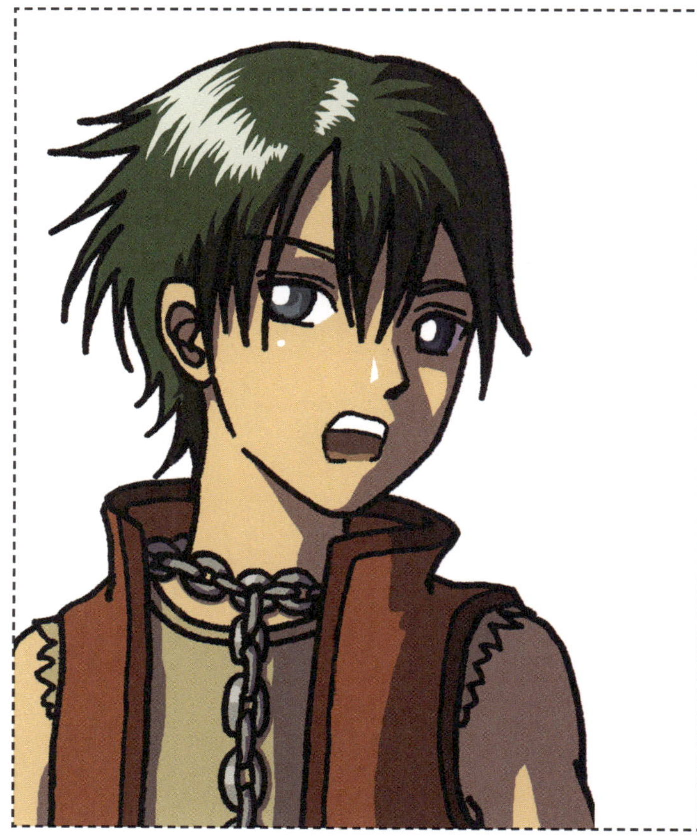

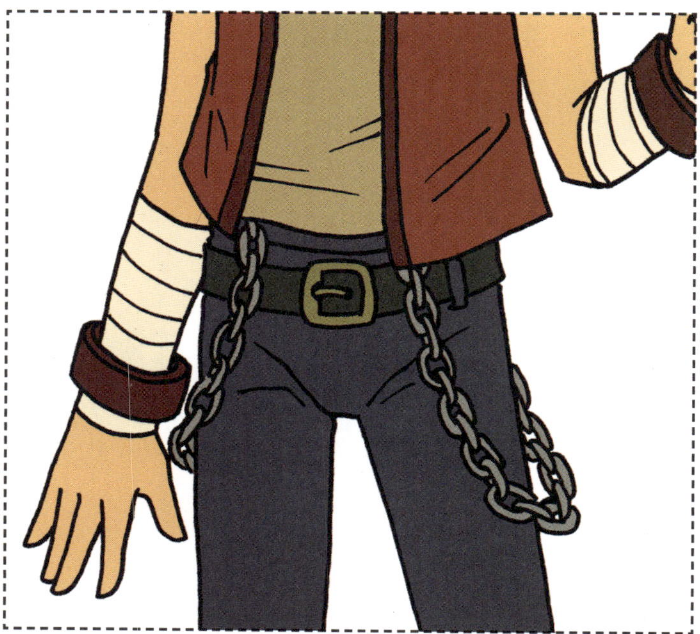

PERSONALITY

- Angry
- Aggressive
- Determined

SETTING

- Contemporary
- Gang or Street
- Action
- Adventure
- Thriller

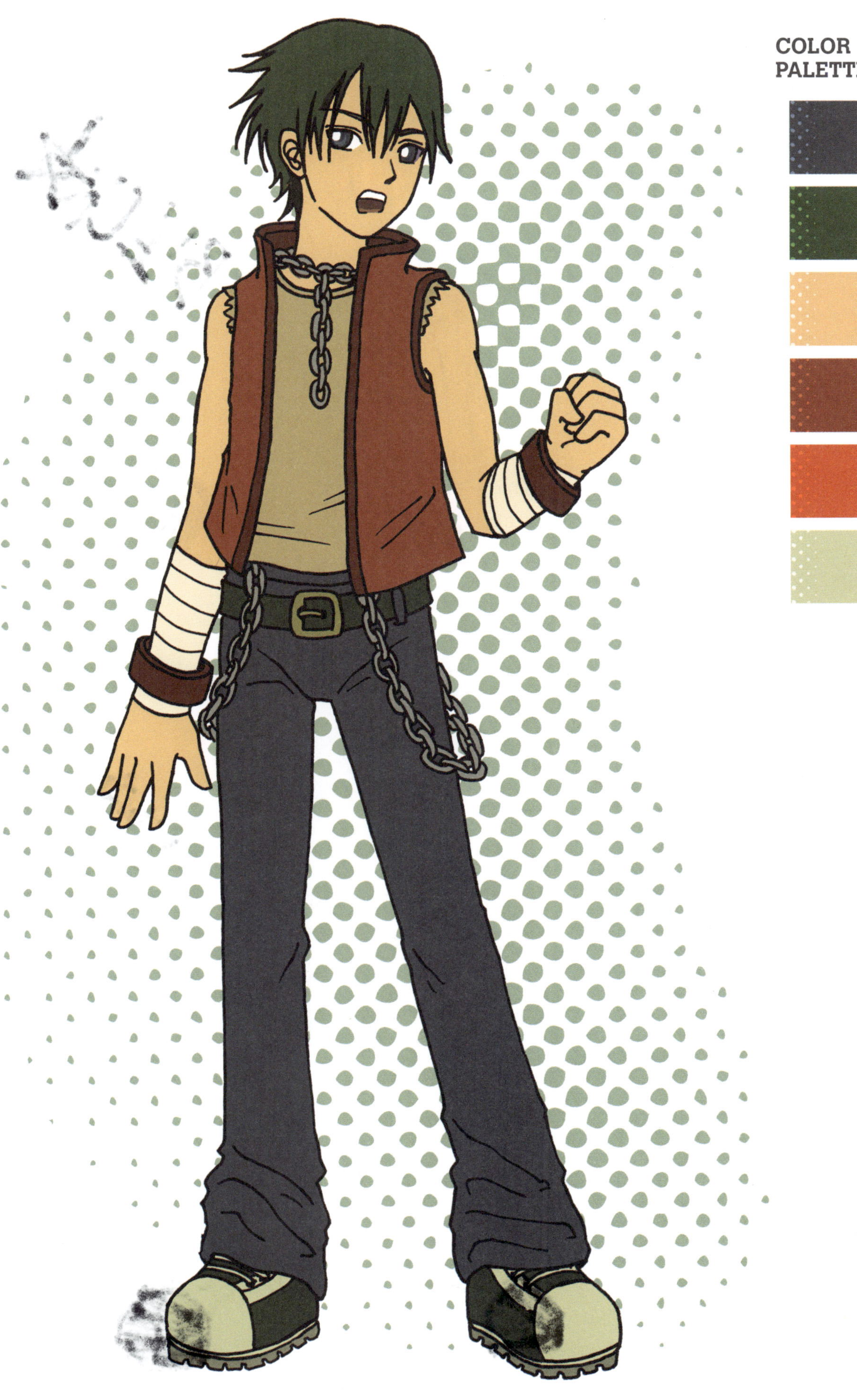

COLOR PALETTE

YOU TRY!

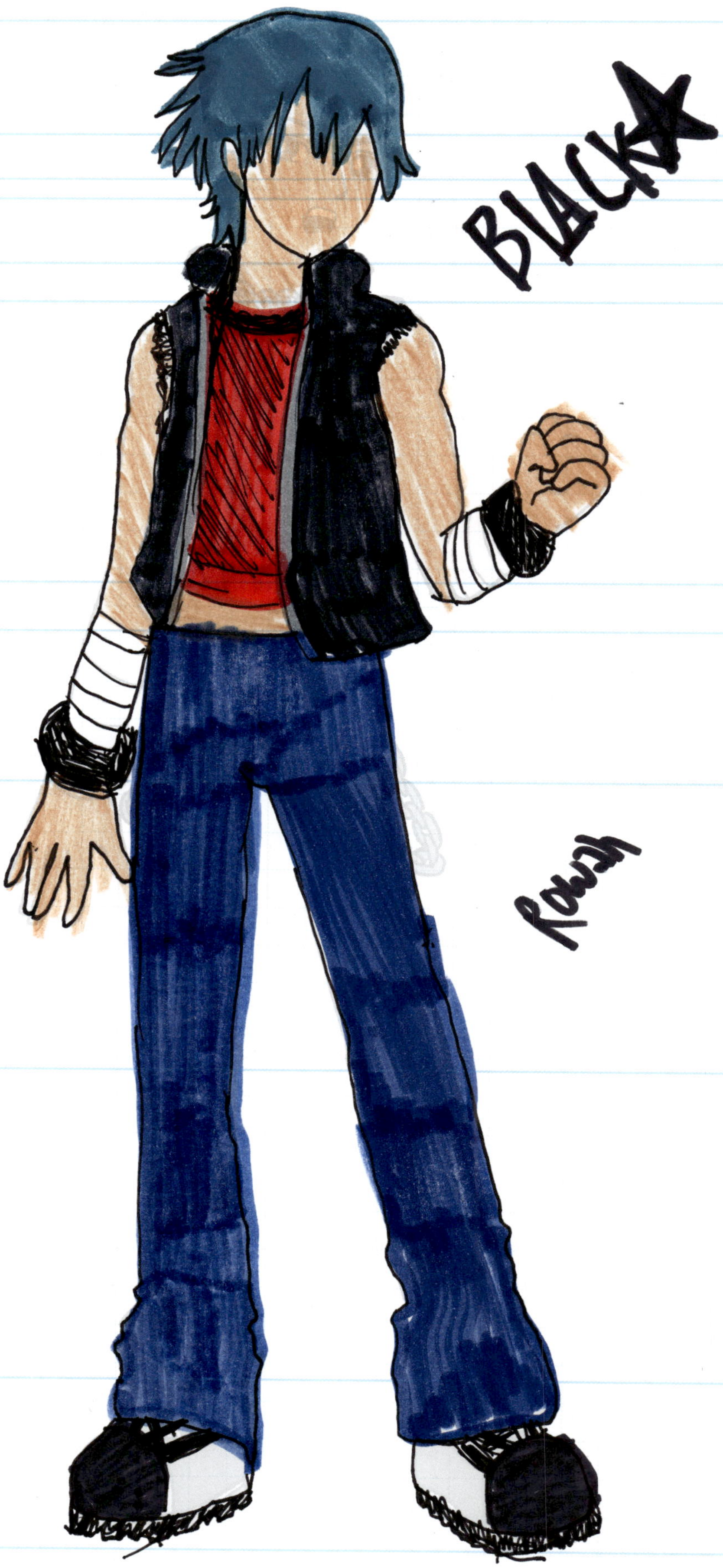

TEENAGE MALE ALTERNATIVE 1

This teenage character probably comes from quite an underprivileged background but finds things in life to be compassionate about. The one hand in his pocket tells us that he has a real lack of regard for authority. He appears self-assured and perhaps arrogant on the outside.

His schoolboy-mod style (pork pie hat and short tie) gives us a clue to his involvement in a subculture or underworld where his stories take place and the type of other characters, perhaps rough and shady, he might be affiliated with.

While his spiky hair and ill-fitting leather jacket have a definite punk sensibility about them, the limited color palette used gives us the sense that he is in fact quite a refined and aesthetic individual. It also helps the character to appear designed.

We need to believe that he is tough and streetwise, but it is important to maintain that this is still our charming and charismatic protagonist. The reader needs to be fond of him. Chiefly, giving him soft and friendly features – large eyes and no lines on his face – creates this notion. He also has strong eyebrows and a slightly comical expression.

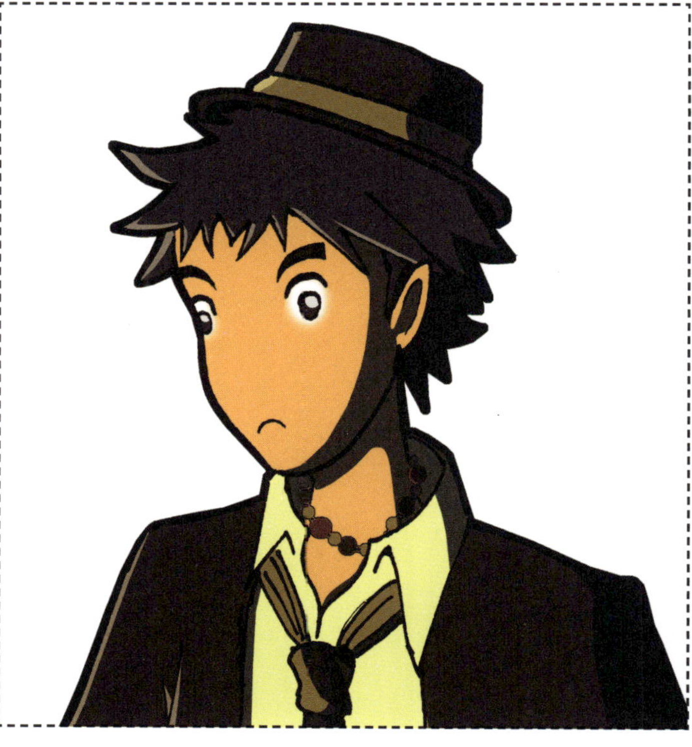

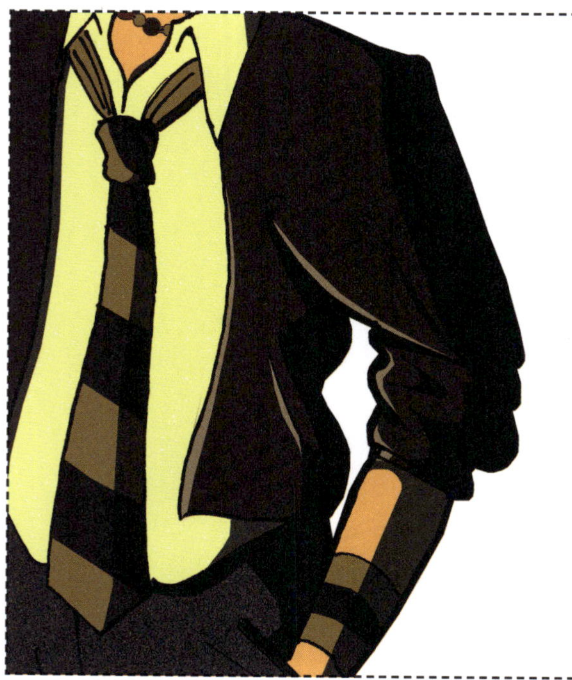

PERSONALITY

- Edgy
- Cynical
- Hard-Nosed
- Compassionate

SETTING

- Contemporary
- Urban
- Seedy Underworld
- City

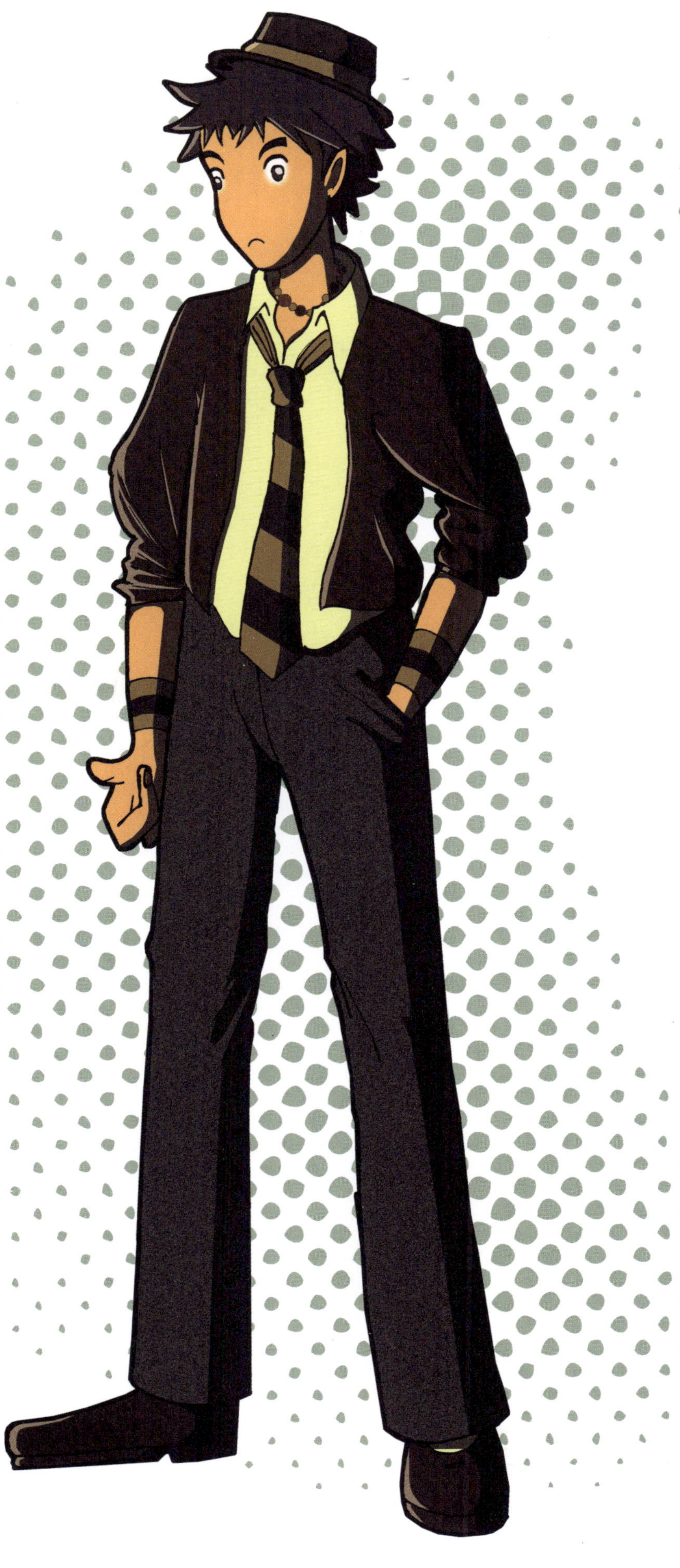

COLOR PALETTE

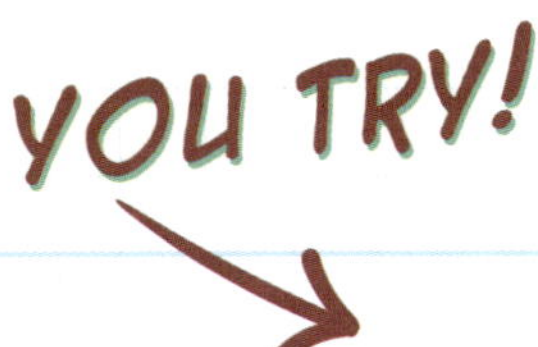
YOU TRY!

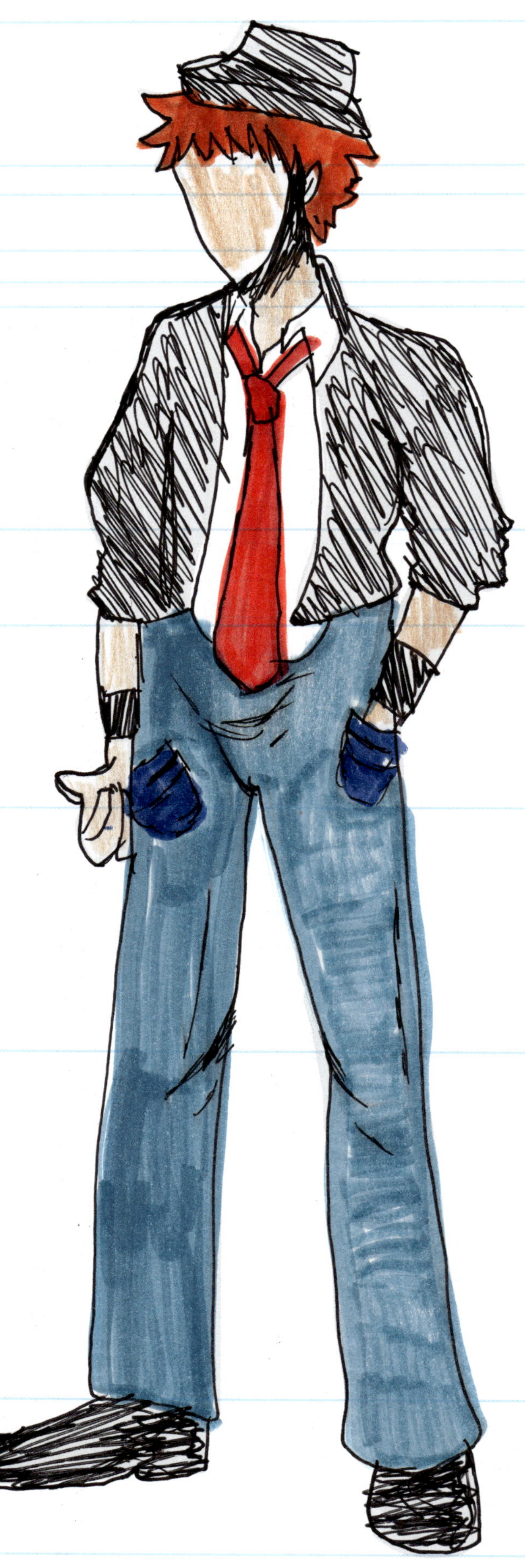

TEENAGE MALE ALTERNATIVE 2

This character is only four head heights tall, as he is drawn in a very exaggerated cartoon style. His proportion set is very deformed: his legs take up 50 percent of his entire height, his torso 25 percent. His limbs are conical, which is unusual for semi-chibi characters.

He's a heroic character from the future who is very happy and optimistic. He has a very open, outgoing pose, which suggests that he is quite approachable, generous, eager to help, and ready for anything!

The strong, bright colors reflect his good nature, reinforcing his character as a hero (this is in contrast to the duller colors usually used for bad guys or more angsty characters). Red shades make him appear full of energy or urgency.

Geometric patterns and stripes appear futuristic and sleek and are an effective tool for adding volume to the character. His arms and legs have similar designs and patterns.

PERSONALITY

- Enthusiastic
- Happy
- Brave
- Loyal
- Kind
- Selfless

SETTING

- Sci-Fi
- City
- Cybernetic Laboratory
- Battles
- Action
- Adventure

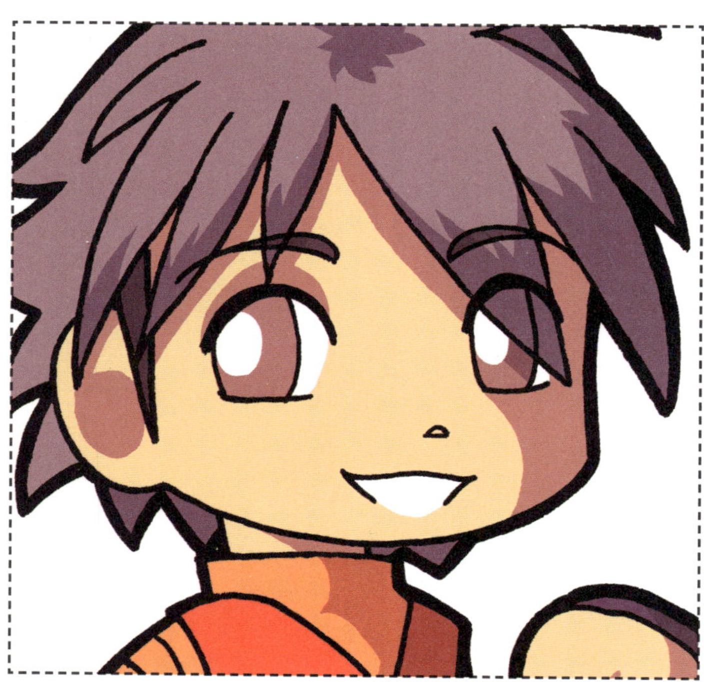

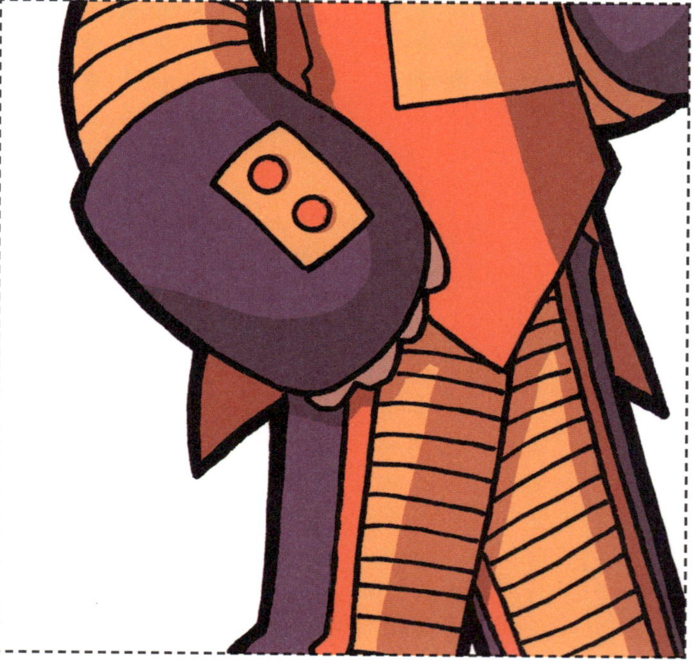

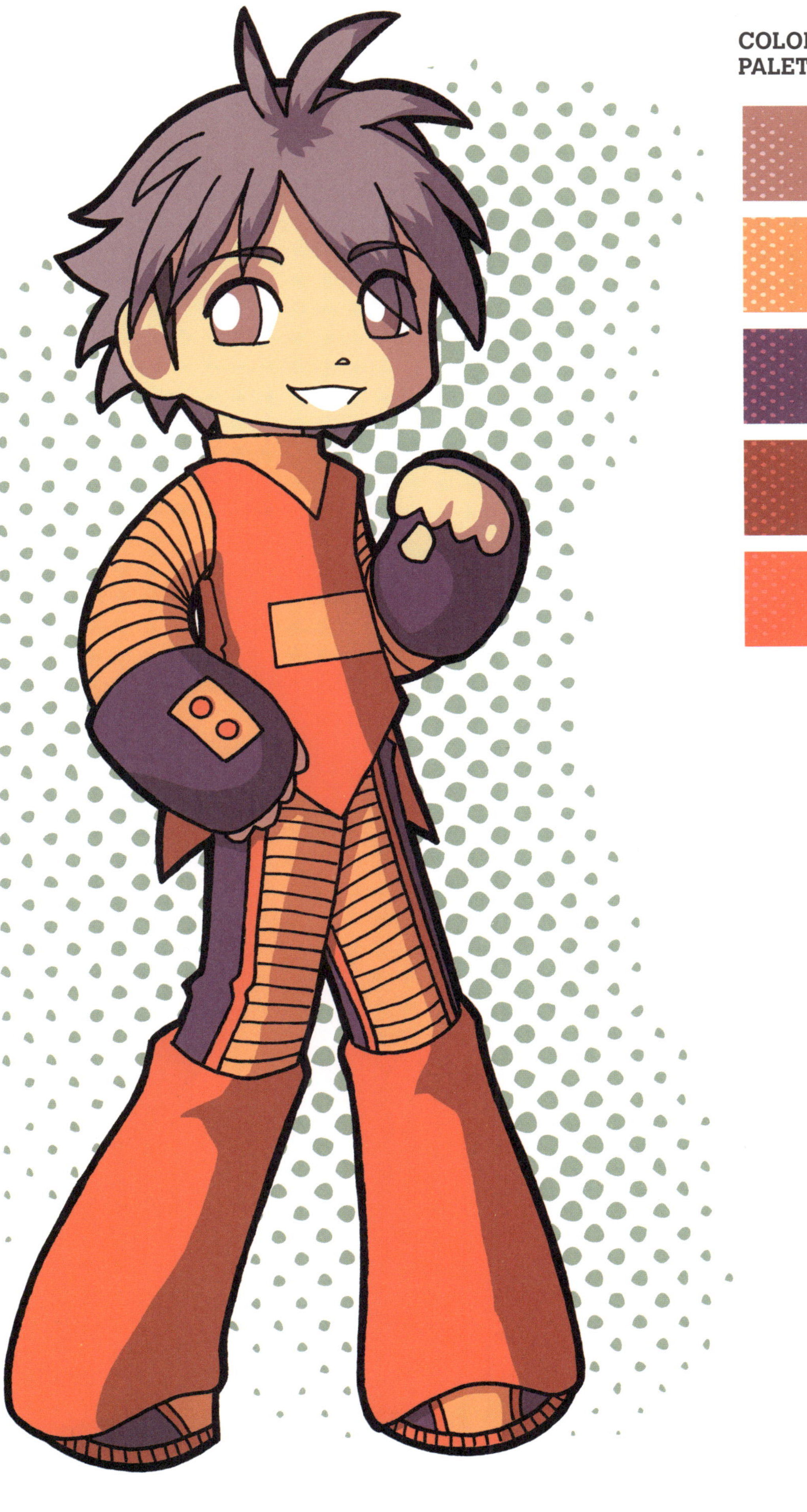

COLOR PALETTE

YOU TRY!

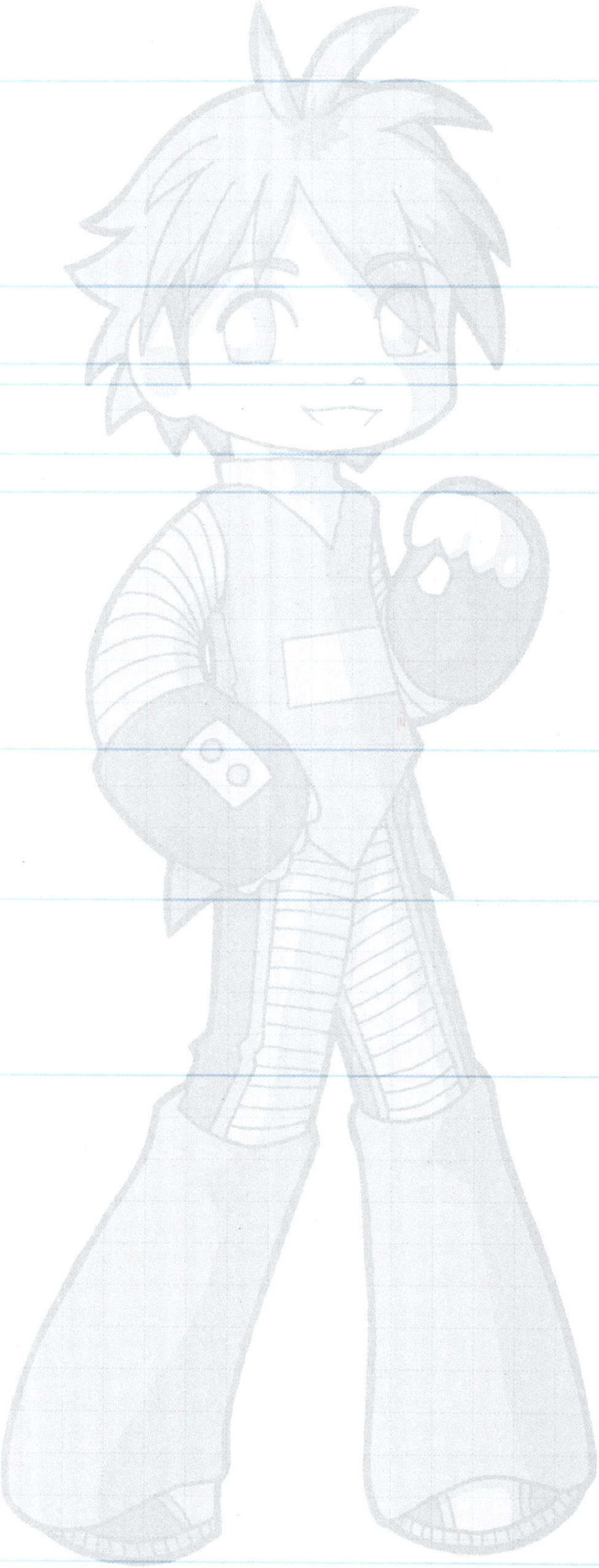

TEENAGE FEMALE

Immensely popular, attractive, and appealing, the teenage girl is ever-present in anime and manga. She is beautiful to look at and still learning about life, playing an essential part in demonstrating the complexities of human emotion.

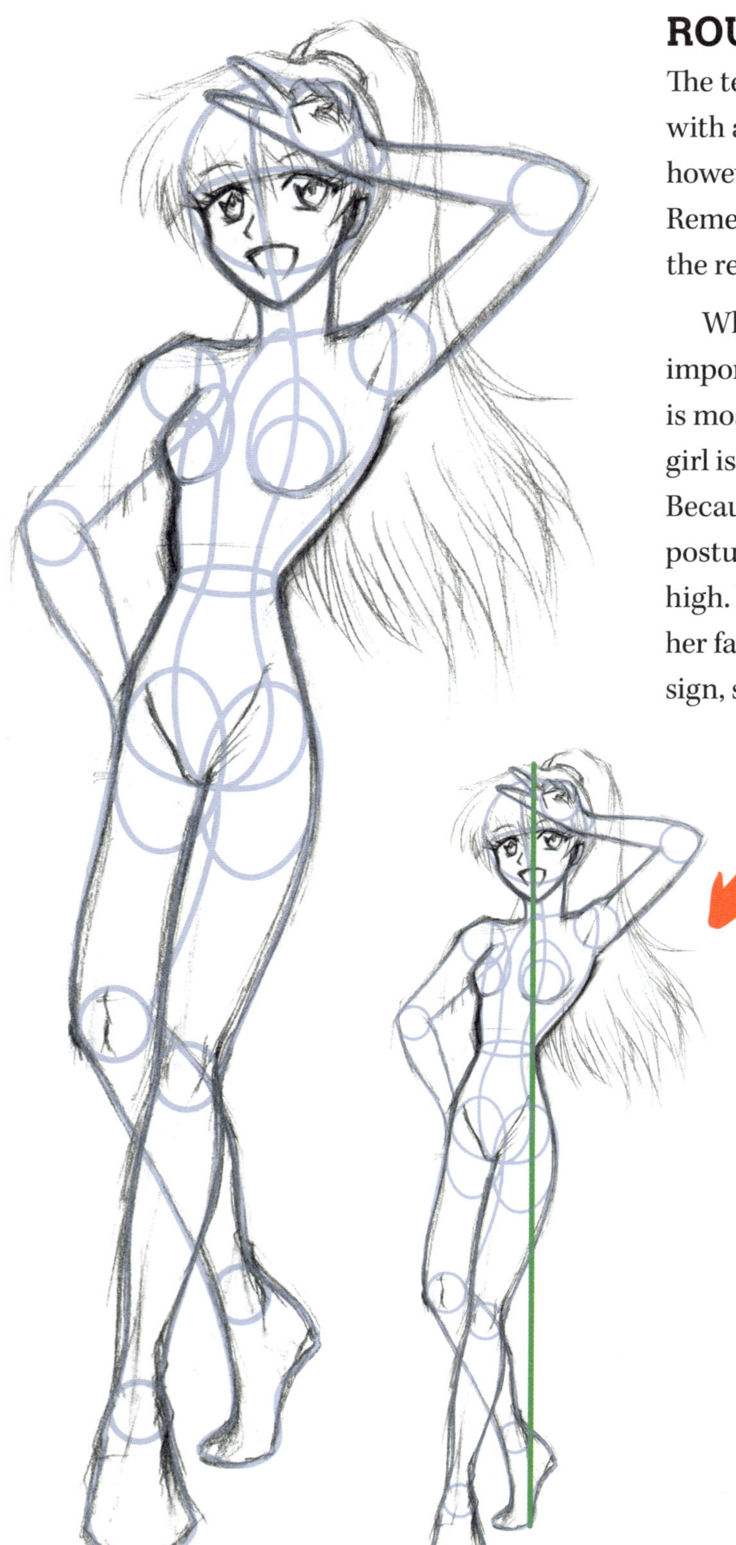

ROUGH SKETCH

The teenage girl still has a rather childlike face with a body approaching that of an adult woman – however, her chest and hips will not be at their fullest. Remember that her overall proportions should be in the region of five to six head lengths.

When designing a teenage girl, it is particularly important to think about her personality because it is most likely to show out of all the characters. This girl is confident about herself and is fun to be around. Because of her positive outlook and friendliness, her posture is very open – shoulders back and head held high. Her hair is tied back – she doesn't need to hide her face, giving a wide smile. Making a peace/victory sign, she enjoys posing for her picture.

When drawing this pose, be very careful with her center of balance. She is leaning back slightly, so one of her feet must be further back to take her weight. Draw the vertical line from her head to the floor to check that her right foot is correctly placed.

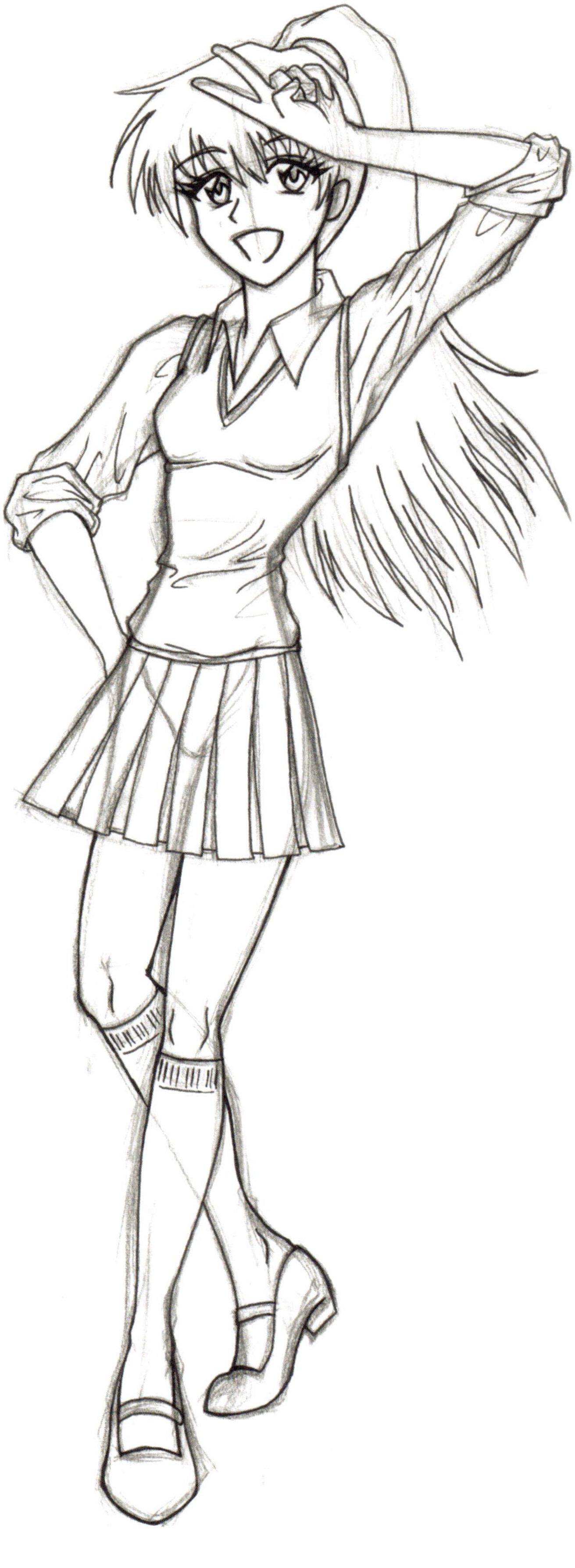

ADDING DETAILS

Because she is a modern-day teenager, she is still in school, so she wears a school uniform of a short pleated skirt, collared blouse, and knitted sweater vest. Her look is enhanced by the knee-high socks and Mary Jane shoes. Even though it is a uniform, she still brings her own touch to it – her sleeves are informally rolled up to her elbows. Don't forget to add folds to her clothing in areas where the fit goes from tight to loose, namely her sleeves, chest, and waistline.

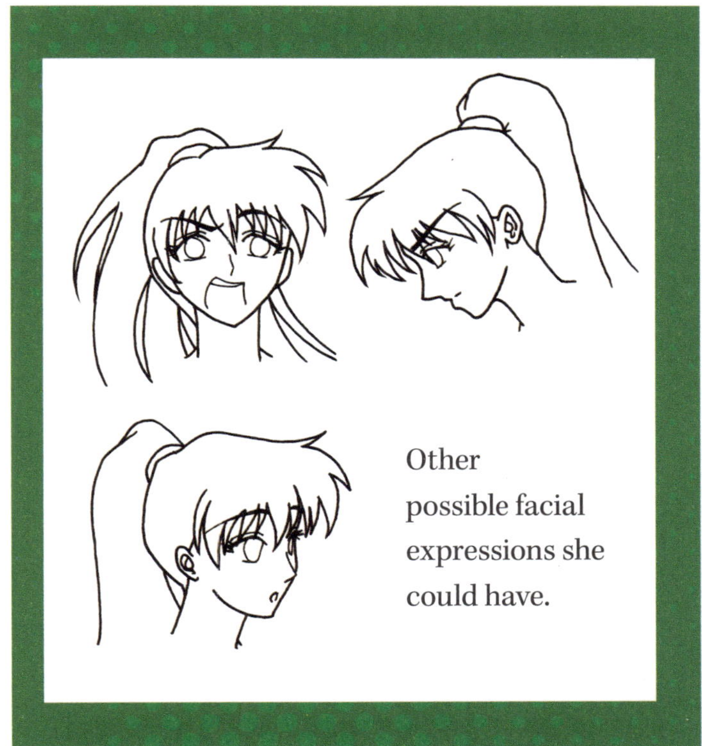

Other possible facial expressions she could have.

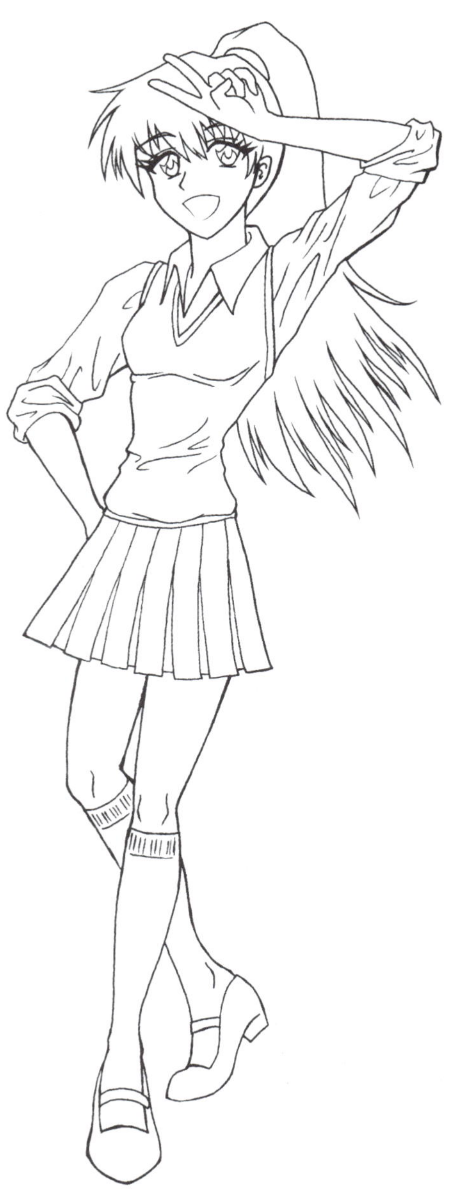

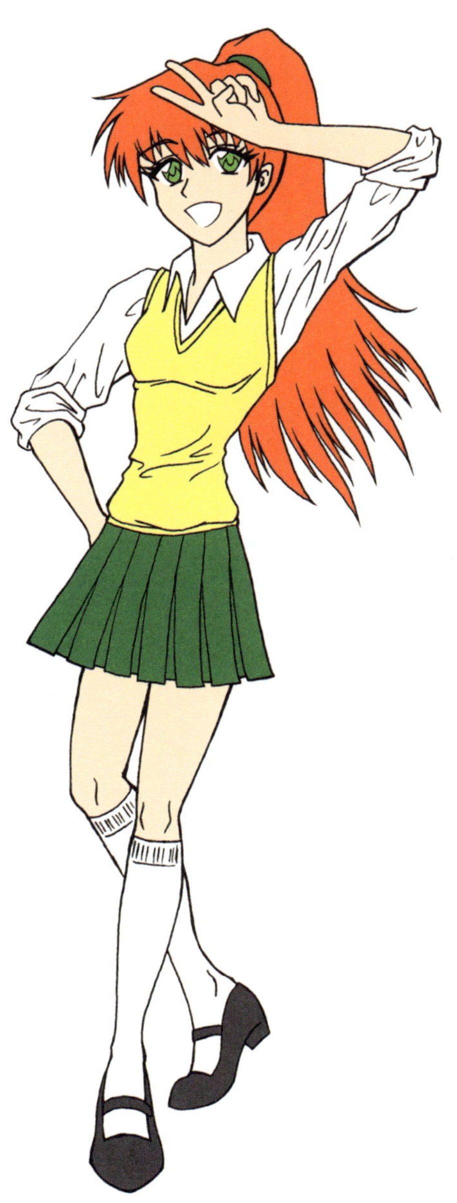

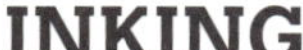

INKING

Clean up the lines carefully in the inking process. Some points to remember when inking:

- Include all the folds in her clothing.
- Lines like these should remain softer and finer than the lines that define real edges. The same principle applies to her skirt – the detail of the panelling of the skirt should be finer than the lines used to define the overall skirt shape.
- Make the ends of her hair pointed. Try to make your lines taper out finely so it adds to the flexible feeling of strands of hair.

BASIC COLORS

Now start adding in the basic colors. Most school uniforms have a policy of white shirts, white socks, and black shoes. Having determined those parts of her outfit, the remainder should offer a good contrast by being colored. Bright and vibrant colors suit this girl's personality. Contrast the shading as well – her skirt is a dark green, but her sweater vest is a light yellow. To tie the whole image together, try using the same color or shade at different ends of her body; for example, her eyes, hair tie, and skirt are all the same green.

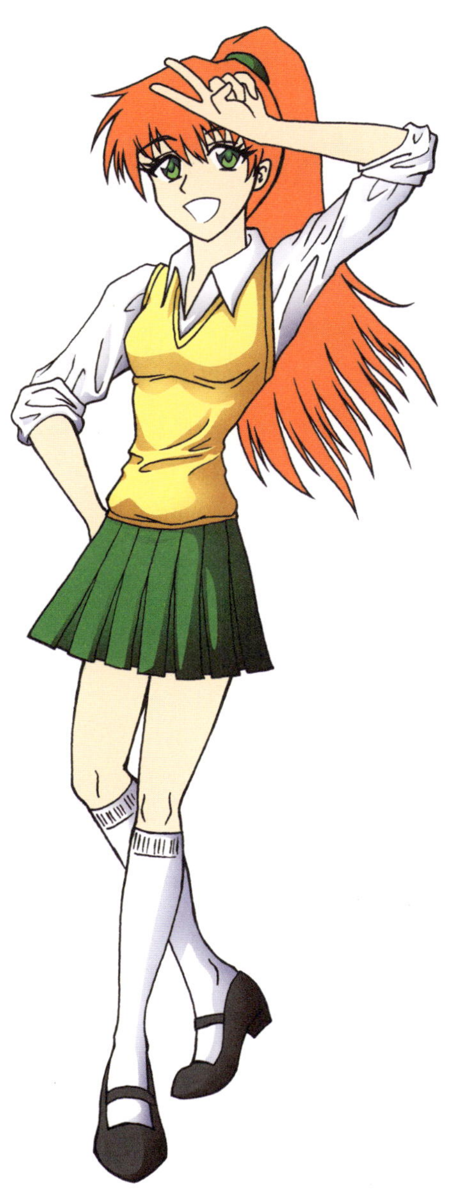

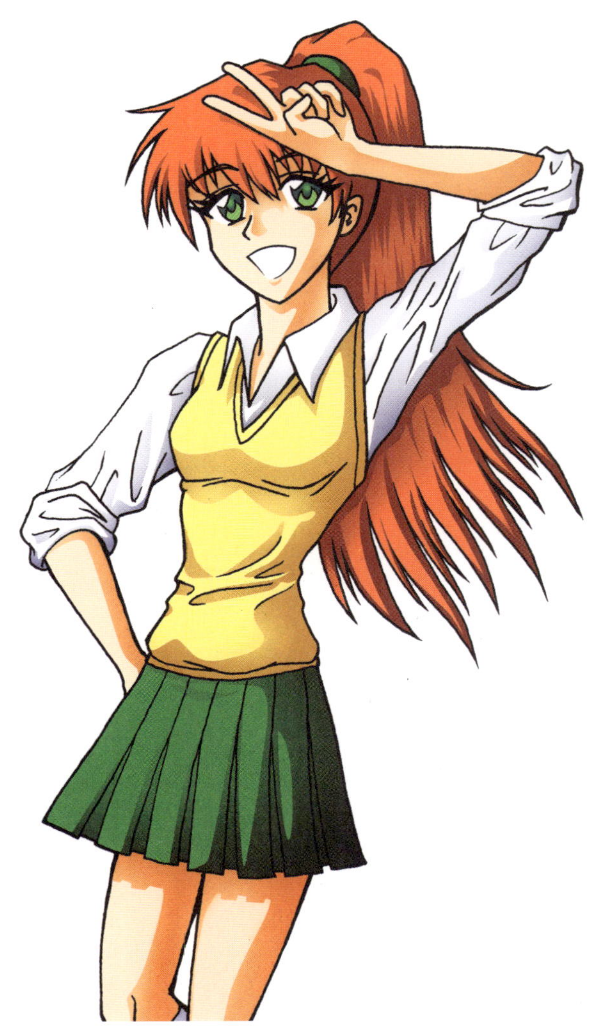

SHADING – CLOTHING

Once you have determined where and how strong the light source is, start shading in the appropriate areas using darker shades of the basic colors. This is a great opportunity to define and add to the folds in the clothing using shadows. Try to vary these shapes between sharp points and rounded curves.

For the shadows on her white blouse, don't be restricted to gray – try a light shade of color. In this case a light blue was used, but other colors such as a pastel pink or beige could look just as good.

SHADING – SKIN AND HAIR

A warm orange-brown suits this girl's skin shadows, matching her ginger hair. A reddish brown was used for the shadows on her hair. The shapes of the shadows really do lend themselves to defining the texture of the surface being shaded. Her smooth skin generally has gently curved shadows, whereas her hair has very thin, long, spiky shadows to emphasize the strands of hair.

Always bear in mind which objects are in front of the light source and which are behind. Her left hand is above her head, therefore her fingers cast a slight shadow on her hair.

When shading her skin, think carefully about the shadows her clothes cast. Note how the shading on her thighs matches the paneled hemline of her skirt.

FINISHING TOUCHES

Bright highlights are mainly required for shiny surfaces. As her clothing is fairly simple and fabric-based, her hair is the only area that needs this. Add highlights to her bangs, the top of her ponytail, and near the ends of her hair.

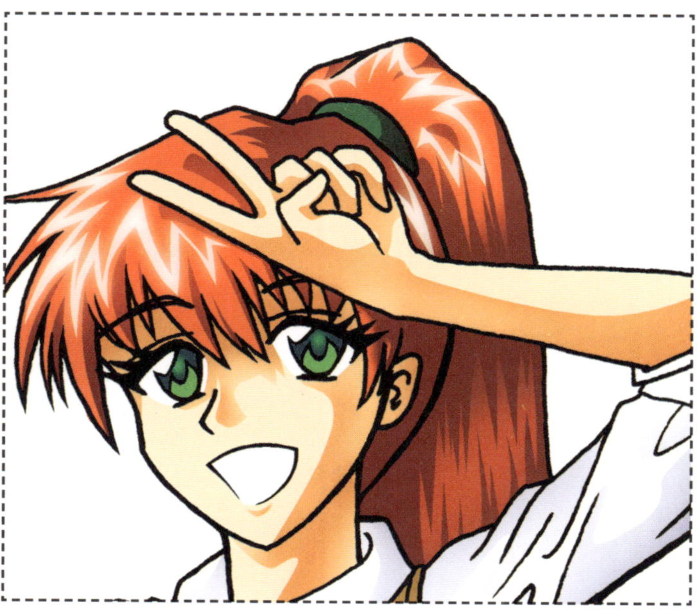

PERSONALITY

- Outgoing
- Boisterous
- Genuine
- Confident
- Loud
- Sporty

SETTING

- Modern
- School
- Shopping Mall
- Comedy
- Romance

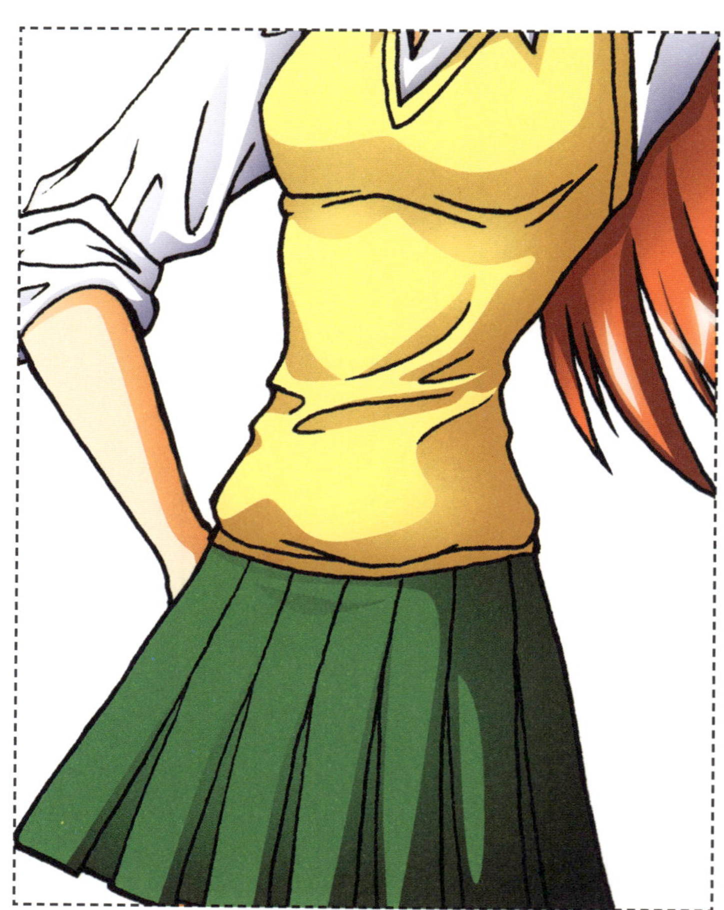

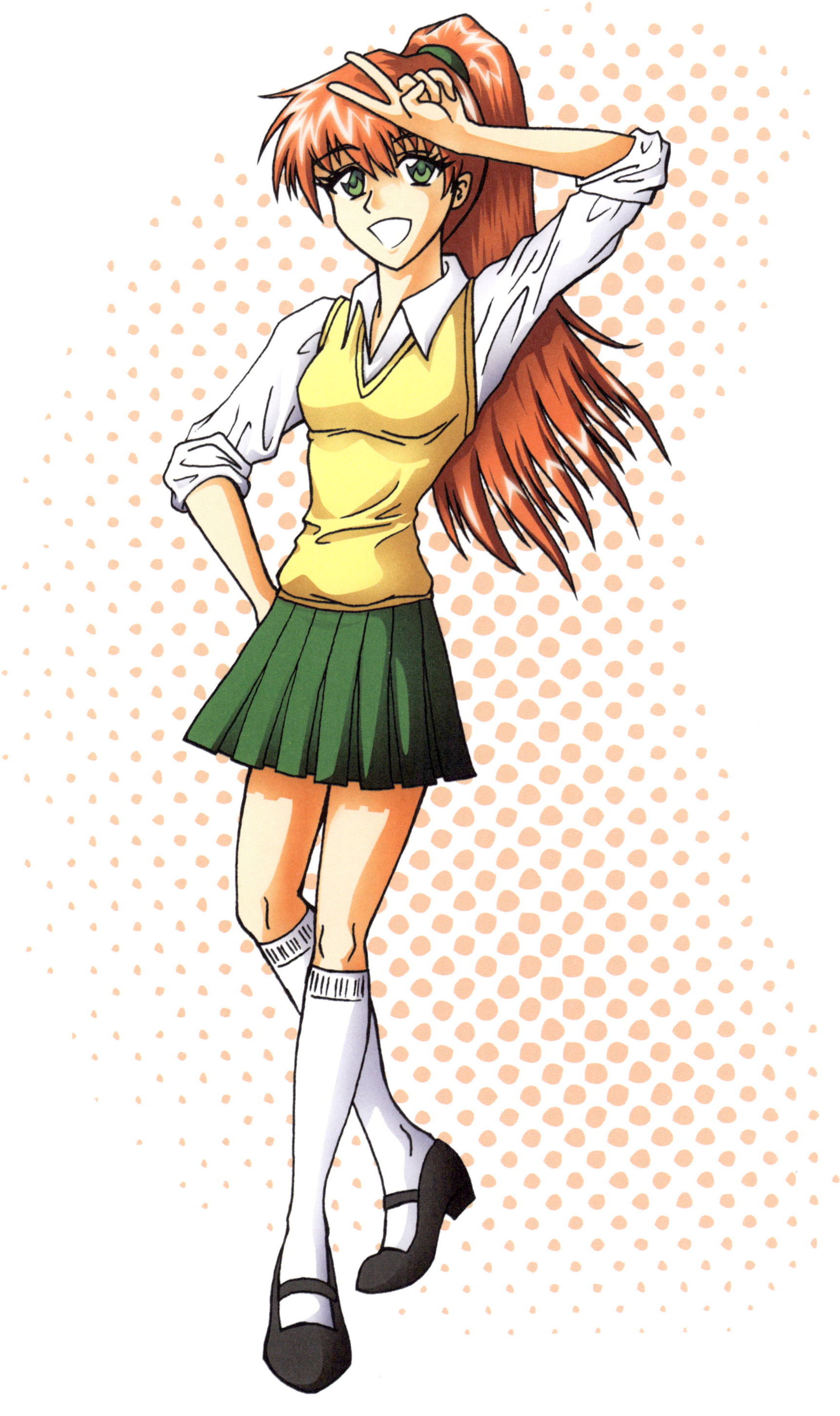

COLOR
PALETTE

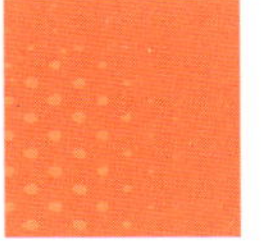

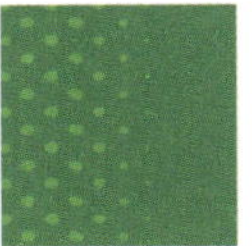
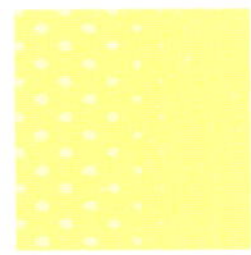
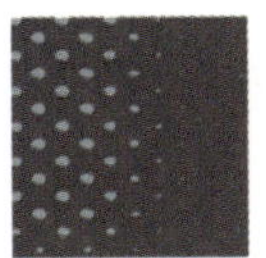

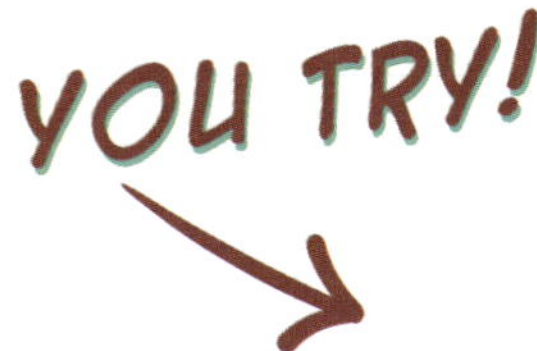
YOU TRY!

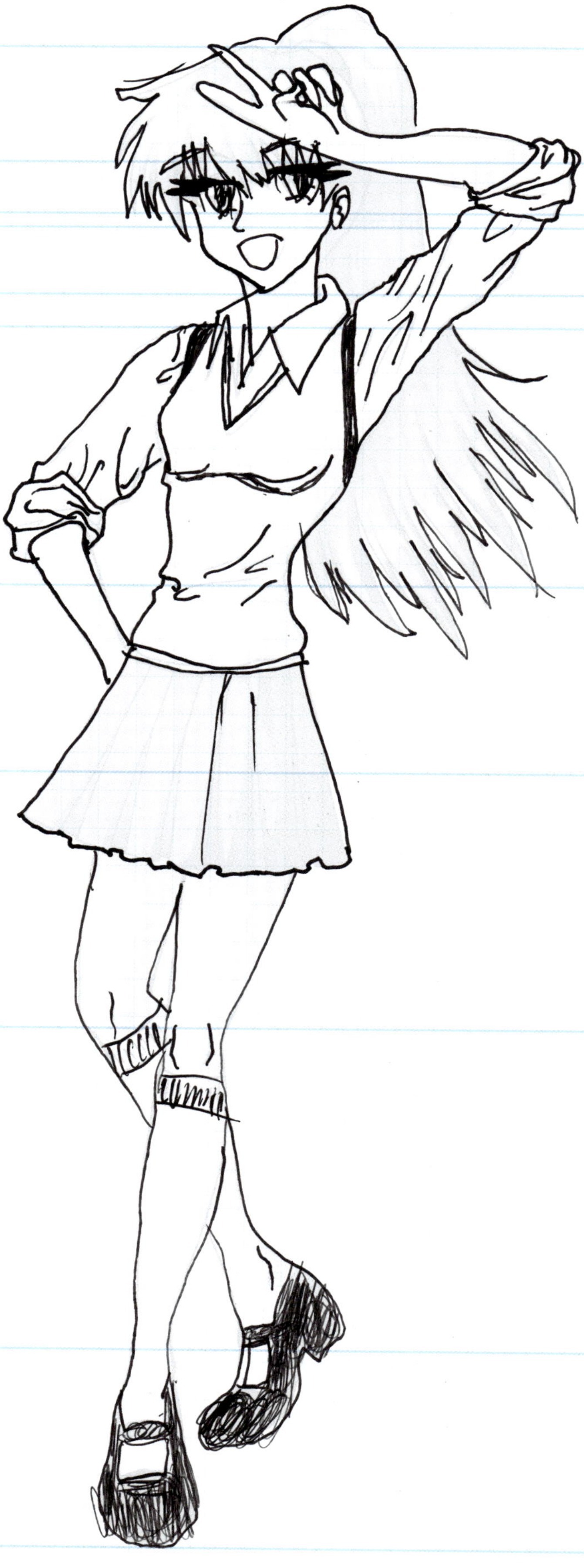

TEENAGE FEMALE ALTERNATIVE 1

This is a highly fashion-conscious modern teenage girl, dressing in the Lolita fashion. This style is worn by many young people in certain areas of Tokyo and is a popular fashion to draw in shoujo and gothic manga.

She is the correct overall height of five to six head lengths, but her head is oversized and her limbs and torso are very skinny. This is a contemporary art style; she looks almost toylike. She still looks correctly balanced due to the fullness of her clothes and her chunky platform shoes. Her stance and the way she holds her bag are very feminine and elegant, with the girlish touch of her toes pointing slightly inward.

The girl is emphasizing her cuteness, so her dress has puffy sleeves and full skirt, heavily accented with lots of ruffles, frills, lace edging, and ribbons. These elements can also be seen in her hairpiece, wristband, and shoes, tying the overall picture together. Take your time when drawing lace to keep the rounded ends evenly spaced and consistently sized.

Pink and white is a popular combination of colors to use in this fashion. Add lots of shadows to the cloth to bring out the ruffles and gathers. Golden locks and blue eyes match very well with her dress, alluding to the romance of fairytale princesses. Her glossy hair is due to the many levels of shading and fine white highlights, blurred slightly to soften the picture.

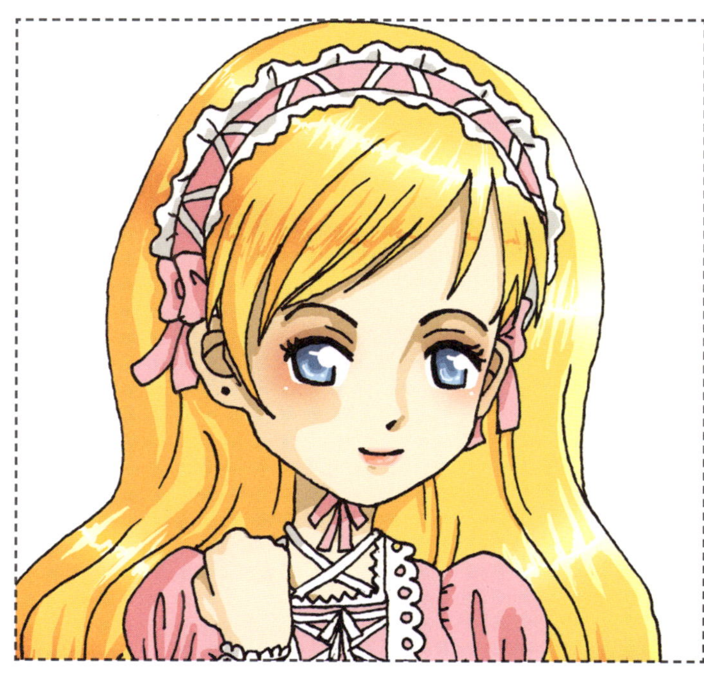

PERSONALITY

- Quiet
- Dignified
- Sweet
- Polite

SETTING

- Shopping Mall
- Garden Party
- Café
- Gallery

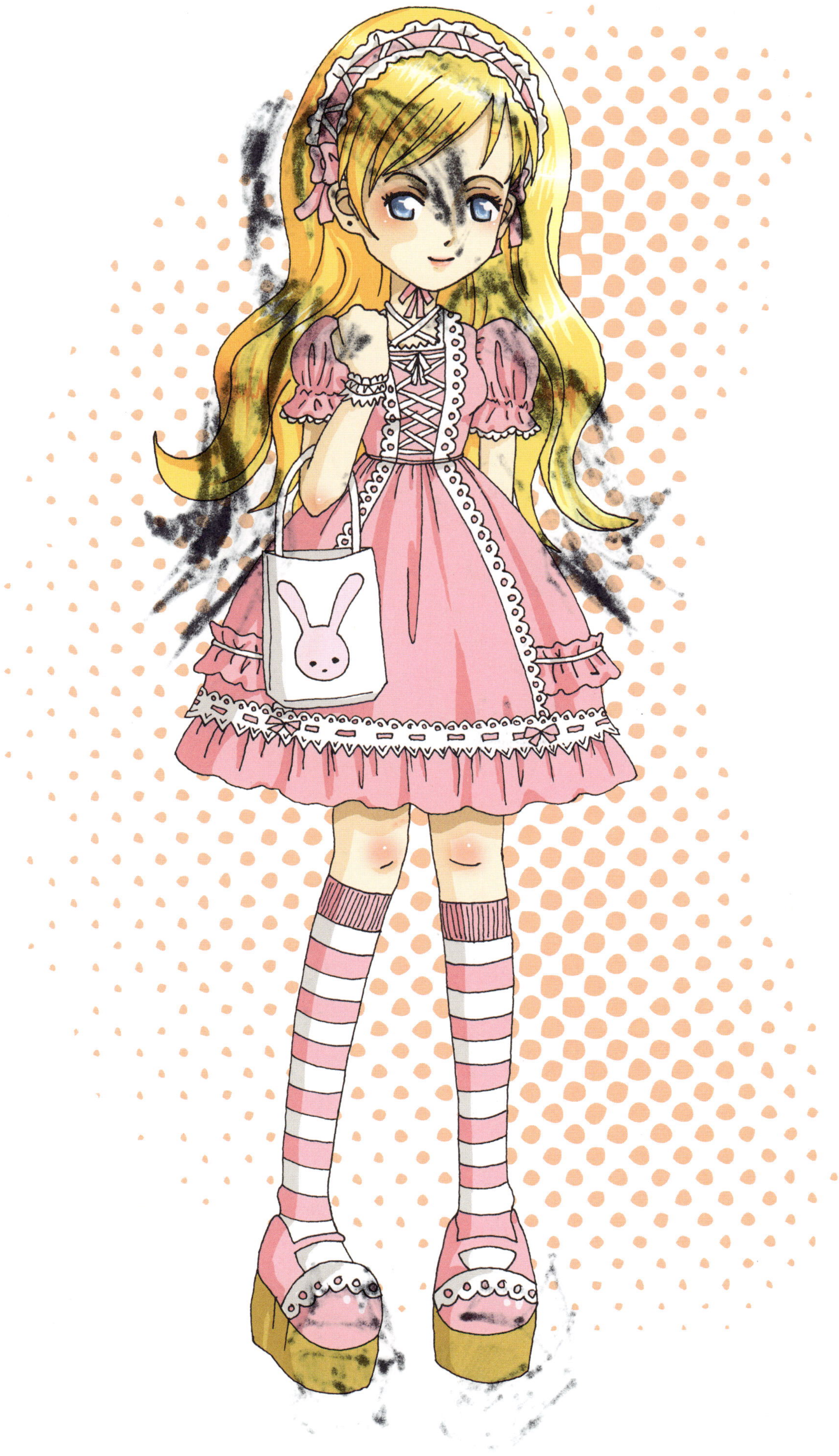

COLOR PALETTE

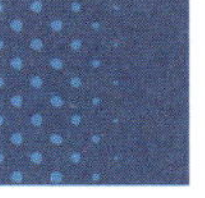

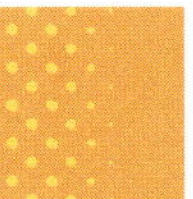

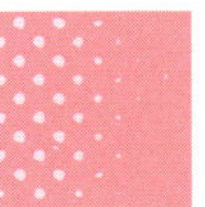

YOU TRY!

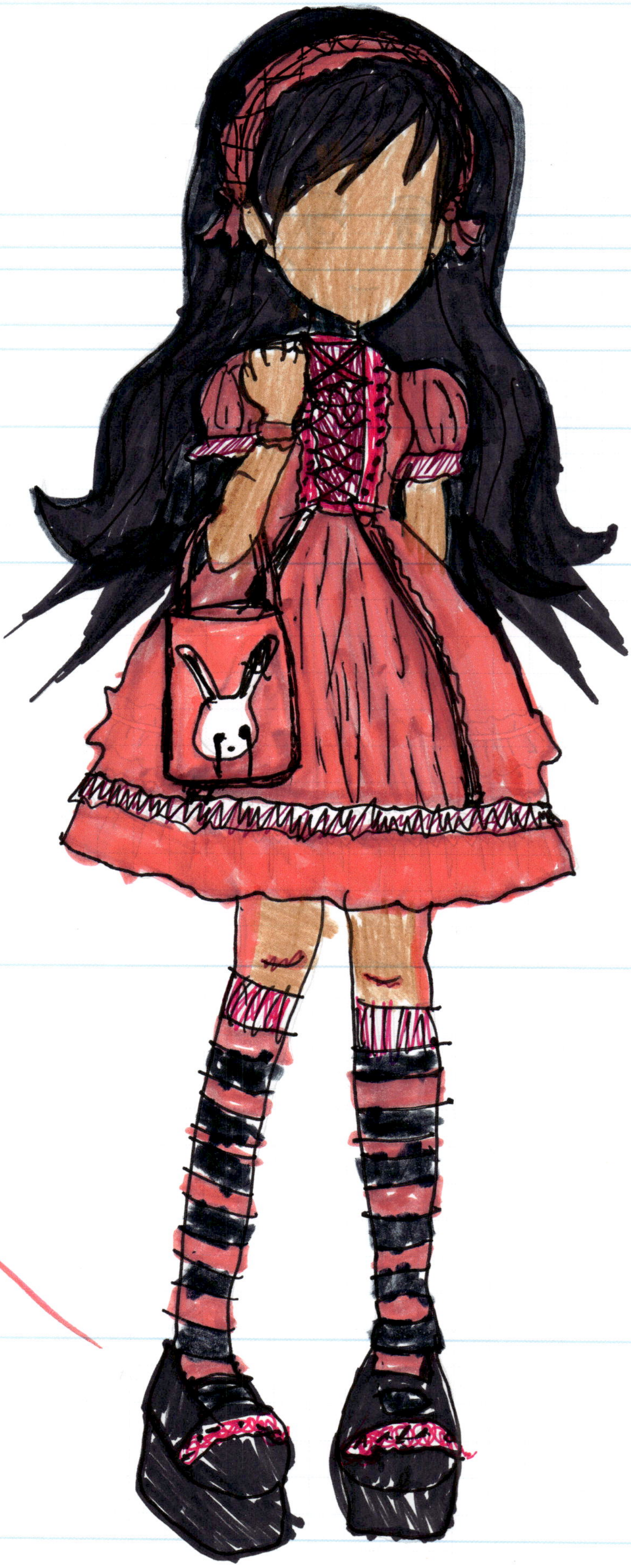

TEENAGE FEMALE ALTERNATIVE 2

In this image our teenage girl is a forest dweller from a fantasy world. Her practical costume is in a medieval style for ranging in the woods, but her unusually long hair and forehead symbol suggest an element of magic.

Her pose is self-assured and knowing. The way in which her hand is placed on her jutting hips expresses a quiet defiance. She's tilting her head down, yet looking up at us with the faint traces of a smile on her lips – a silent challenge, perhaps?

Her clothes are handmade from natural materials, therefore all the seams and stitches are visible, with many of the fastenings in the form of leather string. Note how there are leather ties on her boots, wrist, and hair, creating a harmonious picture. Her hair is not elaborate, simply tied near the ends. Think about placement as well – her hair is blown in front of her slightly, so it flows over one shoulder.

Her entire color scheme is natural and reflective of her environment: forest browns and greens, very earthy. Her hair is a smoky red ocher, unusual yet very natural-looking. On her forehead is a spirit sign, possibly depicting her powers, status, or role in a tribe.

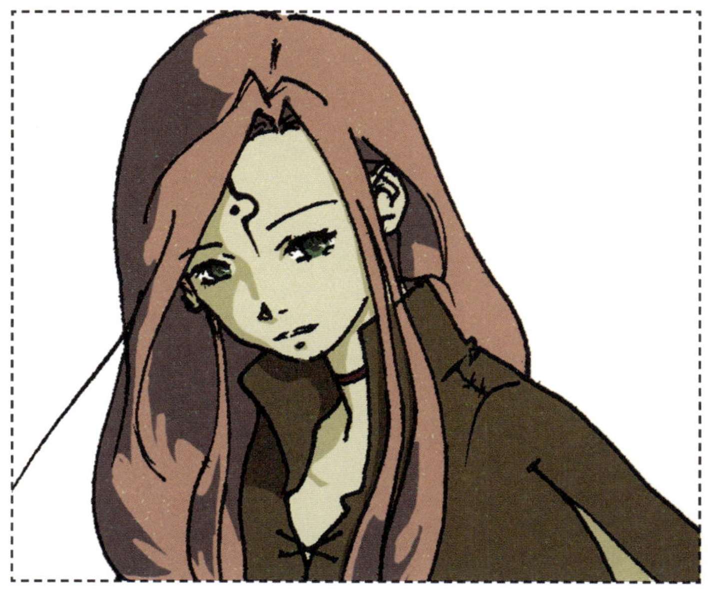

PERSONALITY

- Secretive
- Cheeky
- Independent
- Silent
- Insightful

SETTING

- Fantasy
- Historical
- Drama
- Adventure
- Nature
- Magic

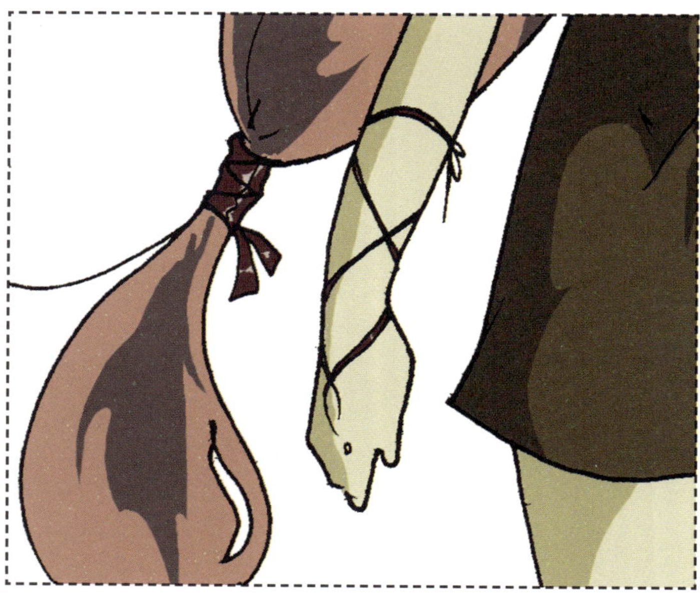

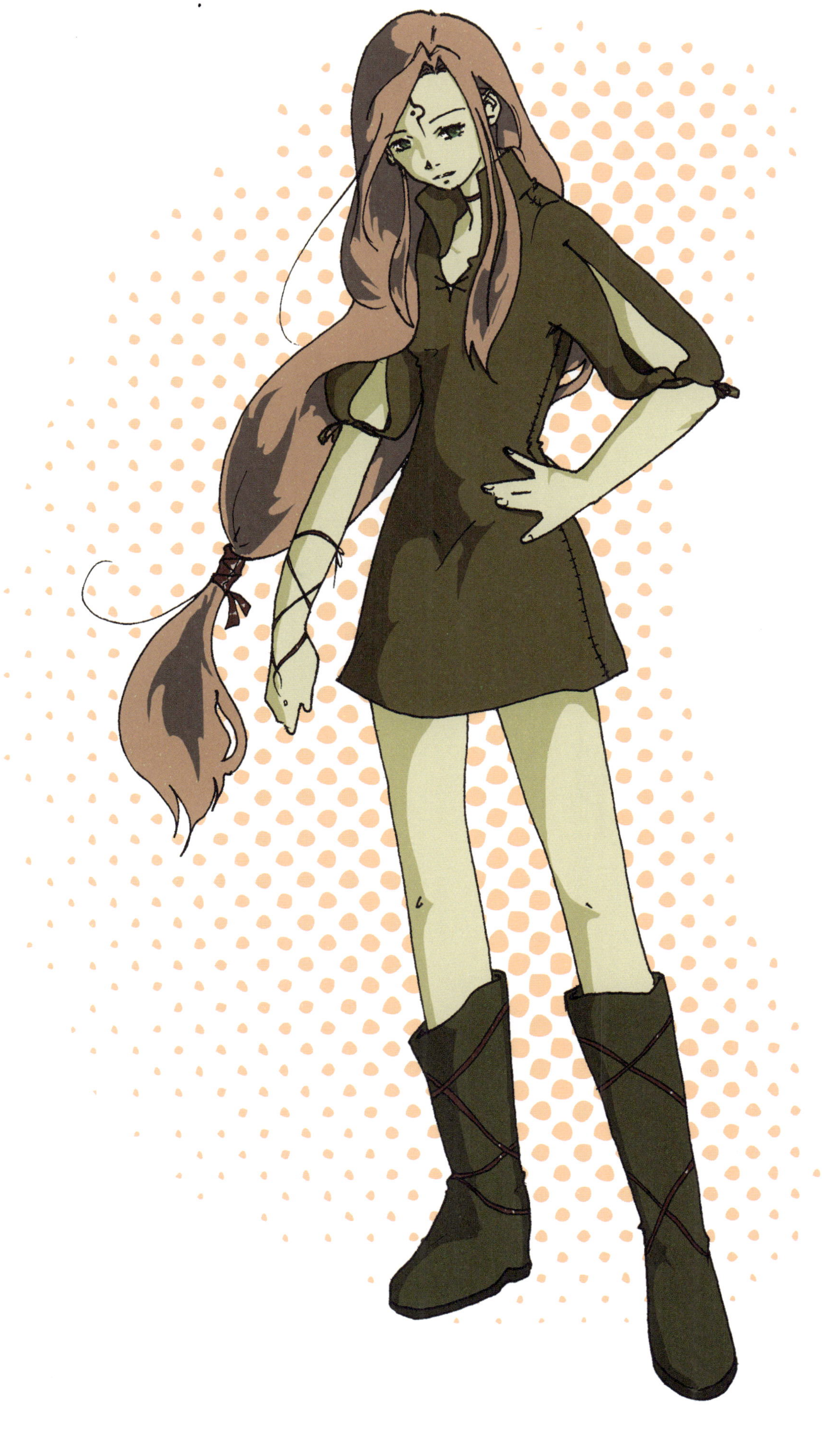

COLOR PALETTE

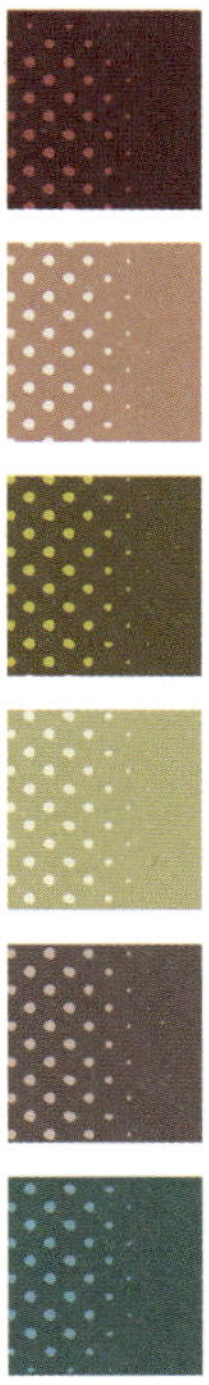

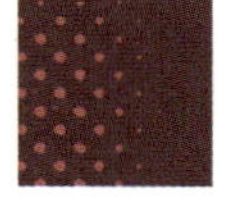
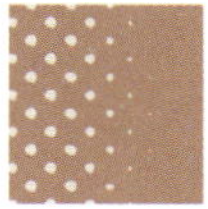
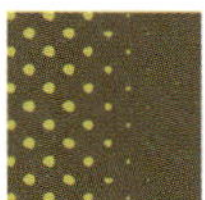

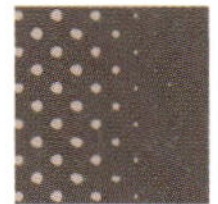
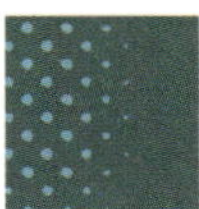

YOU TRY!

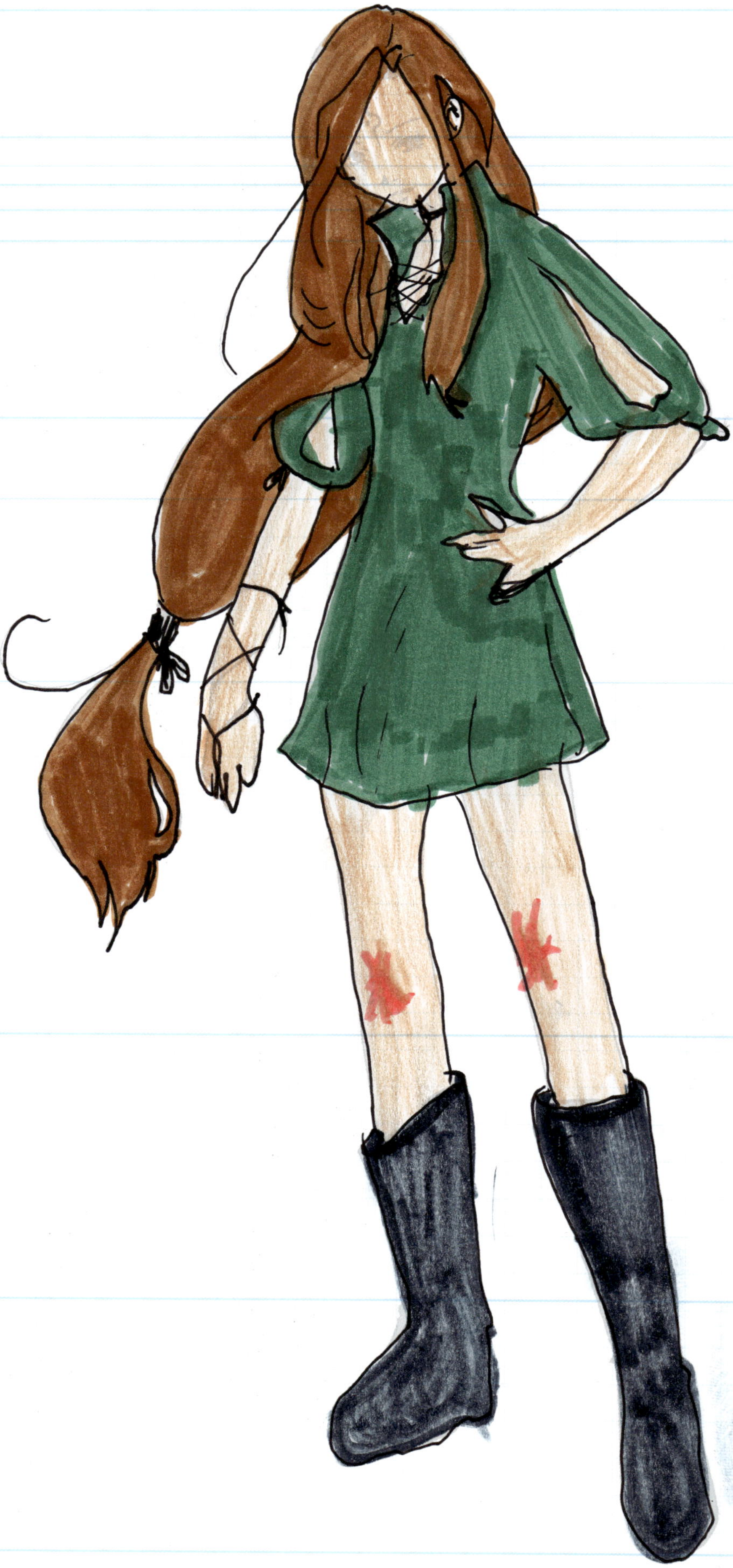

ADULT MALE

Our standard adult male is around seven to eight heads high. Of all the manga character archetypes, he has gone through arguably the largest change. There was a time when he may have been forced into one of two stereotypes: the comedy/gag character or the strong hero. These days the standard adult male is coming of age and has adopted a far more relaxed demeanor. The shoujo revolution has made an impact on his looks, and the need to appeal to both sexes has produced a character who is laid-back, cool, and quick thinking.

ROUGH SKETCH

As always, the sketch and ink stages have been used to ensure that the character's stance is befitting and natural. Our standard male is relaxed, and so his shoulders are loose, hands in pockets. He is standing comfortably, both feet on the ground, and the slightly cocked head implies that his brain is ticking.

FIGURE

As his height would suggest, the standard male is fully matured. His shoulders are broader in order to carry a larger chest area. Even male characters on the slim side will have a fairly broad chest, and the shoulders must always be wider than the upper chest width.

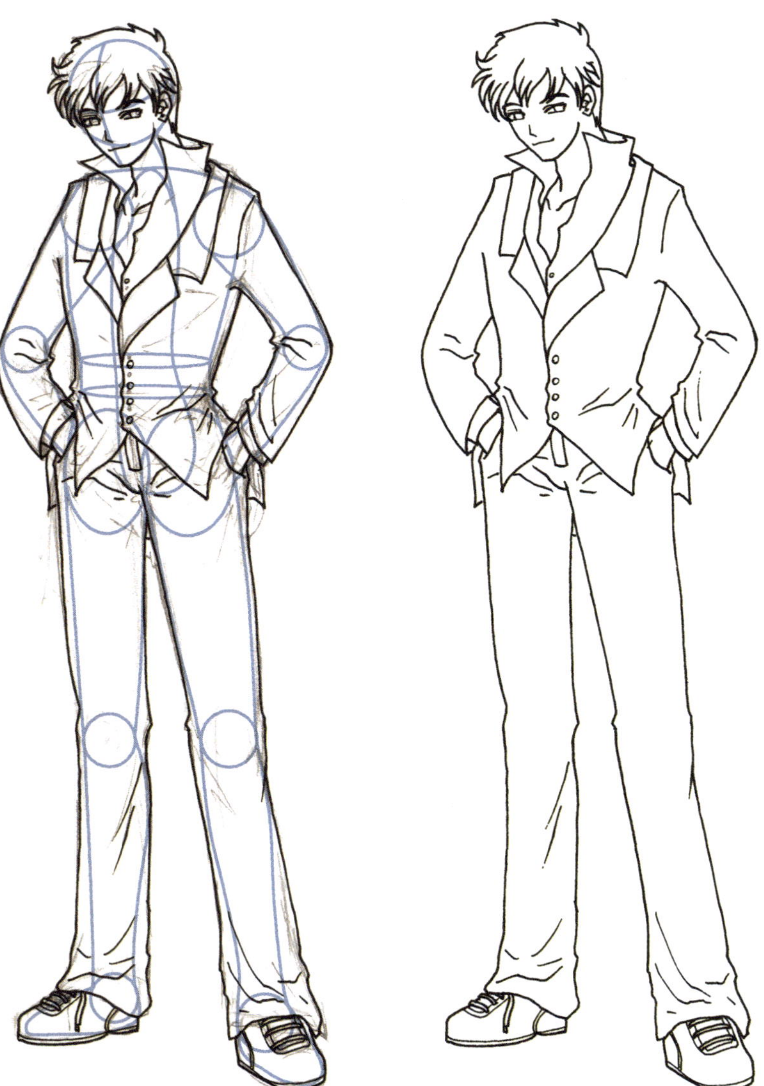

Next, there will be a waistline band, though not as defined as that on a female. There are no hips to curve back out to and so the waist can fall lower. Don't be tempted to give male characters large hips. Unlike the female, the lower body shape of a man is defined by the muscles in his thighs and not by the hip bone. (Refer back to Figures and Proportion on page 46 for a quick reminder.)

If we think more about how this character's personality is reflected in his pose, we can learn a fair bit about him. As said before, his relaxed shoulders and pocketed hands could indeed make him appear casual and at ease. However, when combined with the sly smile and cocked head, we start to get other ideas. It's almost as if this character has something in mind. He seems to be very observant, maybe some form of investigator. Or maybe he's just spied a girl who takes his fancy. Either way, the combination of a casual pose with an active expression can provoke thoughts from an audience. Even if the pose isn't dynamic, the face can be.

Turning to our standard male's attire, our instant thought is that he likes to dress the part. However, when we look a little closer, we can see that the suit he's wearing is quite ill fitting. Adding extra wrinkles and creases to the fabric shows the excess material of his suit. These have been added especially around the areas where the jacket and trousers would naturally crease, namely the elbows, groin, and ankles.

He is wearing a retro-style shirt with its collar turned up. This suggests an element of secrecy and mystery when coupled with his thoughtful expression.

Then of course we have his highly unlikely shoes! What do these suggest about his character? He either wears these shoes out of laziness or maybe the need to move fast when the time calls for it.

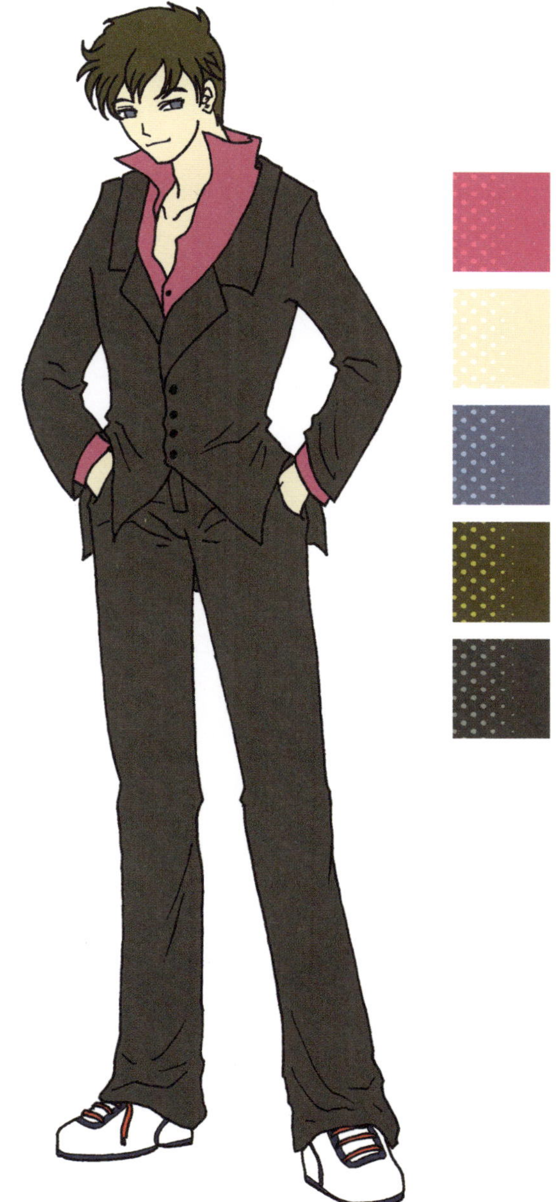

BASIC COLORS

Because our adult male is wearing a standard suit, the likely color is a dark one as chosen. Where the personality shows through is in the choice of shirt. On a design level, this bright pink shirt really lifts the dull color of the suit. On a character level, it speaks volumes about this man's attitude – he's fun, not too worried about being obvious, and quite an extrovert.

This unusual color choice is also reflected in his sneakers. They manage not to suit anything in his outfit, again suggesting that he's not too worried about fashion or appearance.

The skin color chosen for this image is quite pale. This man is not the outdoors type, and so his skin is not tanned.

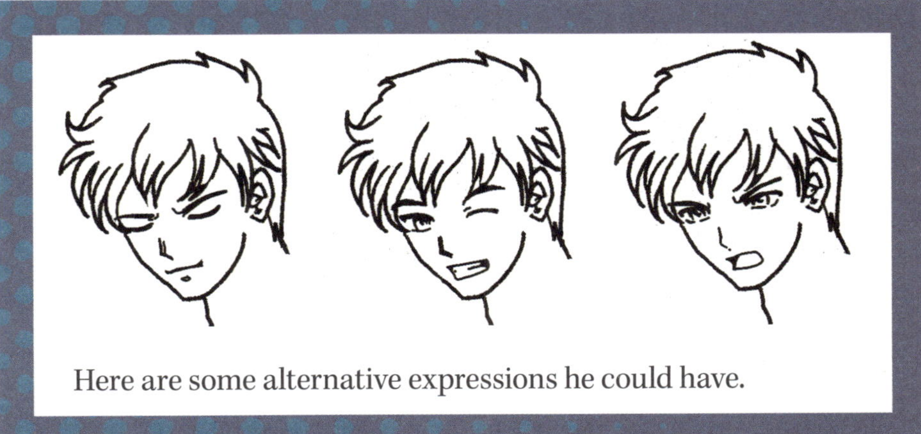

Here are some alternative expressions he could have.

SHADING AND HIGHLIGHTS

Quite large areas of shade have been used that add to the element of mystery in his character. Our light source appears to be somewhere above and to the right of the character. Remember that the heavily creased areas will become especially shaded, as the folds will not allow light through. Though the jacket conceals the frame, shade can be used to define areas such as the chest. By bringing in the line of the shadow, details like the waist and knees can be emphasized even in a heavy piece of clothing like a suit.

There are very few highlights. The fact that the eyes are half closed means that less light would be reflected and so, even here, very little highlight has been added. The slight areas on the hair serve to show further where the light source for the image is.

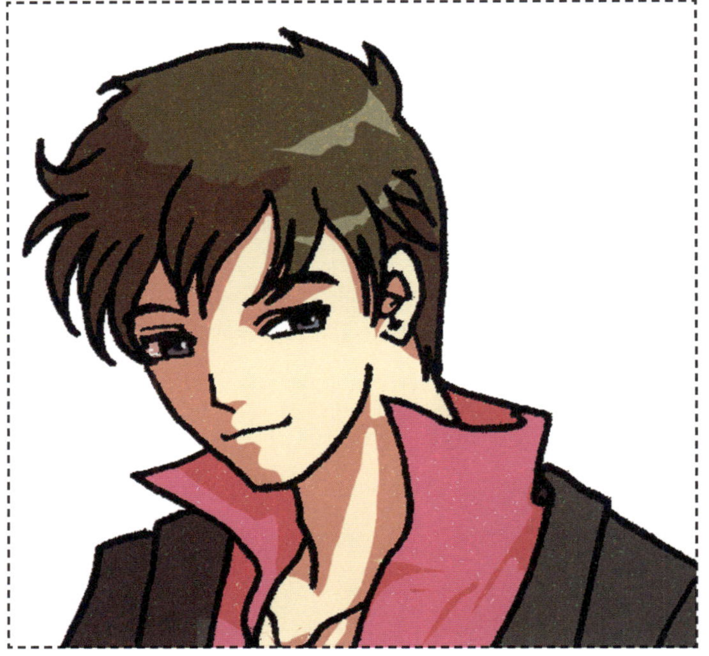

Adding an unusual element to an otherwise standard costume design is an easy and effective way of engaging a reader. Any element of design that can make the observer ask questions is useful in building a character. These sneakers contradict the character's entire outfit and lead us to wonder why he chose to wear them.

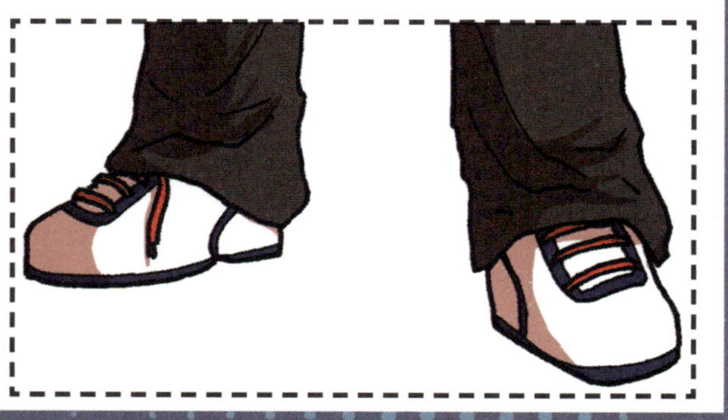

PERSONALITY

- Quick-Witted
- Dry
- Intelligent
- Playful

SETTING

- Nightclub
- Casino
- Detective

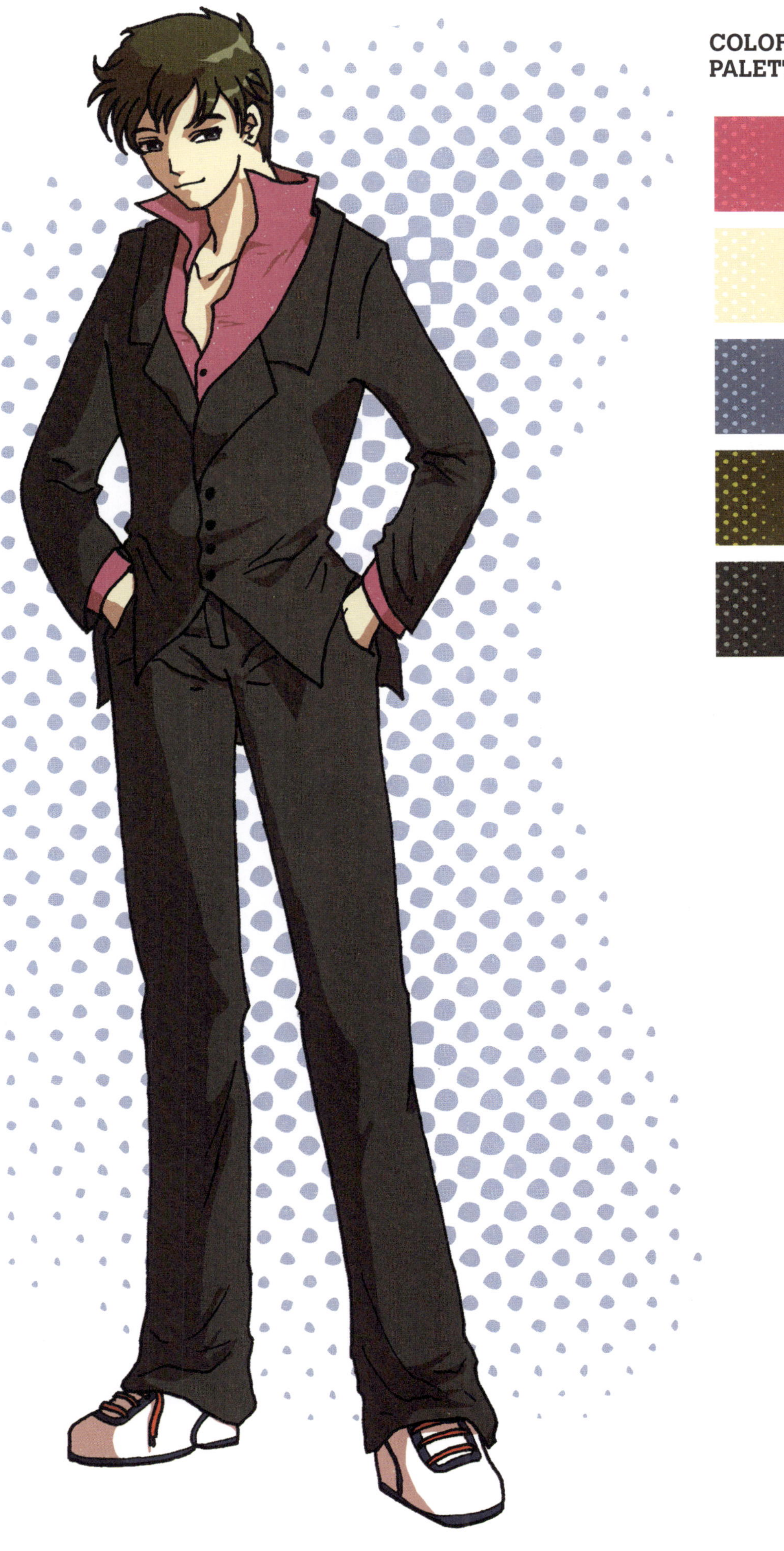

COLOR PALETTE

YOU TRY!

ADULT MALE ALTERNATIVE 1

A traditional samurai warrior with a twist – with his silver hair and indigo eyes, he doesn't exactly seem all Japanese! His true origins are shrouded in mystery. He looks to be a serious type, a man of few words. You can bet his skills with a sword can do all the talking for him!

He is wearing very traditional Japanese attire – a happi/kimono-like top, hakama trousers, and geta sandals. His hairstyle and katana sword are also authentic, in keeping with the historically accurate design. Also common in manga and anime, his top is hanging off one shoulder – it gives an air of self-assurance and skill.

His robes have lots of thick folds to make the fabric look heavy. Take particular care when depicting his musculature, as it is fully on display! Practice drawing thin lines to hint at folds and muscles, and thick lines for true outlines and breaks between clothing, to enhance the three-dimensional look of this piece.

PERSONALITY

- Strong
- Silent
- Intelligent
- Analytical
- Honorable

SETTING

- Japan
- Historical
- Action
- Romance
- Temple
- Duelling Grounds

The colors for his costume are traditional and realistic, so in contrast his hair is a silvery tone. It contrasts nicely with the heavy black line work and complements the other colors. The character's eyes are also not a traditional Asian brown but an intense blue/indigo shade, making him look more mysterious and enigmatic.

Use clean, sharp shadows to emphasize the folds in his clothing. Add soft highlights to his hair, sword scabbard, and chest.

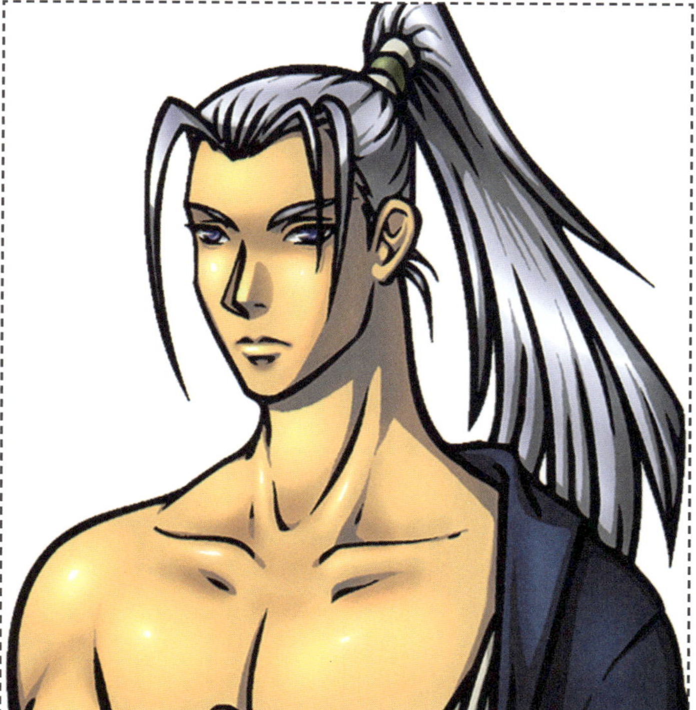

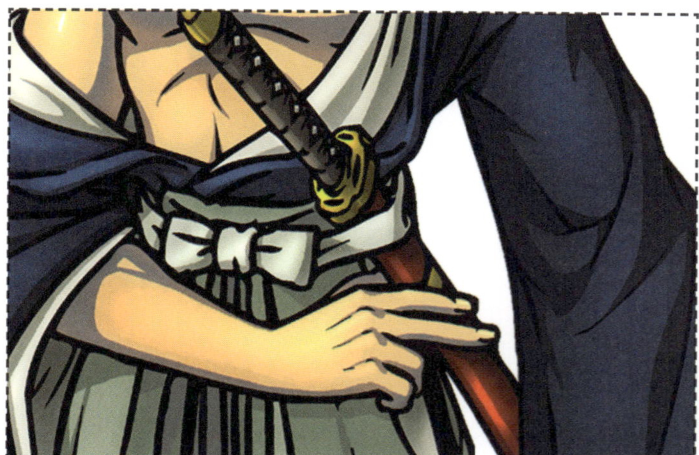

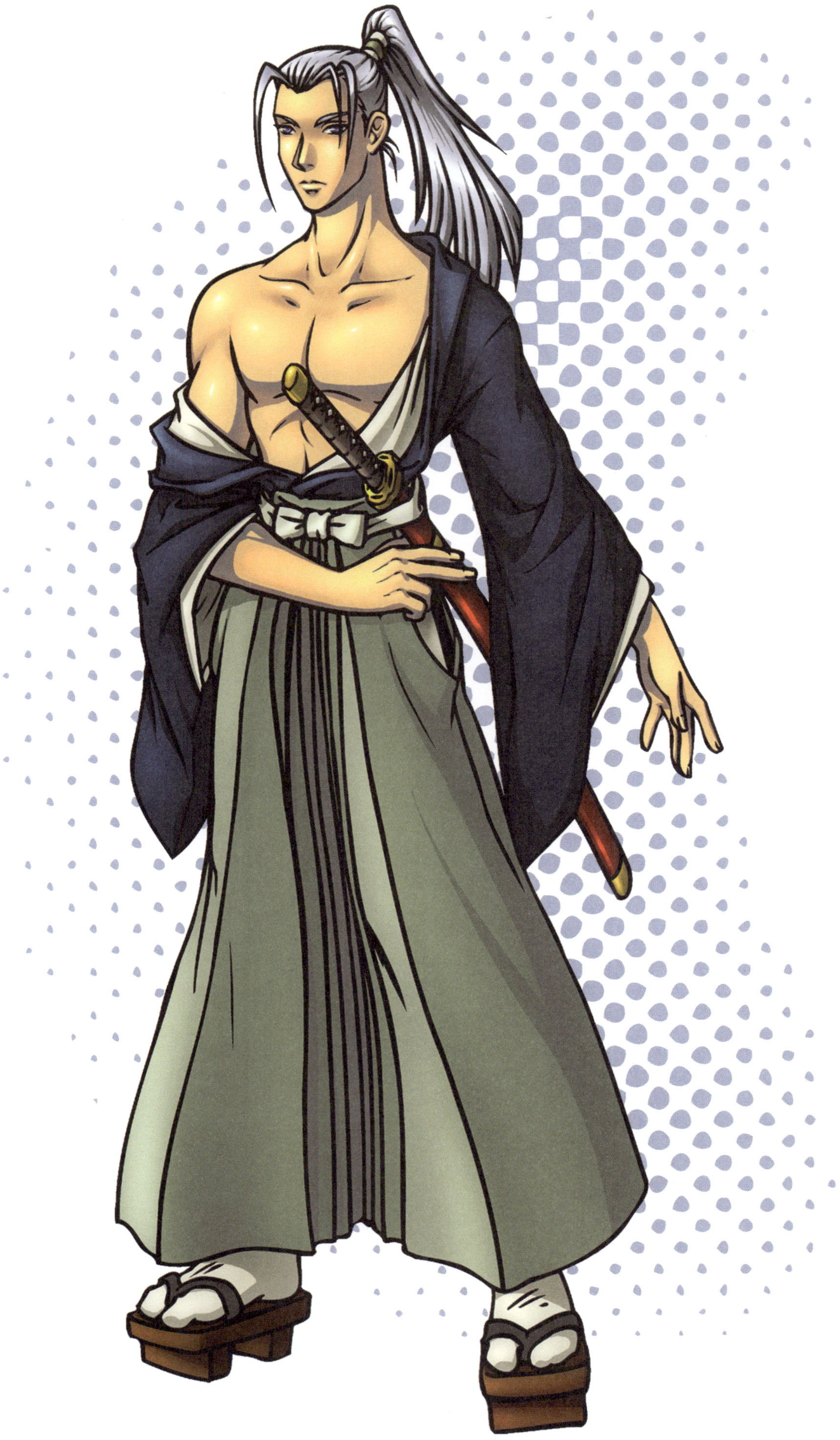

COLOR PALETTE

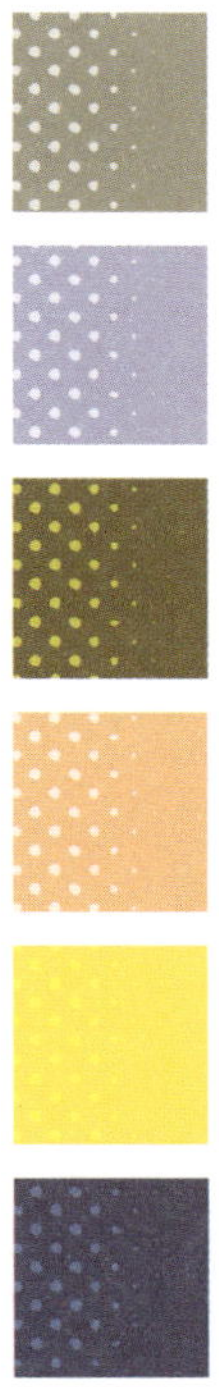

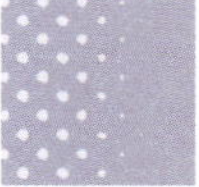

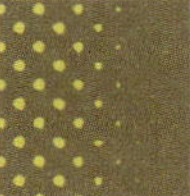

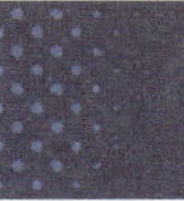

YOU TRY!

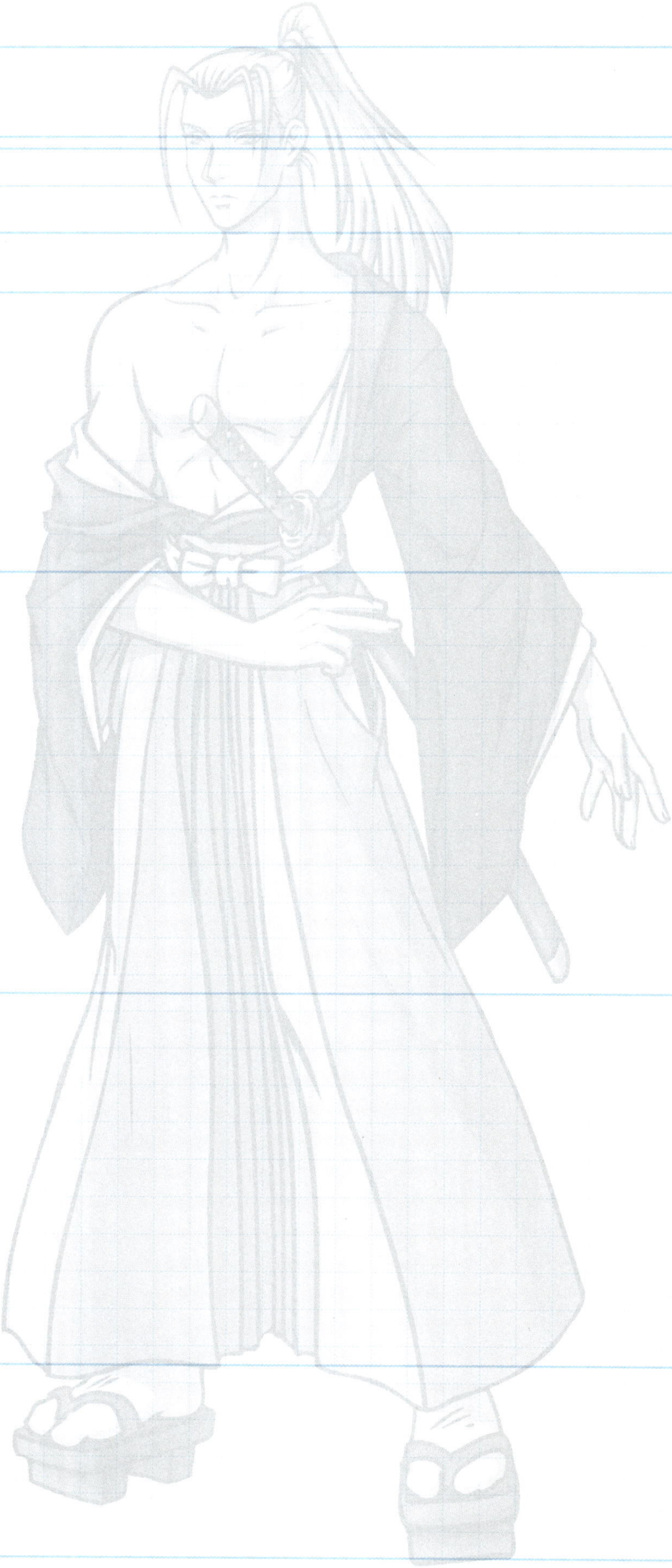

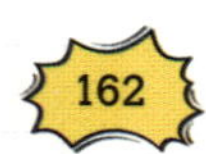

ADULT MALE ALTERNATIVE 2

When creating an adult character, it's important to consider what could be done to make him appear more mature without being too stuffy or boring. This man is definitely not boring – his expression, clothing, and pose all point to a character with lots of attitude.

Using an exaggeratedly tall adult proportion set with tightly defined muscles and bone structure gives him a strong presence and helps to distinguish him from younger, teenage characters. Heavily defined facial features are also important to make a character appear adult, with eyes drawn smaller and much stronger definition of the neck and cheekbones, with chiseling common throughout.

A character such as this presents an air of experience and confidence as he stands bold and fearless with a knowing smile. Although he is youthful and jokey, subtle details, such as the slight squint in his eyes and his firm grip on his pole-like weapon, give the impression of someone not to be crossed.

Sometimes coloring can look very effective without filling in entire areas – the color of his skin is depicted using only colored shadows. His clothes are not only colored but textured as well. Don't forget the small, detailed accessories, such as his yellow-tinted sunglasses, his shiny metal dog-tag necklace, and the buckles and lacing on his chunky boots.

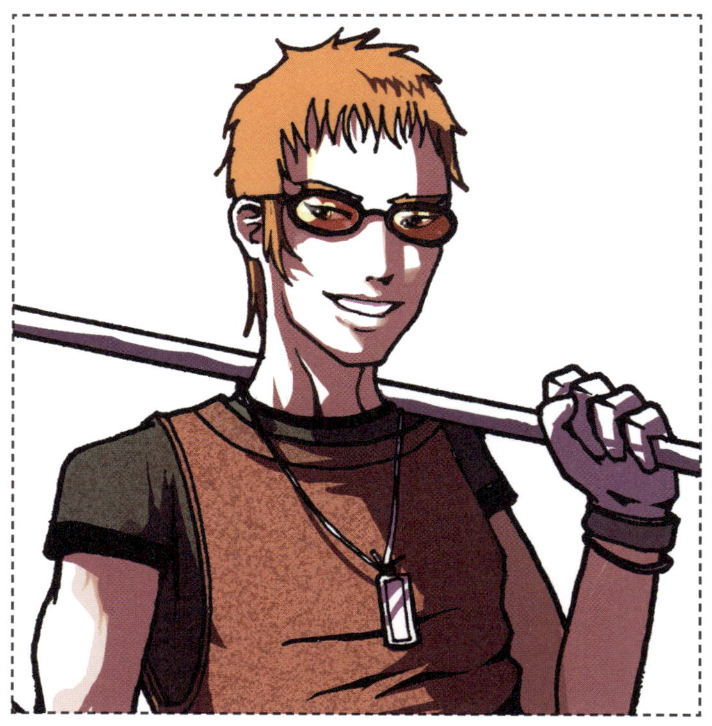

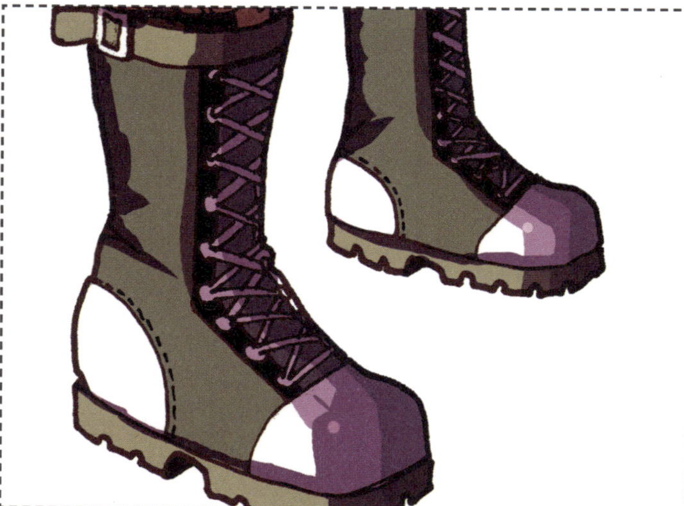

PERSONALITY

- Strong-Willed
- Witty
- Streetwise
- Independent
- Casual
- Cool

SETTING

- Modern
- Action
- Fights
- Gangs
- Street
- Shopping Mall

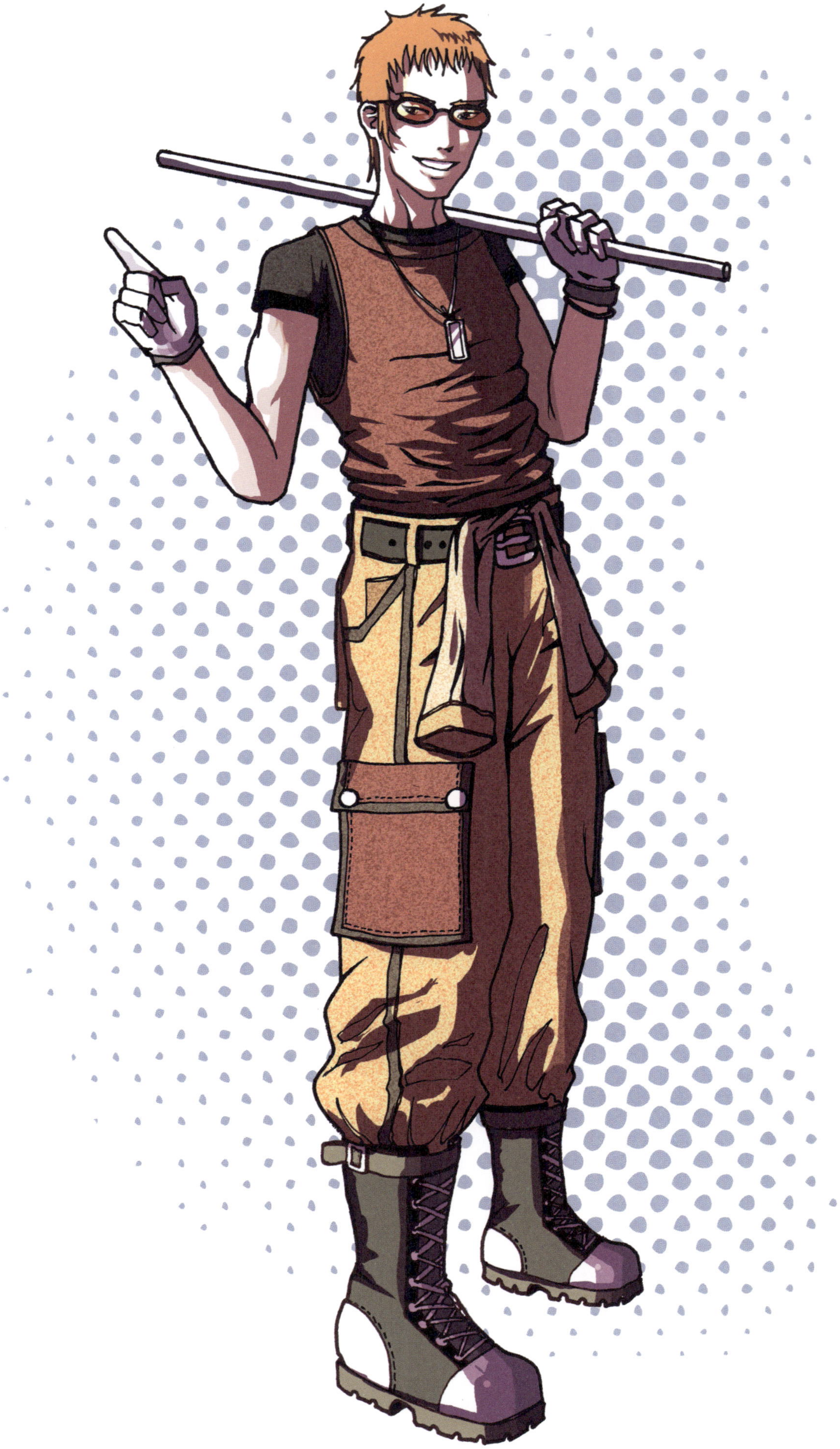

COLOR PALETTE

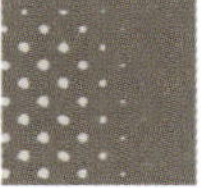
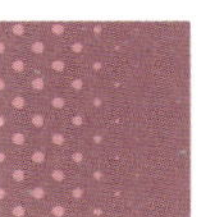
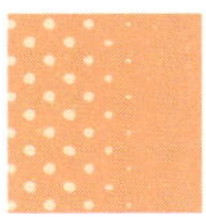
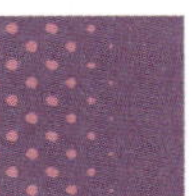
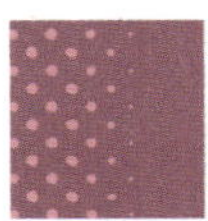
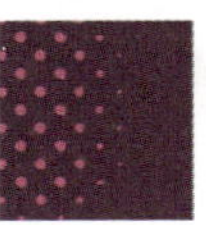

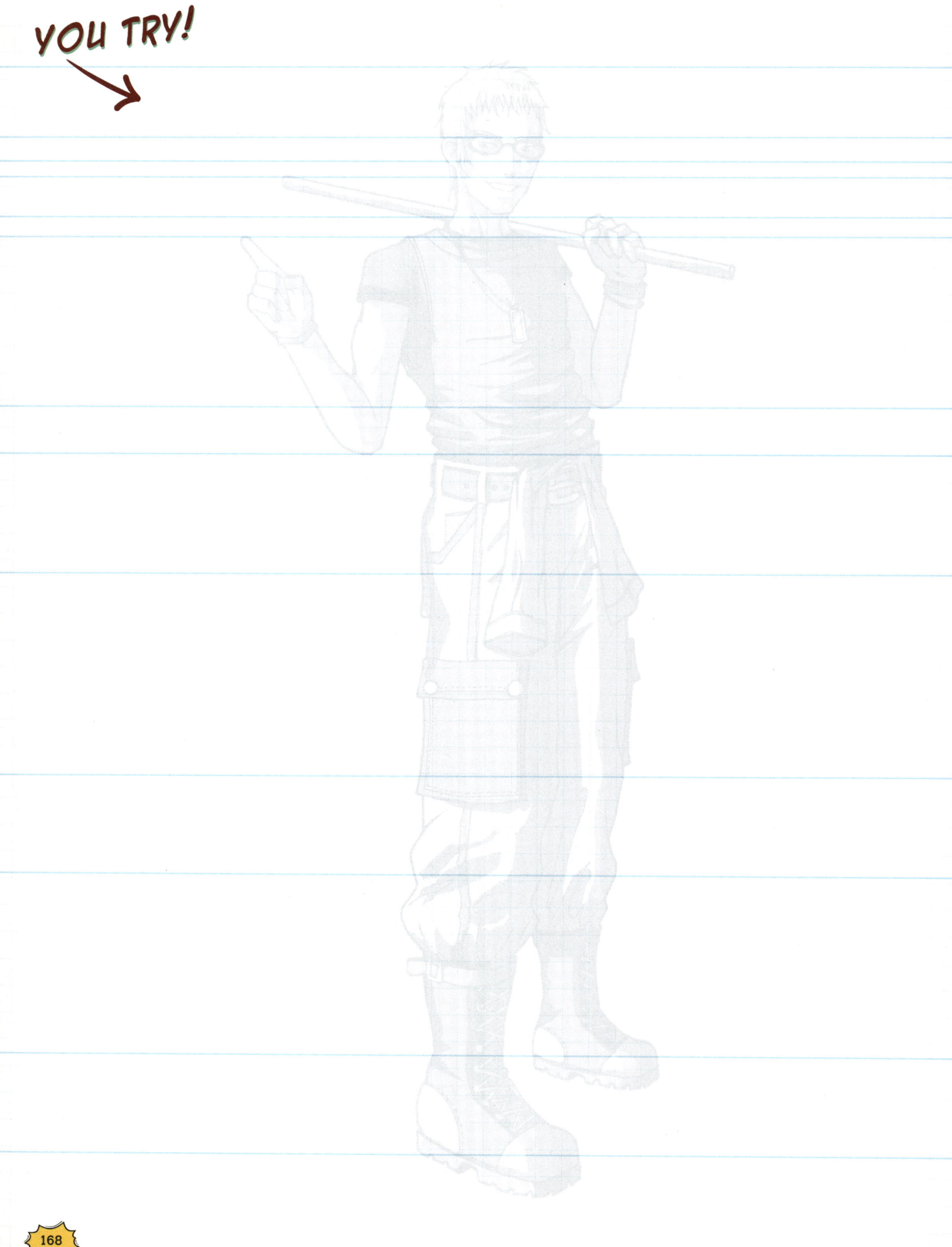
YOU TRY!

ADULT FEMALE

A common character in young women's comics, the adult woman has life experience but retains the fun-loving years of her youth. With many roles in the world of manga, from a big sister icon to a hardworking office type, she is very versatile – supporting the main character in various storylines, as well as being a very interesting and capable character in her own right. In Japan, many young women read manga, which is similar in design to fashion illustration. The themes can range from edgy to contemporary to amusing. Therefore a character that can convey many expressions is very desirable.

ROUGH SKETCH

This lady is feminine but confident. Sketch out a basic skeleton and action line to give her a relaxed pose. She has a less babyish face than a teenage girl, while still retaining wide pupils to show her friendly and welcoming nature. She can be as curvaceous or as athletic as you like. Her proportions here should range from seven to nine head lengths tall when using the usual guidelines.

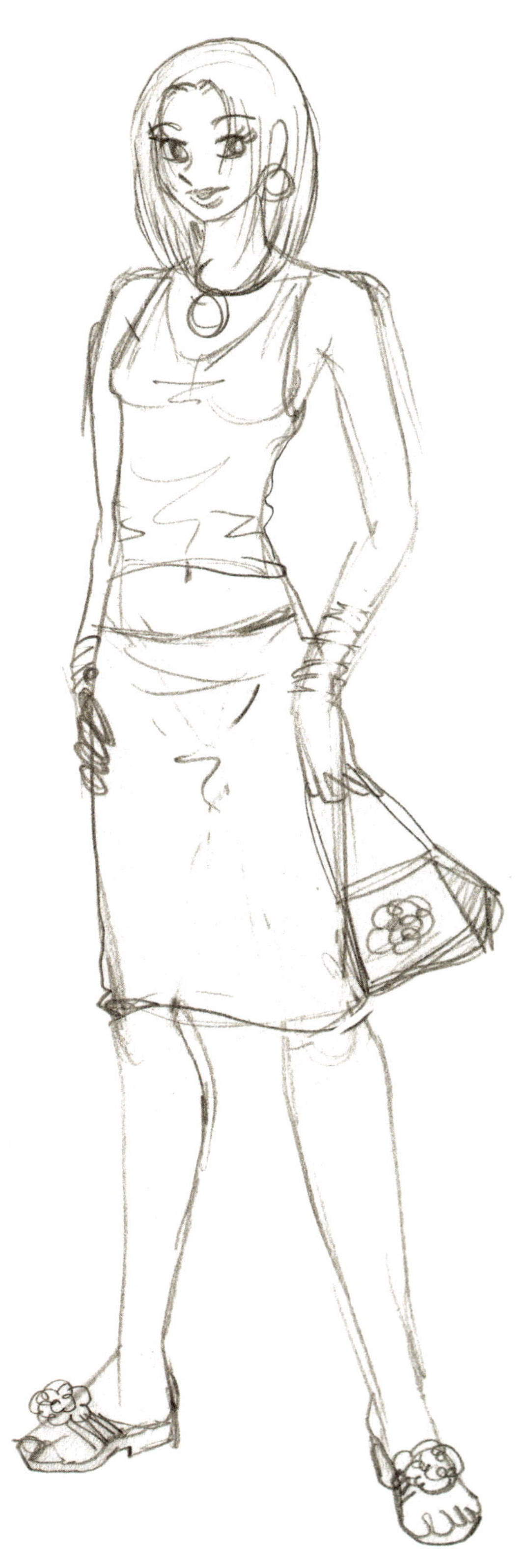

ADDING DETAILS

The hairstyle depicted here is a shoulder-length, straight, layered cut. She has strands of hair over her face, which implies she is sensible but has a fun edge to her nature. She wears simple yet plainly visible accessories: big hoop earrings; a large shell-disc choker; and thin bracelets on each arm. Her handbag aptly matches her summer sandals.

The loose way she holds her handbag implies she may have a gentle aspect to her nature. Her feet are placed slightly apart, which is, unconsciously, a positive, self-assured stance.

Perhaps she is not even an office worker but a student or a mature student. She is possibly a gym-goer, therefore she may be a little body-conscious but can get away with wearing tummy-revealing summer clothes. Her skirt is knee-length and casual; her clothes are fun and fashionable but not in an overtly sexual way, which shows that this character is fun-loving and good-natured.

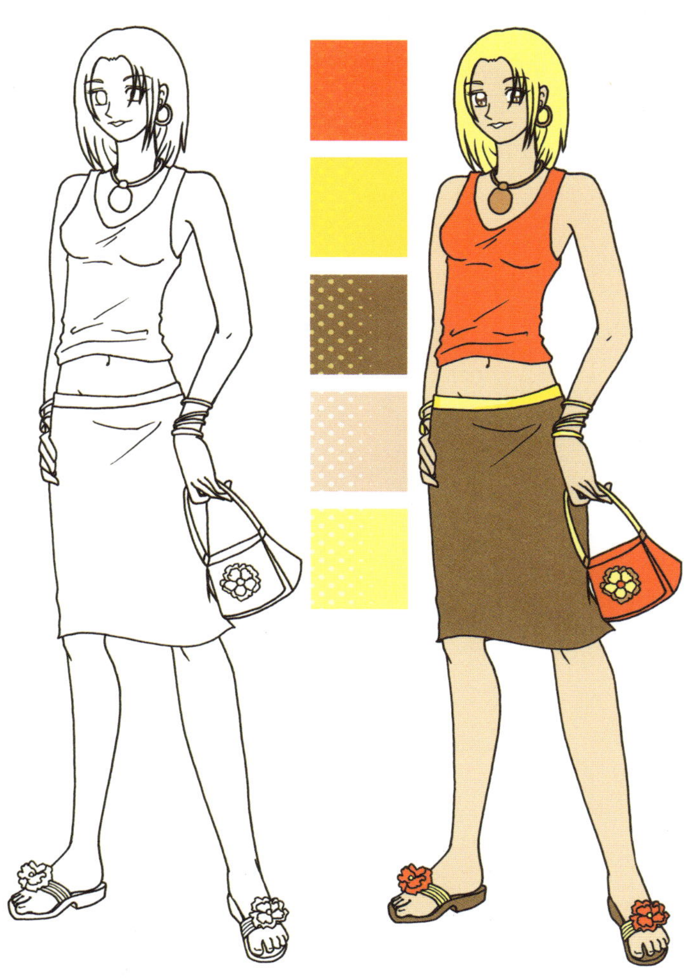

INKING

When inking, it is best to try and remember all of the following points:

- Her hair is layered and choppy; remember that manga hair strands always taper to a sharp point. Her strands are quite thin and fine; the longer the hair, the sleeker this effect should be.
- Place folds and creases accurately and realistically – look at fashion magazines and photos to get a better idea of where creases and folds fall.
- Details like folds and clothing detail can be inked using a finer pen, tapering out to thin lines.

BASIC COLORS

This character is wearing summery clothes that would not look out of place on the beach. The darker tones of the brown skirt and the warm orange top are contrasted slightly by yellow details and the character's blonde hair.

You may like to experiment with skin tones; if this character has been sunbathing, she should have a slightly darker skin hue to show that she is tanned.

For consistency, her brown eyes match her skirt and the soles of her sandals, her orange top matches her orange bag, etc. Her accessories are a neutral color that complements the character's dress sense.

A range of facial expressions that suit this character.

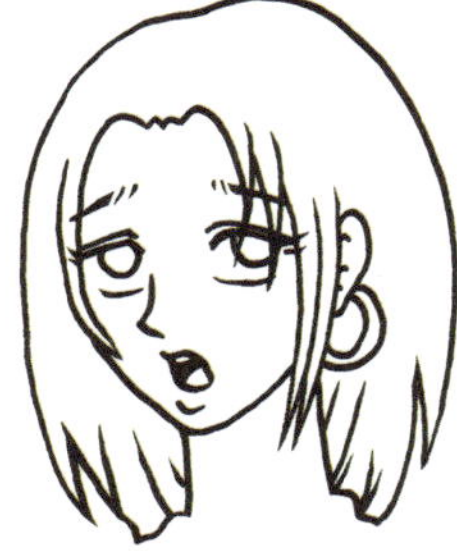

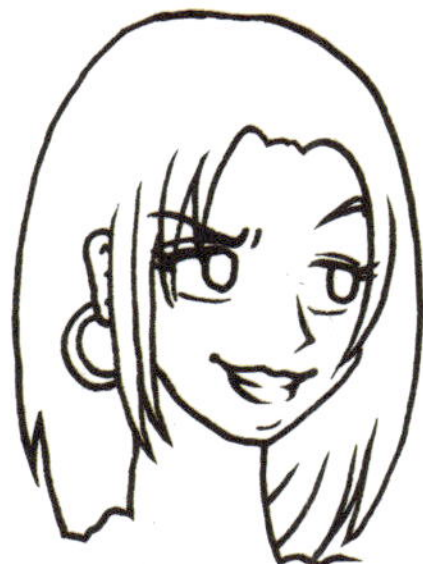

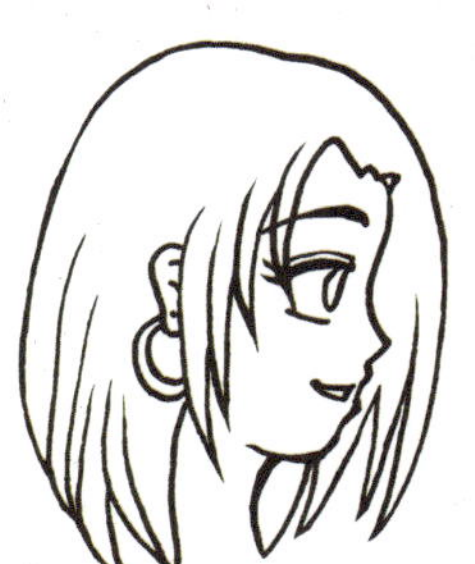

ADULT FEMALE

SHADING

Choose where your light source is coming from. Then make sure you add shadows in the appropriate areas of your character: her skin, her clothes, her hair. This is done using a deeper shade per color used.

You can emphasize the creases and folds by adding and elongating tapered shadows; this is prevalent in the detail used on this character's top at her bustline, near her waist, and also where her hand is holding the bag by her hip. These shadows are quite crisp and pointed; you can alternatively use a softer brush to create softer shadows.

If possible, try to match the shading of the clothes your characters wear with the shading on their skin – note the shadows on her right knee. This adds a consistency to your art. There is more shadow on her skirt on the righthand side, as it is angled away from the light source.

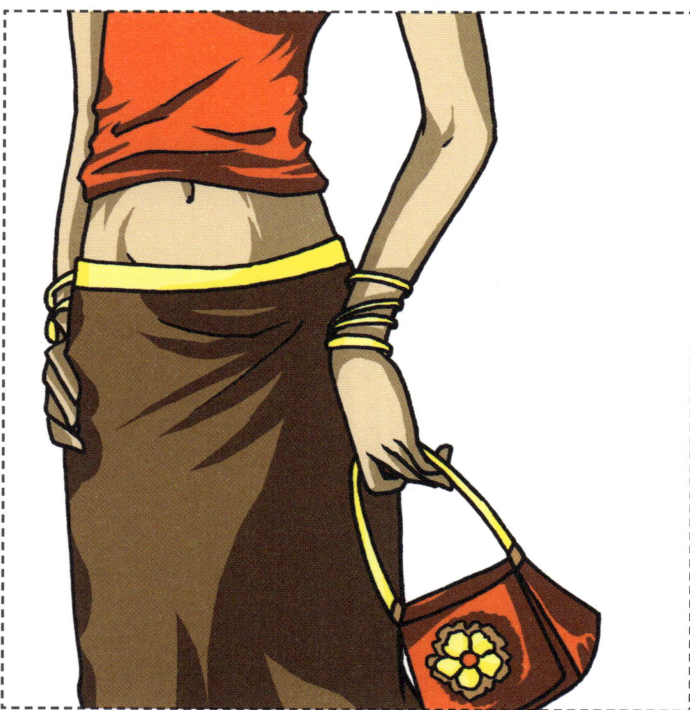

PERSONALITY

- Fun
- Outgoing
- Bubbly
- Hardworking
- Confident
- Determined

SETTING

- Office
- University
- Pub/Bar
- Shopping Mall
- Lecture Hall
- Coffee Shop
- Bookstore

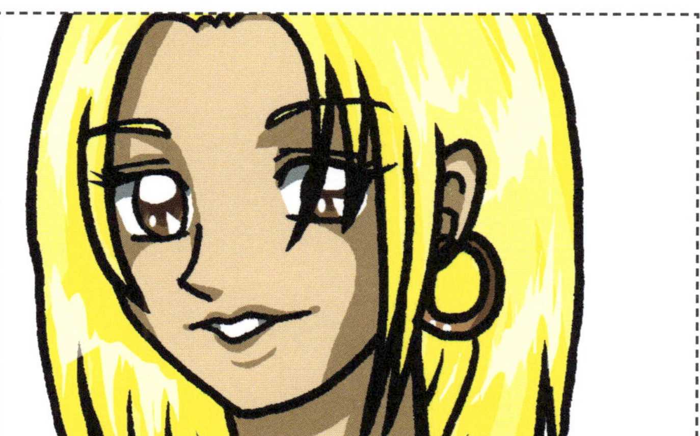

HIGHLIGHTS AND FINISHING TOUCHES

The clothing this character is wearing is made from soft fabrics – even her shoes are made from fibrous materials – so highlighting is not required on her top, skirt, or sandals. As it is summer, she's carrying a canvas bag, so highlights won't be needed here either. Highlights have been added to her shiny jewelry and her smooth hair, although, being blonde, the highlights may not show up unless they are very light or pure white.

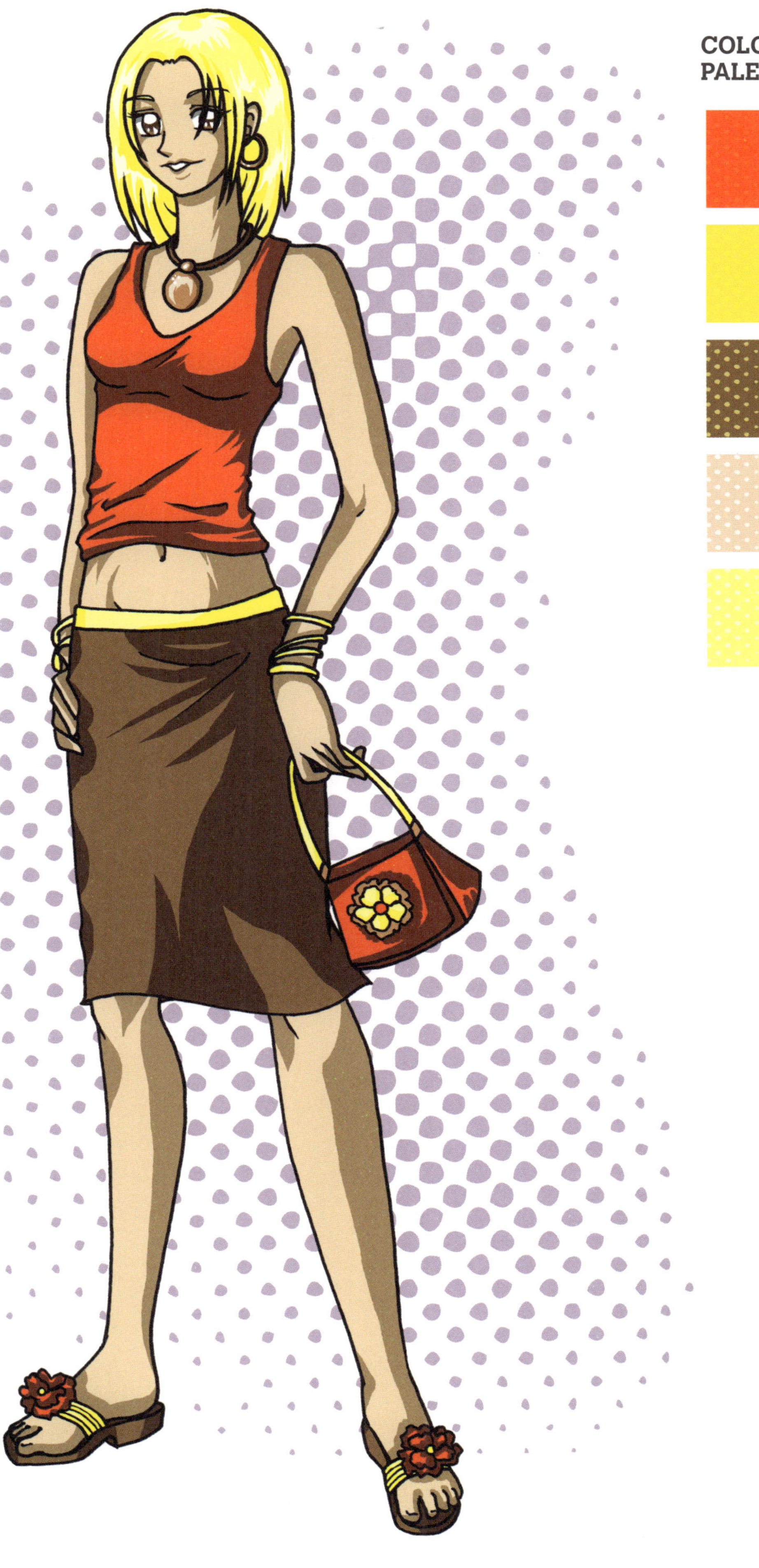

COLOR PALETTE

YOU TRY!

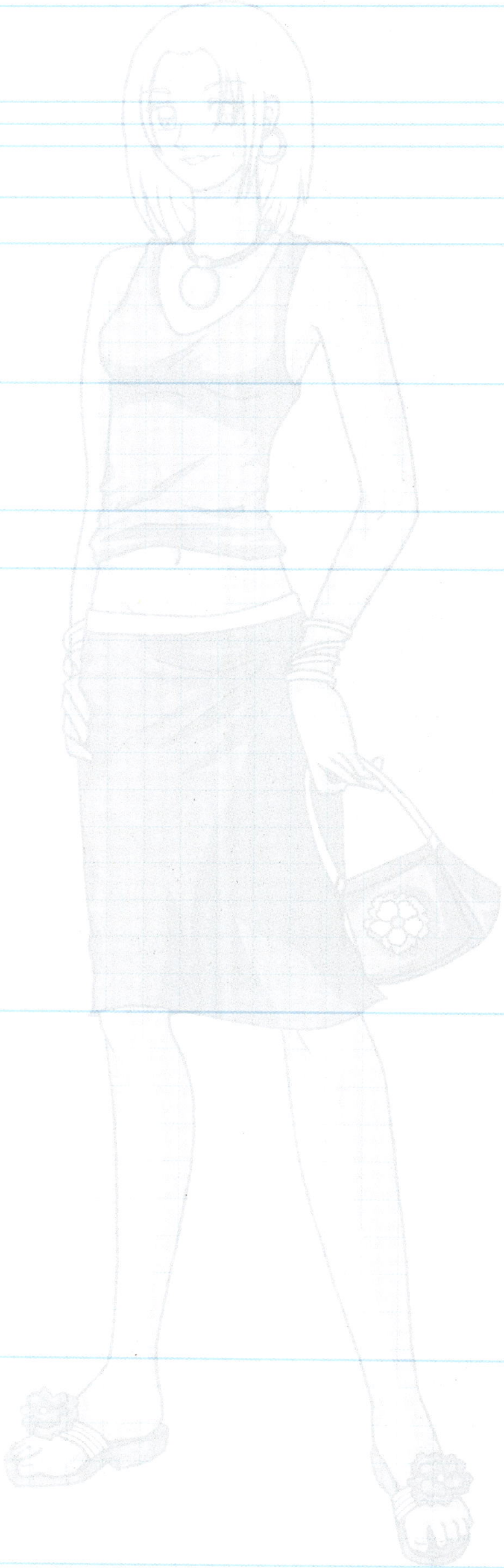

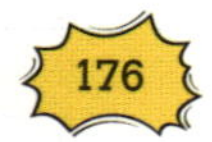

ADULT FEMALE ALTERNATIVE 1

This futuristic woman has just removed her helmet to take in her new surroundings. She is a character that could easily fit into an epic space opera.

She knows she's sexy, making the most of her figure in a tight-fitting suit and by the way she is standing. The details and design of her clothing are futuristic, made of nonfibrous, artificial materials and metallic sections.

It is the coloring of this picture that confirms the otherworldliness of this character. Although she is not old, her hair is white, indicating how different she is from us. The cool color scheme reminds us of the sky and of space, much more appropriate for a space huntress than browns or greens.

The shading really helps to define the materials of her costume – bold, contrasting base colors, shadows, and highlights give her clothes a lot of shine. Look at the metallic areas carefully – start with white leading to light grays, then use a bold streak of dark gray, interspersed with mid-grays. Take particular care with her helmet, as it is not only reflective but also transparent.

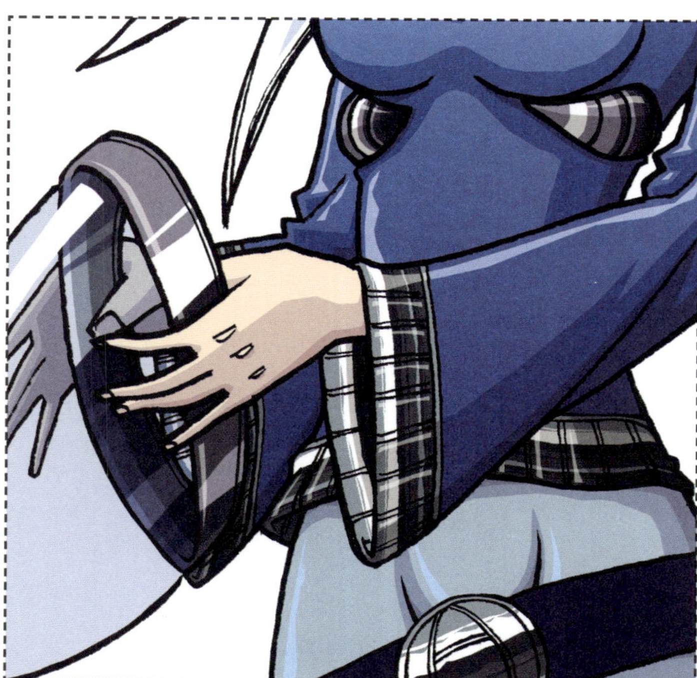

Her calm eyes and wry smile indicate lots of life experience – you can imagine her sighing and rolling her eyes if something annoys her, particularly if it's something she could easily deal with. She looks like someone who will work hard to get a job done, then relax and enjoy herself later.

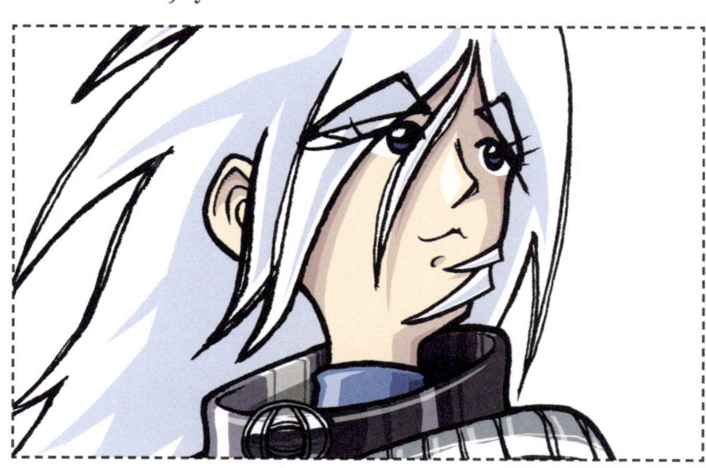

PERSONALITY

- Calm
- Knowledgeable
- Tough
- Cynical
- Independent

SETTING

- Space Station
- Spaceship
- Alien Planet
- Future
- Comedy
- Adventure

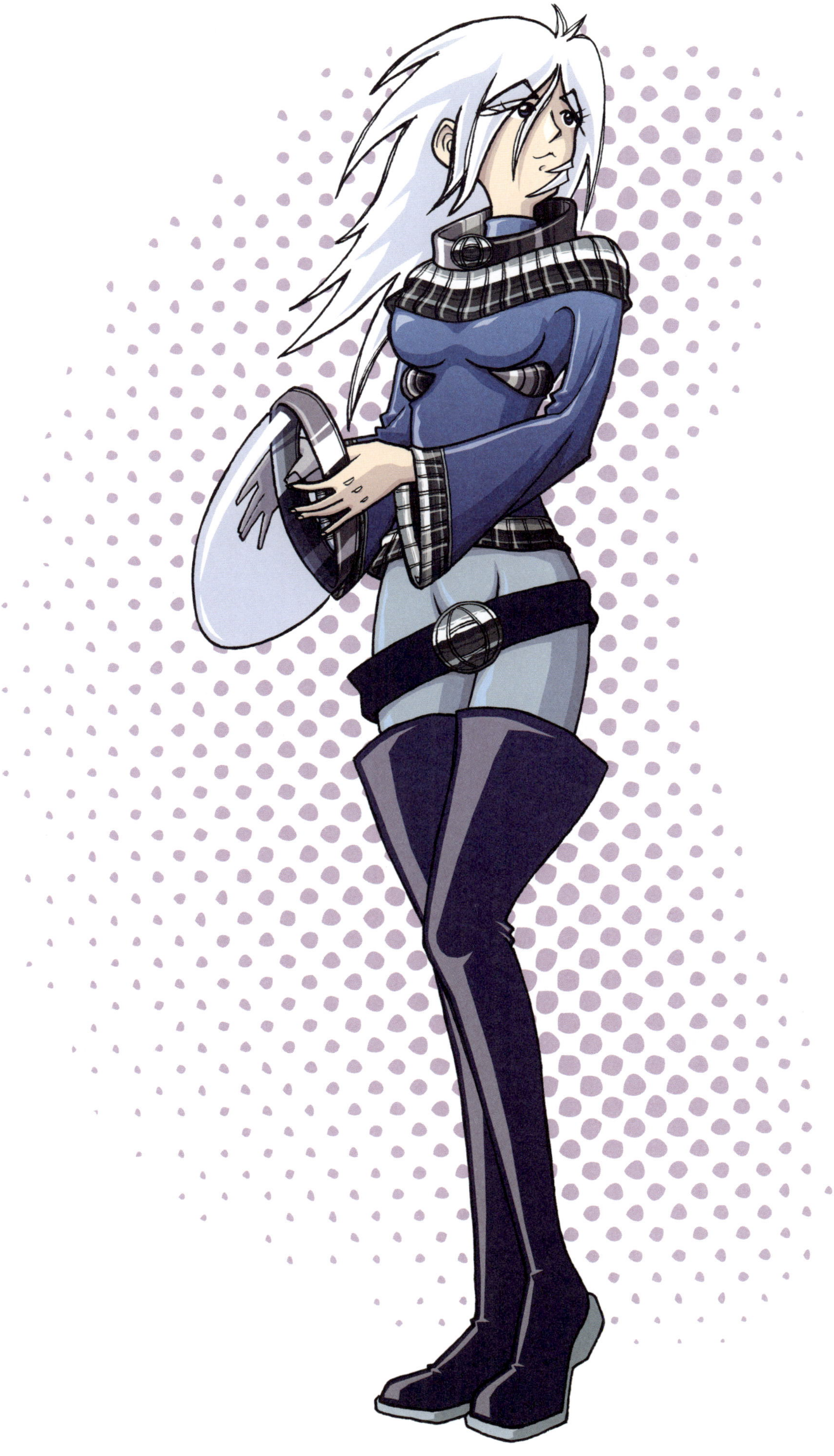

COLOR PALETTE

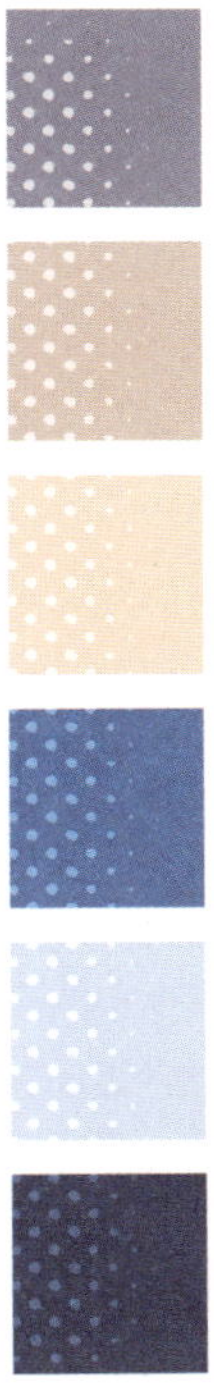

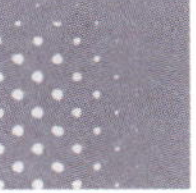

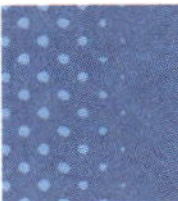

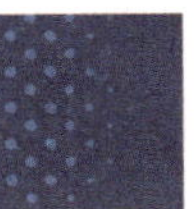

YOU TRY!

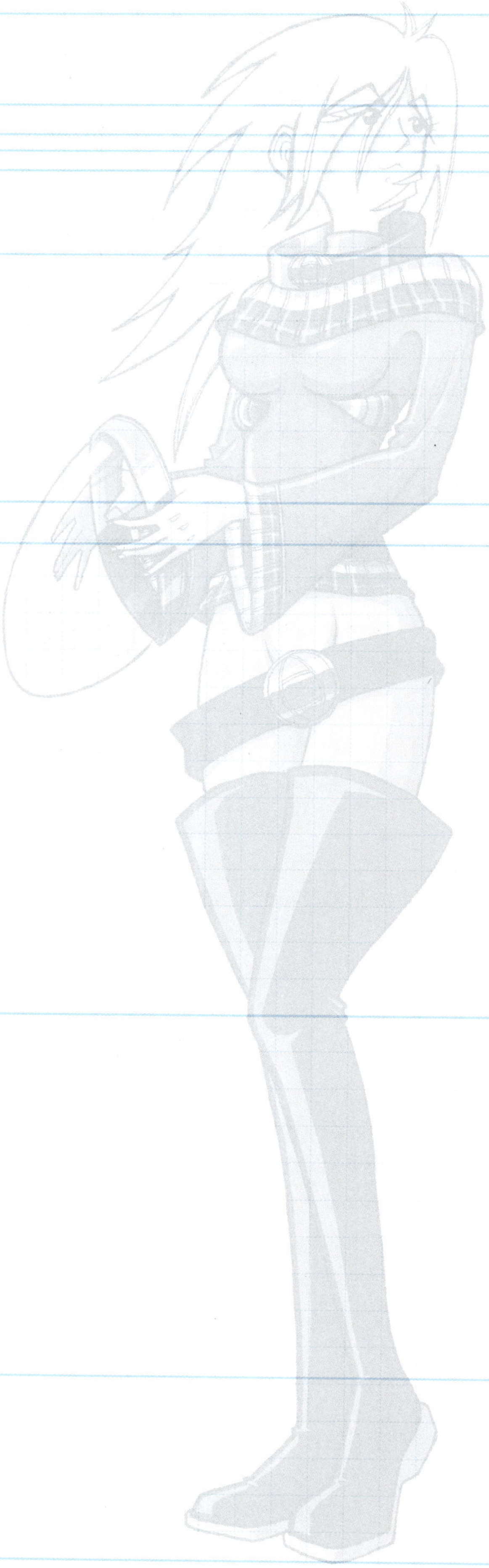

ADULT FEMALE ALTERNATIVE 2

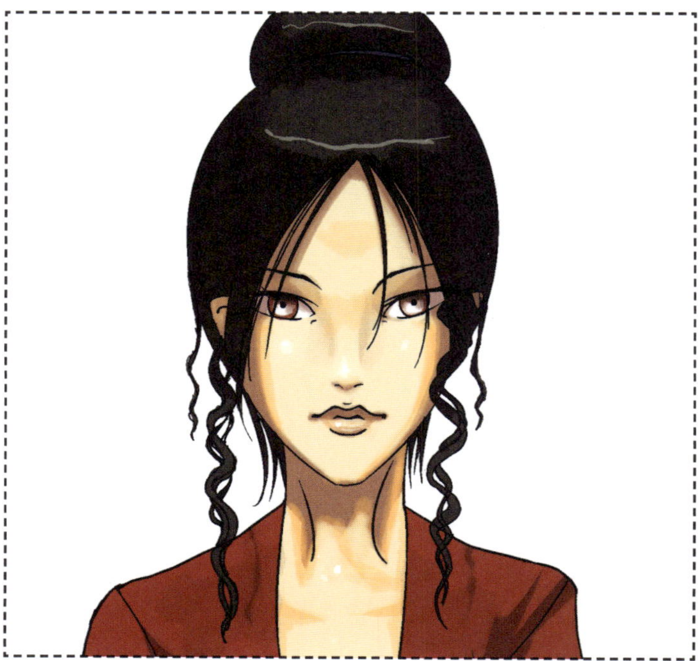

A dangerous woman, this lady is someone you wouldn't want to mess with. She strides purposefully toward us, brandishing her sword, beautiful but deadly.

This character is a modern-day Japanese warrior, wearing kimono-style dress with some contemporary styling that complements her sheer stockings and tightly worn hair. The sword is relatively simple but perfectly matched to work with the costume, along with the matching scabbard. Note the use of very thin, subtle highlights on her stockings, belt, and hair.

Although she is obviously very sexual in nature, due largely to her figure and revealing outfit, the character's pose and expression is completely focused forward without a hint of a smile or a wink. This gives the character a very real sense of purpose and role rather than being a mindless character who is merely dressing up and posing for a photo.

Adult female characters have some distinctive differences from their teenage counterparts. Even with young adults, the physical development shows the difference between women and young teenage girls. A heavy hourglass figure shows off the character's bust considerably but also draws attention to her wide, developed hips. Adult characters tend to be more experienced with their role as well, reflected in the manner of this swordswoman.

PERSONALITY

- Focused
- Cold
- Impersonal
- Ruthless
- Experienced

SETTING

- Japan
- City
- Club
- Street
- Night
- Horror
- Present
- Thriller
- Action
- Gangs
- Yakuza

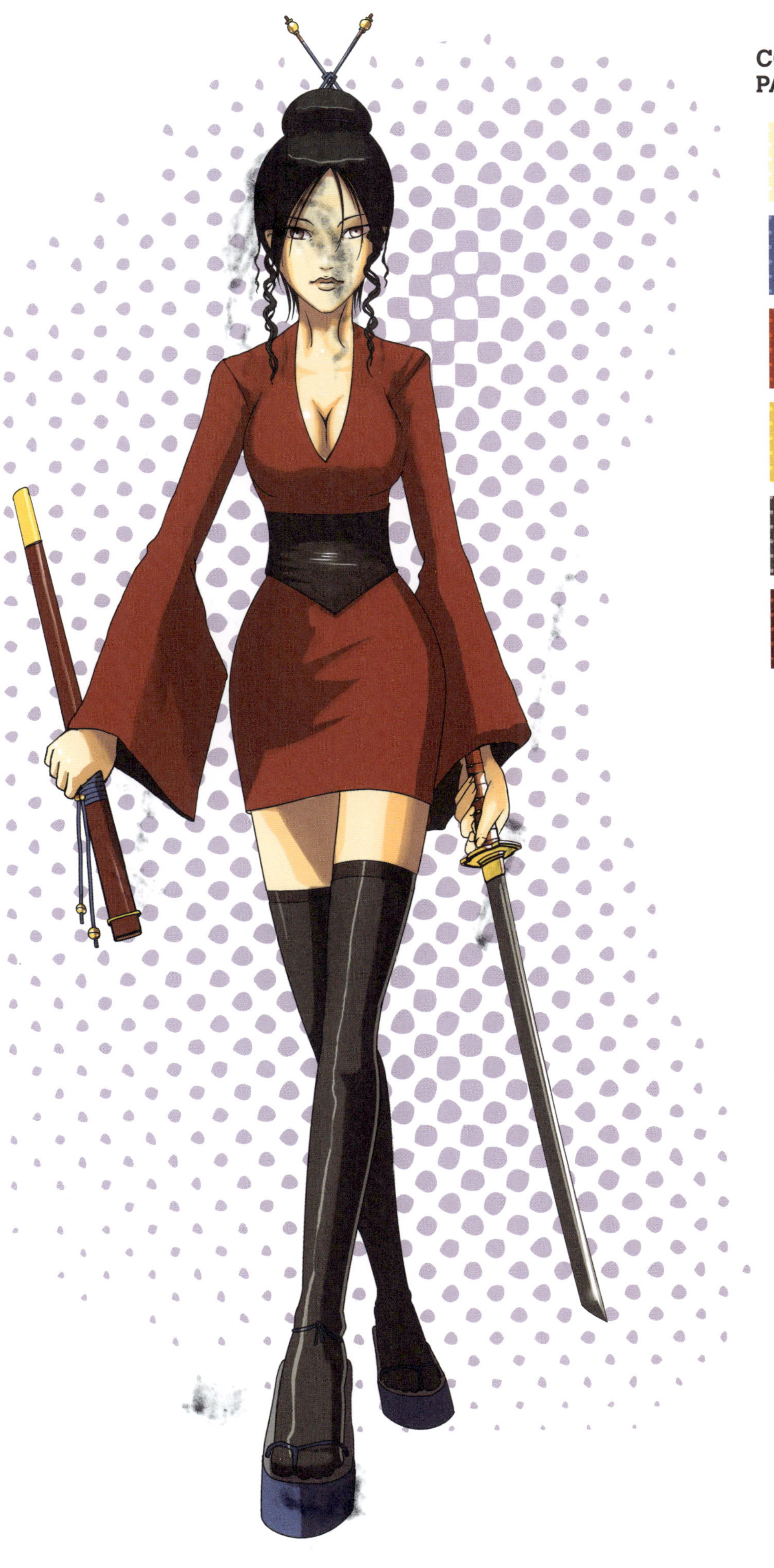

COLOR PALETTE

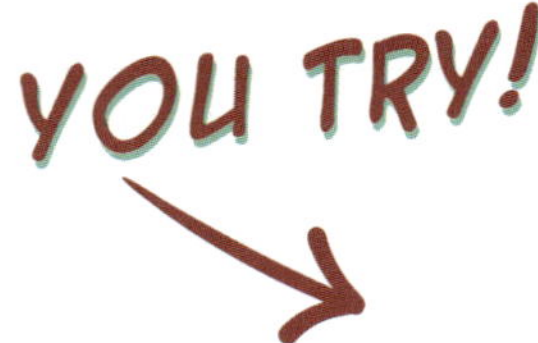
YOU TRY!

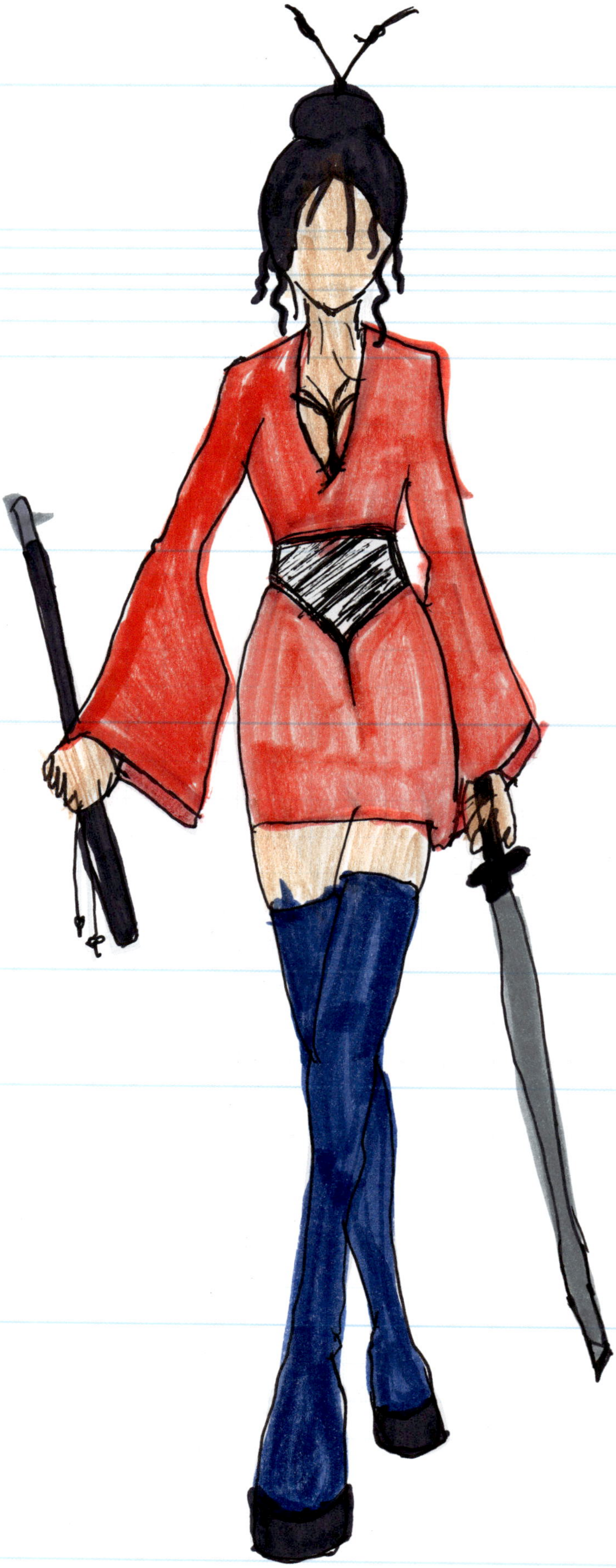

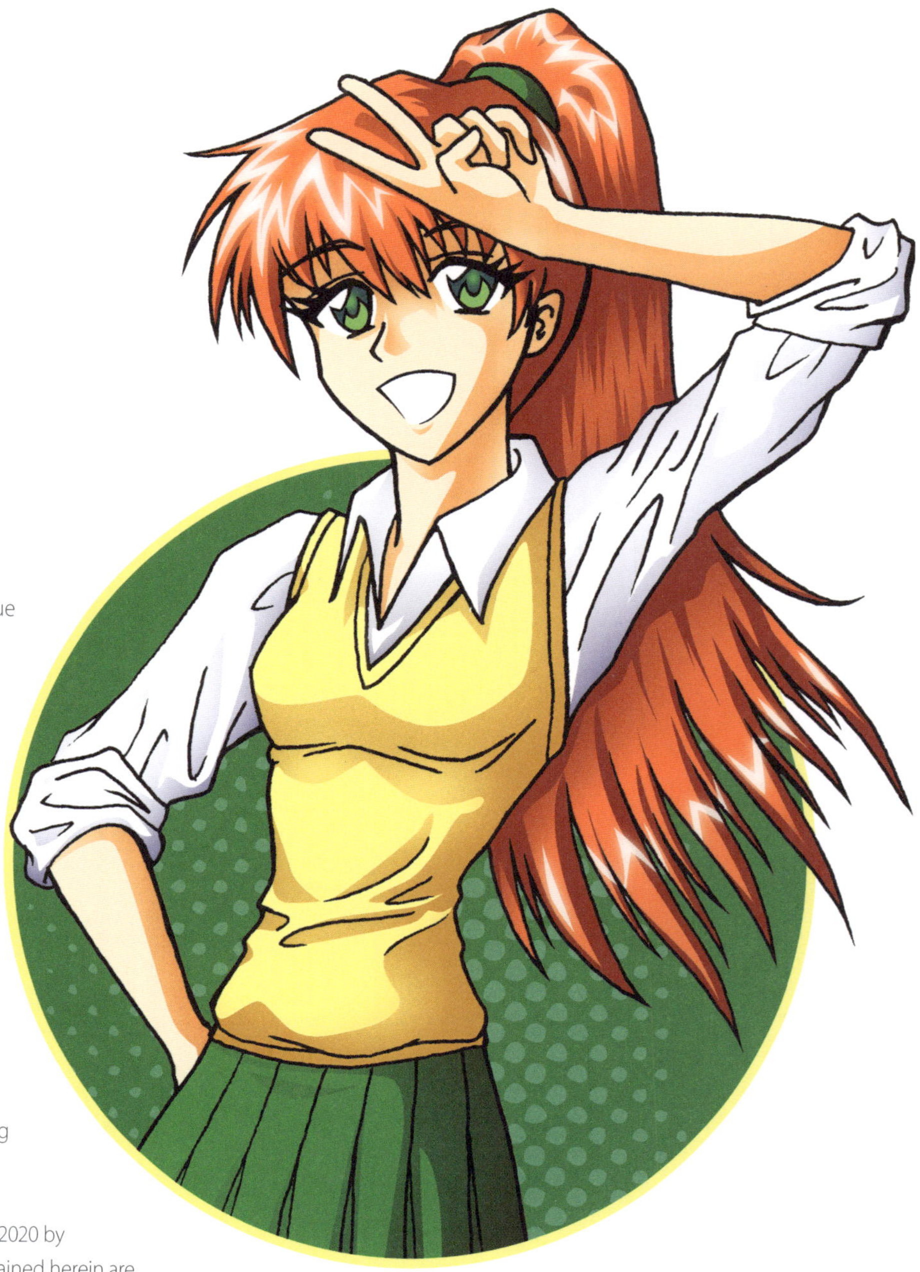

Fox Chapel focuses on providing real value to our customers through the printing and book production process. We strive to select quality paper that is also eco-friendly. This book is printed on archival-quality, acid-free paper that can be expected to last for at least 200 years. It meets the minimum requirements of the American National Standard for Information Sciences—Permanence of Paper for Printed Library Materials, ANSI/NISO Z39.48-1992. This book is printed on paper produced from trees harvested from well-managed forests where measures are taken to protect wildlife, plants, and water quality.

ISBN 978-1-4971-0135-7

To learn more about the other great books from Fox Chapel Publishing, or to find a retailer near you, call toll-free 800-457-9112 or visit us at *www.FoxChapelPublishing.com.*

We are always looking for talented authors. To submit an idea, please send a brief inquiry to acquisitions@foxchapelpublishing.com.

Printed in Singapore
First printing